The New York Times

SURRENDER TO SUNDAY CROSSWORDS
75 Puzzles from the Pages of *The New York Times*

Edited by Will Shortz

ST. MARTIN'S GRIFFIN ⚞ NEW YORK

Celebrate the 100th Anniversary of the Crossword Puzzle!

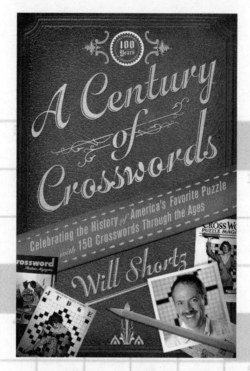

Available Summer 2013

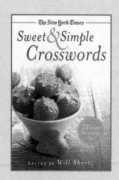   

REAR-END COLLISIONS

ACROSS

1 Spanish girls
7 Label for unmentionables?
15 Burro, e.g.
22 Lower
23 Like some collisions
24 "For real!"
25 Hero of an old Scottish ballad
26 When the pressure's on
27 Avails oneself of
28 Face-offs
29 Bottom line?
30 Yoo follower
31 Heart
32 Godzilla, e.g.
34 Epitome of simplicity
36 One of the "Desperate Housewives"
37 Formal/informal reply to "Who's there?"
41 Daredevil Knievel
42 Lampoons
45 Big media event
47 Hike the price of, perhaps
49 Cultivate, in a way
50 Four front?
52 Snoops (around)
53 Widely popular shows, say
55 Bunting is part of it
59 Old French coin
60 Beknighted souls?
61 Roy of country music
62 Draft pick?
63 An affront
64 Sources of pollen grains
68 Letter-shaped opening in some pistons
69 Diaper wearer
71 Some morning fundraisers
73 "The Closer" airer

74 "___ me!"
78 Last place you'll see a bachelor
79 Jumbo combatants
80 Meyerbeer output
82 Suffered a financial setback, slangily
83 Irk
85 Gen ___
86 Late rallies
88 It involves a trip to the underworld
90 Stares slack-jawed
91 Stuck
92 Al dente, say
95 It's not liquid
96 It's not liquid
97 Blue material
98 Dander
99 Car safety feature
101 Data storage device
106 Was manic
108 Pulls down
109 Decalogue possessive
110 Boxer Ali
111 Mexican cooking ingredients called "flores de calabaza" in Spanish
115 Barely gets
118 ___ rat
119 Echelon
120 Arles affirmatives
121 Murder, ___
122 Special delivery
124 Half brother of Athena
125 1950 film in which Frank Bigelow investigates his own murder
128 Hawaiian souvenir?
130 Kofi of the U.N.
131 Driver's aid
135 Diamond substitute
137 First estate
139 Put into motion
140 Rah-rah
141 Crossed the tarmac
142 Occasions to try out riffs

143 Peeping Tom's home
144 Raga instruments

DOWN

1 OK setting in the summer
2 Go (to)
3 Protected against
4 Clambake dish
5 Skewed
6 Picks up
7 Impress clearly
8 Sewing machine parts
9 Orts
10 Poetic period
11 High-___
12 Letter after delta
13 Tangent, e.g.
14 French weapon
15 Feels for
16 Entertains
17 Diploma, e.g.: Abbr.
18 Neighbor of Mo.
19 Manchester's St. ___ Church
20 "Nobody else is coming"
21 Choir voice
31 E.T.S. offering
32 Former Ford offering, for short
33 Runs through
35 Doesn't get taught a lesson?
36 Aberdeen hillside
37 Dirt
38 Storytelling Studs
39 New York lake
40 Freezes over
43 They might be held at a sewage plant
44 Members of a Connecticut tribe
45 Aisle or window, e.g.: Abbr.
46 Part of a medical bill
48 Pharmaceutical company that developed Metamucil and Dramamine

51 Clump of grass
54 Toy piano sound
56 Remedy for acid reflux
57 Seasonal helper
58 Petitions
61 Request
63 Unmoving machine parts
64 Cross
65 88-Across, for one
66 Part of a.m.
67 Scottish inventor and road builder John Loudon ___
68 Hooked (up)
69 J.F.K., e.g.
70 Very serious, as an accident
72 Habitual teeth grinding
73 Aligned
75 Change, as keyboard keys
76 Dos + tres
77 Newsworthy 1950s trial, informally
80 Item of winter sports equipment
81 Climb, as a rope
84 Road designer, e.g.: Abbr.
86 Italian turnover
87 Confine
89 Water in the Oise
90 Attendee
92 Primarily
93 Syrian's neighbor
94 "Side by Side by Sondheim," e.g.
96 Poetry contests
97 Area near Little Italy
99 Bank offerings, in brief
100 Change in Mexico
101 It can help you get inside someone's head
102 Followed
103 Jamaican coffee liqueur

by Mike Nothnagel and Byron Walden

104 Bonnie and Clyde contemporary
105 Item at a bakery
107 Corn unit
112 Hamlet confidant
113 Many Bics
114 Medical suffix
116 Put in someone's care
117 Political writings
123 Zhou ___
124 Collect
125 Cartoon character voiced by Mel Blanc
126 Airing
127 Yearn (for)
129 Unhip
131 Rule that ended in 1947
132 South American tuber
133 Bills are in it: Abbr.
134 Italian actress Eleonora
135 Bencher's target
136 Barbarian
138 Gridiron figs.

2 TWO-FOR-ONE SPECIAL

ACROSS

1 Border-crossing necessities
4 Black cloud formers
9 Unresponsive state
13 A flat equivalent
19 Hitchcock thriller set in Brazil
21 It's all downhill from here
22 Nation bordering Svizzera
23 Ordeal that's no big deal?
25 Gaze upon
26 It's much followed in North Africa
27 Large cloth sign with nothing on it?
29 Toy hammer?
34 Ending with sex or symbol
35 Seek redress from
36 "Anything ___?"
37 Potential pet
38 Smartphone buy
40 Swine's diet
42 Full range
43 For ___
45 "So that's your game!"
46 Gulf of Oman port
50 Soft yet easily breakable "Star Trek" creature?
56 Available
57 "Save Me" singer Mann
58 Break in logic
59 Fire starter?
60 Magic, for instance
63 Refresher
64 European of the Iron Age
65 In days gone by
66 Hemispherical computer add-on?
68 "Ride 'em, cowboy!," e.g.?
70 In its current state
71 "As if that weren't enough . . ."
72 Perpetually, to Pope
73 What only one Best Picture winner has had
74 In the distance
75 Dieter's target
76 "The cat's meow" or "a dog's life"
78 "___ Eyes" (1969 hit for the Guess Who)
79 Big house that's not as big?
82 Site of one of the Seven Wonders
83 Rower's need
84 "I hate the Moor" speaker
85 Young builder's supply
87 Point of rotation
90 See 71-Across
91 Floors
92 Casino souvenir
96 "Entourage" agent Gold
97 Back stroke?
99 Goddess of gas?
102 Get part of one's shirt under control?
106 Poppies, e.g.
107 Undamaged
108 What the Gorgon Stheno does in Greek myth?
113 Render unproductive?
114 Dressage gait
115 Noisy water heater
116 Old Soviet naval base site
117 Vodka brand
118 "Borrow"
119 Rubber-stamps

DOWN

1 Early enough
2 At the back
3 Ones going on a long walk?
4 Old machinery coating
5 Actress Vardalos
6 ___ Mail
7 "You know better!"
8 Belarus, once: Abbr.
9 Venae ___ (large blood vessels)
10 It can make you dizzy
11 Yom Kippur War politician
12 Revolutionary device?
13 Longtime Redskins coach Joe
14 The Andrea Doria, for one
15 Chemistry Nobelist Otto
16 King of Naples in "The Tempest"
17 Cheese off
18 Baseball team once owned by Ray Kroc
20 Like kiwi fruit
24 With proficiency
28 Pinch
30 Exam administered four times a yr.
31 "Lou Grant" production co.
32 Caribbean resort island
33 Army heads
38 Pledge of Allegiance finisher
39 Like most canned tomatoes
41 Defensive return
42 Reacted to shocking news
43 "Watch your ___!"
44 Took a few seconds?
45 Podium personage
46 They're not popular in offices
47 ___ oneself (share private thoughts)
48 Workhorse's quality
49 Phoebe of "Drop Dead Fred"
51 Sunni sermonizer
52 Communication system of old
53 Exchanged, as words
54 Reckless driver's loss, possibly
55 Becomes clear
61 More copious
62 Wisdom tooth, e.g.
64 Caesar's first wife
65 Maker of Bug-B-Gon
67 Adds, as to a recording
68 Print shop unit
69 Salty language
72 Interrupter of Dagwood's naps
75 Kentucky Derby and Epsom Oaks, for two
76 Old sofa's problem
77 Concerned about the environment
80 Can of Newcastle
81 Young chap
82 ___ Bud, schoolgirl in "The Mystery of Edwin Drood"
86 M.A. seeker's test
87 Director and star of "Looking for Richard"
88 Free of creases
89 Shaw defined it as "insufficient temptation"

by Patrick Berry

90 Disney subsidiary
91 Drive-___
92 Holder of plunder
93 Regarding this matter
94 How Sam's Club buys goods
95 Free tickets
98 Extremist
99 George Jetson's boy
100 Scrumptious
101 Outside shot?
103 Cry often made while snapping the fingers
104 Elects
105 Read but never post
109 "Too many to list" abbr.
110 Poseidon's domain
111 Launch platform
112 Record with many beats: Abbr.

3 Of Course!

ACROSS

1 Drop
5 Diagnostic test, of a sort
9 Crosswise, when 18-Across
14 ___ bean
18 See 9-Across
19 Augusta National Golf Club, for the Masters
20 Class, abroad
21 SST component
22 Golf club repositioning?
25 "I bet I'll know it"
26 Botanical holder
27 Stock price movement
28 Yonder
30 Cloths with repeating patterns
32 When to get in, briefly
34 Three-time Best Director in the 1930s
37 Jennifer of tennis
40 Hole in one?
44 Take out ___ (get some assistance at the bank)
45 Stance
47 According to
48 Shoot two under
49 Comment after hitting a tee shot out of bounds?
53 Insect named for the Virgin Mary
55 Multiuse W.W. II vessel
56 Where tumblers can be found
57 Brightest star in Orion
60 "I do"
61 Ex-Jet Boomer
64 Pilfer
66 Uniform: Prefix
69 Wedge shot from a worn-out practice range platform?
75 Equal
76 Continental coins
77 Disappearance of 7/2/1937
79 Wait to play
82 100 kopecks
84 Like 20% of Israel
86 Start of an attention-getting call
87 Put through
90 Use one club for all 18 holes?
95 "That's ___!"
96 Topper
99 Old-time actress Talbot or Naldi
100 Words to the left of the White House flag on a $20 bill
101 Course not listed in the guidebooks?
104 Ones on a circuit
107 Untrue
108 Robert Frost's middle name
109 "Now We Are Six" author
111 Like some columns
113 Spelling aid?
115 Newly districted
119 Fragment
122 Woods stowed in the rear of a golf cart?
125 Action Man : U.K. :: ___ : U.S.
126 Long Island airport site
127 Legislative excess
128 Any of seven Danish kings
129 Revenuer
130 Loses
131 Sleighful
132 Reagan and others

DOWN

1 There are 336 dimples on a typical golf ball, for instance
2 1970s Wimbledon victor over Connors
3 Meager
4 Terrestrial decapod
5 Aussie chick
6 "Chill!"
7 Inits. in bowling lanes
8 Swell
9 Operating in either of two ways
10 Carnival worker
11 Suffix with Milan
12 On the line
13 Protection from bug bites
14 Duffer's shots?
15 Whichever
16 Enthusiasm
17 Whiz
21 Attacked from the air
23 Not fine
24 Knocked
29 Prefix with management
31 ___ center
33 Shirt
35 Sport named for a British boarding school
36 "I haven't ___"
37 TV option
38 Milano of "Charmed"
39 Like works of Kipling and Browning
41 Light start?
42 Director ___ C. Kenton
43 They might help produce a blowout
46 Annoy
50 Secretive couple
51 Pro ___
52 Iroquois foes
54 Cassim's brother in a classic tale
58 Investors' news, briefly
59 Come together
62 "Caught you!"
63 Military title?
64 Pharynx affliction
65 One-word query
67 Certain 35mm camera
68 "Lo-o-ovely!"
70 Second of 12: Abbr.
71 Suffix with ear or arm
72 Valued
73 ___ Lake (one of New York's Finger Lakes)
74 Swedish coins
78 Lincoln in-laws
79 Often-filtered material
80 Shaw who wrote "Rich Man, Poor Man"
81 Location of many organs
83 Org. with boats
84 Lawyer: Abbr.
85 Violate a peace treaty, maybe
88 Club thrown in disgust?
89 Installment
91 Anonymous: Abbr.
92 Herbal tea
93 Early Wagner opera
94 Quick survey
97 Like a real-estate deal that doesn't involve a mortgage

by Patrick Merrell

98 Crusty one
102 Oui's opposite
103 Object of curiosity on the first day of school
105 Put on the line
106 Some postal workers
110 Novelize, e.g.
112 University of Miami mascot
114 Egyptian menaces
116 Nephew of Caligula
117 Country in a Thomas Moore poem
118 Mil. awards
119 ___ Pepper
120 That guy
121 Hit Steely Dan album
123 The Indians, on sports tickers
124 As well

4 IN-NUENDOS

ACROSS

1 Split the tab
8 Left
15 McEnroe rival
19 Under development?
20 Put on microfiche, maybe
21 Golfer with an "army"
22 1997 Will Smith/ Tommy Lee Jones flick
24 Van Gogh or Monet vista
25 "Frosty" air?
26 Knicks star Anthony, to fans
27 Hikers' wear
29 General refusal?
31 Attention getter
35 Bishop's locale
36 Preventive measure, proverbially
40 Yesteryear
41 Huge, to Hugo
42 Prima donnas' features
46 Skip over water, as stones
49 Some game
51 Headstone phrase
55 Camaro ___-Z
57 Fraction of a min.
59 Phony: Prefix
60 Commercial suffix with Power
61 Baskin-Robbins unit
63 Smooths
67 Athlete wearing a calligraphic "D" logo
69 Lurid 1979 film about John Dillinger's girlfriend, with "The"
76 Went downhill fast
77 Misses part of a movie, maybe
78 Contortionist's bendy part
79 Letter seen twice in Philadelphia
81 Stray sounds?
84 Blocks (up)
87 Masculine principle
88 "To be on the safe side . . ."
93 Bank take-back
95 Seasonal potation
96 Hook hand
97 Stone-pushing Winter Olympian
99 Japanese native
101 Golf ace
109 Rogers's partner
112 Swiss cheese concoction
113 ___ driver
114 The Royal Game of India
117 Russia's ___ Mountains
119 "There is ___!"
120 Refuges
121 One who looks friendly but isn't
126 31-Across, for one
127 Like some bad language
128 Hammy, say
129 Compos mentis
130 Spouse's acquiescence
131 Perched

DOWN

1 Designer Versace
2 Hoofing it
3 Coercion
4 Multipurpose
5 Private investigator, in slang
6 Do a semester's worth of studying in one night, say
7 Breakfast items often eaten with spoons
8 "Amscray!"
9 Total
10 "Bad Moon Rising" band, for short
11 Yellowfin tuna
12 OFF! target
13 Ex-senator Bayh
14 Reply to "Gracias"
15 Security crises
16 Where skaters skate
17 Where skaters skate
18 V components
21 Org.
23 Big name in the diamond business?
28 Set (against)
30 It's often slanted
32 What [wink wink] may signify
33 ___ about (approximately)
34 Dungeons & Dragons figure
37 "Dianetics" author ___ Hubbard
38 "Want me to draw you ___?"
39 Bedews
43 Certain angel
44 ___ school
45 Canonized mlle.
46 45, e.g.
47 Western U.S. gas brand
48 Locale for many a lounge chair
50 Lounge lizard's look
52 Sasquatch's kin
53 Torpedo
54 Does some yard work
56 Pan handler
58 Virginia athlete, informally
62 Get ready
64 What a texter of ":-(" might be
65 "Xanadu" group, for short
66 "Oh yeah? ___ who?!"
68 Glimpse
70 Retainers, e.g.
71 N.B.A. forward Lamar ___
72 "Game of Thrones" protagonist ___ Stark
73 Father of a grand duke
74 Word on a cornerstone
75 Person with a safe job?
79 Sleepers
80 Run nicely
82 Home of the Texas Sports Hall of Fame
83 Leave thunderstruck
85 Tyrannosaurus rex, archetypally
86 Prepare, as cotton candy
89 "Wake up and smell the coffee!"
90 Not kosher
91 Cockney greeting
92 Head turner
94 Cross to bear
98 Dieter
100 Deutsch marks?
102 Percussion instrument with a pedal
103 Afore
104 Wiggle room
105 "Why not?!"
106 Quits, slangily

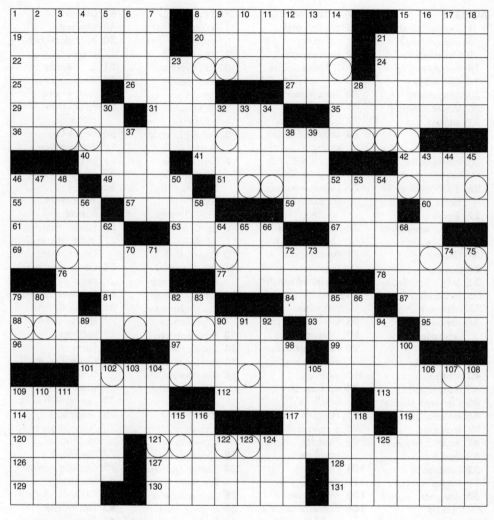

by Daniel A. Finan

5 FIX-A-TION

ACROSS

1 [That is correct!]
5 Overconfident
9 Not edited for TV
14 Bengay targets
19 Old switch attachment?
20 Whom mateys address
21 Jinx
22 Underfunded
23 Following the rules?
26 2009 "Survivor" locale
27 Traveling, say
28 R.S.V.P. component
29 Ladle cradle
31 Unbending
34 Astringent
35 St. ___ (malt liquor brand named after an Irish nun)
36 Variety of arbitrating techniques?
39 Observance
41 Vinegar, for one
42 Hummingbird food
43 Car rental freebie
46 Universal Human Rights Mo.
47 Sault ___ Marie
49 Scraps
52 Fertilization targets
53 Title under a photo of rain?
57 Whole tone, e.g.
58 Propose a date to
61 Fishing aids
62 A person might hang one on a road
63 Subject of paintings by Corot and Manet
64 Montgomery of "The Young Lions"
65 Peru's ___ Trail
66 Colo. ___, Colo.

67 British smell
68 Skipjack and albacore
69 Montemezzi's "L'Amore ___ Tre Re"
70 Restaurateur Toots
71 Some fighters
72 Societies: Abbr.
73 Detergent factory, e.g.?
76 Rock Island and Reading: Abbr.
77 Depression at the mouth of a volcano
78 "Galaxy Quest" characters, in brief
79 Arrangement provider
82 Keyboard features
84 Wedding proposal?
88 Gin flavorer
89 Units in physics
90 "$100 per dozen plus shipping," e.g.?
94 ___ Lang of Smallville
96 Hoopster Gilmore
98 Second best
99 Place for hangings
101 Fr. firm
102 Annoys
105 Mobile homes?
106 Enthronement of a metalworker?
110 They're sometimes found on belts
111 Sleep disruption
112 ___ Reader (bimonthly magazine)
113 Ad in, e.g.
114 Titleholder
115 E-6 officers in the U.S.A.F.
116 Burn
117 Duff

DOWN

1 So-called "style moderne"
2 Press
3 O.K. to put in one's mouth
4 Retire
5 Harum-___ (reckless)
6 Dallas player, for short
7 Grp. with the old slogan "A deadline every minute"
8 Early Christian
9 The Golden Bears, briefly
10 Cuckoo bird
11 "It's digestible" sloganeer, once
12 Event won five straight times by Roger Federer
13 Pervading tone
14 Society: Abbr.
15 Red Cross, e.g.
16 Being forced into a smaller house, say?
17 Having an irregularly gnawed edge
18 Recap numbers
24 Former Australian P.M. Kevin
25 ___ the heart of
30 Comic Conan
32 Take for another year, say
33 Commercial suffix with Gator
34 Inflate
36 Batty
37 Hail, e.g.
38 Cheerios
40 "___ showtime!"
43 Is too much
44 Amsterdam in New York
45 Credentials

47 Latches
48 Little one
50 A drunk might be in one
51 ___ Nevada
53 Some sleepers
54 Party of nine
55 Family secret, perhaps
56 Windy City transportation inits.
57 Brougham, e.g.
58 Cast
59 Wet cement mixture
60 Passing reference in the "I Have a Dream" speech?
63 Goes off on one's own
65 The Beatles, once
66 Who sells seashells by the seashore
70 Rash
71 Classic Parker Brothers card game
73 Dances with spins
74 Tough tests
75 "Grand" backdrop for "Shane"
77 Gear tooth
79 Opposite number
80 Moreover
81 Outlaw's refuge
83 Thorny bush
85 "Hamlet" courtier
86 Watery
87 Work on a tan
88 Say "Th-th-th-that's all, folks," e.g.
90 Leaves without an answer
91 Intending
92 19th-century Swedish writer Esaias ___
93 Vicinity
94 Milk: Prefix

by Kelsey Blakley

95 It might be presented with a bow

97 Met again, as a legislature

100 It disappeared on Dec. 26, 1991

101 Alternative to Chuck

103 Word repeated in an "Animal House" chant

104 Corker

107 Lunar New Year

108 Travel plan: Abbr.

109 Off ___ tangent

6 LETTING GO OF

ACROSS

1 Spiderwoman?
8 Phony laugh
14 Possible barrier to romance
20 Dwells
21 Natural gas component
22 Wife of Alexander the Great
23 Diet?
25 Tea, e.g.
26 Plains Indian
27 Part of the Dept. of Justice
28 Wee creature
30 Sign on a British restroom door
31 Be very successful at fishing?
34 Site
36 Actor Paul of "American Graffiti"
37 Do a clerk's work at a morgue?
42 Unborn, after "in"
46 Cardinal from New York
48 Prussian pronoun
49 Something further?
50 Throw large bank notes around?
55 O
58 It begins "Forasmuch as many have taken in hand . . ."
59 What sisters often are
60 Net
62 ___ Dame
63 "___ mentioned . . ."
64 How albums may be stored
65 Beige
66 Conditional construct in programming
67 Take advantage of good Samaritans?
72 Desert homes
74 Amount in the back of a pickup, e.g.
75 Cloudless
76 Bunny man, for short
79 Bathroom fixture
80 Abbr. in many a party invitation
81 It may be broken on a ranch
83 Kind of bean
84 It may be raw
86 Forge some personal notes?
89 Director Lee
90 Edwards or Andrews: Abbr.
92 Whatchamacallit?
93 Breaking sports news, maybe
94 Outdo one's buddies?
98 Cloudless
102 #2 in a prosecutor's off.
103 Be a sadistic masseuse?
108 Without enough money
111 Coca-Cola brand
114 Wee, to a Scot
115 Anent
116 Dr. Seuss title character
118 Send for a special bridal accessory?
121 Breakout
122 Swank do
123 Chorus, e.g.
124 Thin in supply
125 Like many a Broadway play
126 One getting roasted or toasted

DOWN

1 Chile de ___ (hot pepper)
2 Lariat
3 ___ Martin, British sports car
4 Given a ticket
5 "Good" cholesterol, for short
6 Razz
7 Regard
8 ___-haw
9 Held off
10 Baba au ___
11 Overhead light?
12 Ali trainer Dundee
13 Some sports footwear
14 Word in the MGM logo
15 Owner of YouTube
16 Go over
17 Put on weight
18 Cadaver study: Abbr.
19 Mates
24 Tennis champ Mandlikova
29 Director's "start"
32 Garden ___
33 Statistics method for checking means
35 "Excuse me"
37 Heavy-handed measure
38 Next at bat
39 Faddish 1970s footwear
40 Eat up, so to speak
41 Film director Stanley
42 Where Bertrand Russell taught philosophy, for short
43 Some crosses
44 They're mushed
45 Itinerary abbr.
47 Many an anesthetic
51 Oscar winner Tom
52 Response to a shot, maybe
53 Too much
54 Gandhi garment
56 Figure out
57 Foldable furniture
61 Seek election to
64 Adams with the 1991 hit "Get Here"
65 Windup
66 One way to be trapped during winter
68 "Yeah, sure"
69 It may be set with candlelight
70 Relatively safe investment
71 Frontiersman Boone, informally
72 Award-winning British sitcom, to fans
73 Moon of Saturn
77 Brontë heroine
78 Unfading
80 Is suitable for
81 HVAC measure
82 Veg-O-Matic maker
83 500 initials
85 Needlefish
87 Abbr. in trig
88 Gang land
91 It helps support a canopy
95 ___ sauce
96 Camera settings
97 Like some minds and margins
99 Sot
100 Tangle up

by Paula Gamache and Ed Stein

101 Slowly
103 Georges who wrote "Life: A User's Manual"
104 Slowly
105 Animal or vegetable fat, e.g.
106 Volume unit
107 Play (around)
108 Steve Perry hit "__ Mine"
109 O.R. or E.R. site
110 Ocean menace
112 Peculiar: Prefix
113 Trillion: Prefix
117 Born as
119 Vietnamese holiday
120 Mrs. Romney

7   INFRACTIONS

ACROSS

1 It has eyes that can't see
5 Flips
13 Student of morality
20 Philippine money
21 Pacific strings
22 Fine word for libraries?
23 With 26-Across, like grandchildren
25 Beach bottles
26 See 23-Across
27 Deck out
28 Bad record part, for short
29 "For shame!"
30 Ancient parting place
33 With 44-Across, execute, in a way
36 Keen observer
40 Prefix with cycle
41 Pond fish
43 ___-d'Or, Québec
44 See 33-Across
45 With 50-Across, euphoric
48 Ankle bone
50 See 45-Across
51 Product with the old ad catchphrase "Mother, please, I'd rather do it myself!"
53 Faith that celebrates both Jesus and Muhammad
57 Superlatively strong
61 Initially
64 Scaredy-cat, maybe
65 Sacred music composer ___ Pärt
67 Trig inverse
68 County subdivision: Abbr.

71 With 77-Across, high-end retail chain
74 Neighbor of Bulg.
75 Botanical beards
77 See 71-Across
78 Grove
80 Political party that won 39 electoral votes in 1948
82 "Apparently"
86 Panache
87 They're fit for kings and queens
90 Poet who wrote "In the room the women come and go / Talking of Michelangelo"
91 What's left behind
94 With 103-Across, 1999 Shyamalan thriller
98 Part of AARP: Abbr.
101 Fury
102 ___ Records (old music label)
103 See 94-Across
104 What's left
105 With 112-Across, compromise
108 Later
111 Abbr. on many food labels
112 See 105-Across
113 Ancient Balkan region
115 Stinko
120 Like some interpretations
122 With 127-Across, classical work that's the source of the European Union's anthem
125 Dancer Duncan
126 Military depots
127 See 122-Across
128 They have scales

129 Gave, as a hot potato
130 Peter, e.g.

DOWN

1 Bind
2 Phnom ___
3 Possible candidate for rehab
4 Old Italian magistrate
5 Word with top or pop
6 Fine, in old slang
7 "1984" superpower
8 Blue-gray
9 Be fooled
10 Et ___ (and others)
11 "Star Trek: T.N.G." role
12 "The Mary Tyler Moore Show" Emmy winner
13 The West was part of it
14 Promises
15 Become fixed
16 The Rams of the N.C.A.A.
17 "Ditto!"
18 George Bush's chief of staff John
19 Person doing a practice run
24 Poetic "always"
31 Biblical suffix
32 Dr. ___
34 ___-garde
35 Neighbors of C notes
36 What letting off steam might result in
37 Operating without ___
38 Zigzagged
39 Trouser parts
42 ___ mission
46 New faces on bases

47 Brewer's vessel
48 Gherman ___, cosmonaut who was the second human to orbit the earth
49 Jobs for dentists
52 Venae ___
54 Musical with the song "Easy to Be Hard"
55 The Piazzale Michelangelo affords a view of it
56 Detail
58 R&B singer Hayes
59 Glacial formation
60 Part of A.B.S.: Abbr.
62 World capital once occupied by France
63 Fly off the handle
65 Flavor akin to fennel
66 Quickly accelerate
68 Iotas
69 Order in the court
70 Sprite
72 ___ same mind
73 Prefix with resort
76 Muted
79 Fisher with a grig
81 Agitated, after "in"
82 Beijing-to-Shanghai dir.
83 One from Germany
84 Nature's pillow?
85 Put back
88 And everything else, for short
89 Death personified, in ancient Greece
92 Colonial service
93 Colored parts
95 Bonelike
96 "Henry & June" role

by Tracy Gray

97 Outside: Prefix
98 2009 Hilary Swank biopic
99 Gender offender
100 Like a nasal membrane
102 Rescued damsel's cry

106 Others, in Oaxaca
107 Up
109 Cousin of rust
110 Korean money
114 Sleep stages
116 "Freedom ___ free"
117 ___ Lowry, children's writer

118 City in Sicily
119 Silhouette on many a yellow sign
121 Child-care author LeShan
123 Cat scanner?
124 "___ Beso"

A-V Club

ACROSS

1 Something you willingly part with?
7 Air Force college athlete
13 Calm
20 Tied up
21 Nervous
22 Fixes
23 Have, say
25 Record collection?
26 Protector of the dead, in Egyptian myth
27 As a result
28 Seek (out)
30 Easy run
31 Slowly
33 It runs down the neck
35 Title role for Kilmer and Costner
37 In accordance with
38 They're likely to blow
44 Keglers' org.
47 A state symbol
48 No laughing matter, e.g.
49 Savanna grazer
53 Insensitive
55 Turkeys
56 At a glance
58 "Friends" friend
59 Ridicules
60 Reciprocally
61 Bismarck-to-Grand Forks dir.
62 Some acting awards
63 Decidedly eligible, in a way
64 Invoice abbr.
65 Not seeing eye to eye
68 End of the main part of the Constitution

71 Flashed hand signal
72 Canadian Indian
73 Bit of a jam
74 "Either you do it ___ will"
75 Often-dried fruit
78 Get-rich-quick scheme?
79 Nix
82 Annual quartet
83 ___ Bornes (classic card game)
84 Certain link
85 10 kilogauss
86 Sister ___, 1920s-'30s evangelist
87 Noted ring family
88 Foreign one
89 Electrical pioneer
94 Crib cry
97 Mex. women
98 Bit of a jam
99 Valuable violin
103 "Zip-___-Doo-Dah"
105 Two-finger keyboard shortcut in Windows
109 Itinerary info
111 "Love ___"
112 Old country name from the Portuguese for "beautiful"
114 Common houseplant with colorful blooms
117 Competitor at a hippodrome
118 Speaker of the line "He thinks too much: such men are dangerous"
119 Store, as corn
120 Kind of organ or overload
121 Some of them are marching
122 Got in the end

DOWN

1 In-box contents
2 Pickle
3 Botulin, e.g.
4 Record label for the Kinks and Pink
5 Abbr. to the left of a number
6 Falco of "The Sopranos"
7 Pardoned
8 Tom, Dick or Harry
9 Part of the Pentateuch: Abbr.
10 Alphabet quartet
11 No Mr. Nice Guy
12 Wyo. neighbor
13 Like Quito and La Paz
14 Place to see una ópera
15 Wager
16 Bibliographical abbr.
17 Greek with a storied life
18 Brunch serving
19 Word often preceded by poly-
24 Multitudes
29 Bawl out
32 Kind of surprise
34 Shiver-inducing stare
36 Shakespeare contemporary
39 Steadfast
40 Locker rooms often have them
41 Romeo's "two blushing pilgrims"
42 Bldg. directory listings
43 Microchannel
44 Narc's find
45 Dickensian cry
46 Some succulents
50 Brandy, for one
51 1920s Olympic track gold medalist Paavo ___

52 Tooth: Prefix
54 Yakutsk's river
55 Parry
56 Newsman Roger
57 Bric-a-___
59 Intense hankering
60 Setup, of a sort
62 Bakery display
63 Tub-thump
65 Sailor's cry
66 Portable home
67 Desktop feature
68 They come out of the head
69 One of Egypt's plagues
70 Arrow shooter
73 Like a shoe
76 Cancún, por ejemplo
77 Barbecue blocks
78 Portray
79 Go easily (through)
80 Hi-tech special effects
81 French ___
83 Actress Farrow
84 "Just for the taste of it" or "Just do it"
86 ___ U.S. atty.
87 Embodiments
90 Golf pencil's lack
91 It might go up via an escalator
92 Like some garages
93 No more than
94 Drifts
95 Not just esteem
96 "Great blue" creature
100 On again
101 Singer with the multiplatinum albums "19" and "21"
102 Was sweet (on)
104 CPR pros
106 Crunchy munchie

by Alex Vratsanos

107 Beginning to cry?
108 Born's partner
110 Cinematographer Nykvist
113 Oklahoma Indian
115 Sussex suffix
116 Like Haydn's Symphony No. 12 or 29

ACROSS

1 One waiting in France
7 "Who's there?" response
12 Hank Aaron led the N.L. in them four times
16 British pols
19 Mark who won the 1998 Masters
20 Alternative energy option
21 ". . . there ___ square"
22 Maximum
23 Slogan for medical marijuana activists?
26 Portuguese "she"
27 Tattoos, slangily
28 More than a quarter of academic circles?
29 Alias
30 "No surprise to me"
32 Like unworn tires
36 Persians who protect their feet?
40 Took a break around one, say
42 Was halting
43 Plant, of a sort
44 Author
45 Not straight
48 "___ Beso" (Paul Anka hit)
49 Big twit?
50 Entitlement to cross the stream first?
54 Conductor Toscanini
56 Singer DiFranco
57 Start of a "White Album" title
58 Pod-based entity
59 People who avoid social networking, maybe
63 Mixologist's measure
65 My ___, Vietnam
66 It was published four years before "Moby-Dick"
68 "Snowy" bird
69 "If you can't behave on this tour, I swear you'll be sorry!"?
75 Forerunner of euchre
76 Smack
77 ___ culpa
78 State for which a Springsteen album is named: Abbr.
79 Hunt's co-star on "Mad About You"
81 Error indicator
82 Largest campus of Long Island Univ.
85 The title of this puzzle, e.g.
86 One + one?
88 Big part of the dairy business?
90 Like much of Pindar's work
93 [Smack!]
94 Revolver
95 Tragic E.R. status
96 Cartoon pet of note
97 Melodic
99 Play double Dutch, say
104 Lost subject of a hit Beatles song?
108 Working as a store clerk
109 Disney princess
110 Part of a newspaper: Abbr.
111 Jobs creation
113 OBs, e.g.
114 Vietnam Veterans Memorial designer
115 Clothing-free version of the national pastime?
122 Dark meat piece
123 Feminine suffix
124 Pitch
125 Simplified language form
126 Pompous person
127 "I'll have what ___ having"
128 Itching
129 City near Clearwater, informally

DOWN

1 Chaperon
2 Supreme Egyptian god
3 Offended the nose
4 "Dog"
5 Choice words?
6 "I don't think so"
7 Part of a chain, maybe
8 Studio sign
9 Trudge through wet snow, say
10 Dallas pro baller
11 "We'll teach you to drink deep ___ you depart": Hamlet
12 "Tommy," e.g.
13 Most inclusive
14 It has many servers
15 "___ I care!"
16 Famously temperamental court figure
17 Stout alternative
18 Salmon, at times
24 Powered in either of two ways
25 Chicago mayor Emanuel
31 World leader beginning December 2011
33 "Kubla Khan" river
34 On account of
35 Make magnificent
37 French "she"
38 Take a load off
39 Two-time N.L. batting champ Lefty
41 Obama's birthplace
46 Whit
47 Hardly sharp
50 Josh of "How I Met Your Mother"
51 Where to conform, per an expression
52 Jason who's a five-time baseball All-Star
53 Deception
54 Ages and ages
55 Director Nicolas
58 Car in "Gone in 60 Seconds"
60 City down the lake from Buffalo, N.Y.
61 Oklahoma state tree
62 "Tristram Shandy" novelist
64 Something you might tap in
67 Mayo, e.g.
70 Projectionist's unit
71 Scrape
72 Drives
73 Big suits
74 Entered slowly
80 Steel support for concrete
81 People with reservations in Florida
83 Minute
84 Some Camaro roofs
87 Swollen, as veins
88 Dynasty for Confucius
89 ___ avis
90 Big maker of smoothies and energy bars
91 Accounts with keys?

by Ben Tausig

92 Extra ones might be dramatic
94 News Corp. paper
98 Look like a creep?
100 Grammy-winning Radiohead album of 2000
101 Prime years for rocking?
102 Consent form
103 Dead Sea Scrolls writer
105 Cary of "Robin Hood: Men in Tights"
106 Made whoopee
107 Some blades
112 With a sure hand
116 "You mean . . . what?"
117 Surveillance org.
118 "Star Trek: Voyager" airer
119 D.J.'s purchases
120 Tanked
121 Economic stat

ACROSS

1 Course preparer
5 Close shave
11 John Lennon song that ends "I love you, yeah, yeah, now and forever"
16 Deck (out)
19 Tops
20 Like some church matters
21 Monster slain by Hercules
22 Lead-in to meter
23 Chocolat, say?
26 Shorten, with "off"
27 In the limelight
28 HBO competitor
29 Emphatic denial
31 Home to the Minutemen, informally
33 When repeated, an old New Orleans tune
35 Word repeated four times in the last line of Shakespeare's "All the world's a stage" speech
36 Polyester fabric
39 Macho drag queen?
46 Shield border
47 Make, as a copy of a CD
48 Stop on a line
49 Dockworkers' org.
50 Like literary classics?
54 Call to the bar?
56 Weirdo
57 Earth goddess
58 Bobby who sang "Take Good Care of My Baby"
60 Hall-of-Fame pitcher Joss
61 Unsurprisingly
63 Skinny?
65 Discreet signal
68 Like a centaur?
70 "Don't let that youngster get off without paying!"?
75 Rural setting
76 Had way too much of
78 Words from a con man
79 Given a number, maybe
83 Flushed
84 Baseball's strikeout king
85 Go (for)
86 Unbiased account?
89 Announcement made by a transplant surgeon, perhaps?
92 British isle
93 Allan-___ (figure in the Robin Hood legend)
95 Omelette ingredient
96 Middling grades
97 Stigmatize a "great" king?
100 Hankering
102 Salon selection
103 Twin killings, on a diamond: Abbr.
104 Went off course
106 Part of the inn crowd?
110 Access requirement, maybe
114 Old-fashioned ingredient
118 Big collection agcy.
119 Two reasons to avoid a dog kennel?
122 Apt name for a 1-Across?
123 Unenthusiastic
124 Maximum
125 Bar mixer
126 Rx amt.
127 Wonderland message
128 "Are you kidding me?"
129 Ocho minus cinco

DOWN

1 Roman censor
2 Game ender, at times
3 Chemical endings
4 Given prominence
5 "A diamond is forever," e.g.
6 Saint-Germain-des-Prés sights
7 Ohio or Colorado: Abbr.
8 Some tennis winners
9 Head line?
10 Lanchester on the screen
11 Little genius
12 Olive ___
13 Mid 16th-century year
14 God with a shield
15 Launch party?
16 Was duplicitous
17 Former co-host of "The View"
18 Lose it
24 ___-shanter
25 Of no interest
30 See 32-Down: Abbr.
32 Native of 30-Down
34 It's solid yellow
36 Take a peke?
37 Excitement
38 Debate ender
40 Do more than threaten, say
41 Pilgrim
42 Anesthetized
43 Tore
44 Like some dorms
45 Title town of a Longfellow poem
51 Chihuahua drink
52 Tandoor-baked bread
53 Where heroes are made
55 Elaine of "Seinfeld"
59 Represented
62 Outlaw Belle who is said to have harbored Jesse James
63 Many a Little League coach
64 River to the Rhône
66 When many German steins are lifted
67 They get bigger when you smile
69 Hit the runway
71 Astronomical distance: Abbr.
72 Refrain syllables
73 Easter activity
74 Abhor
77 Actor Alain
80 Barely
81 "I did it!"
82 It's grounded every Saturday
84 Prepare, as some Mexican-style beans
86 Aesop, notably
87 Places for gates
88 "That makes sense"
90 Saturn S.U.V.
91 Conclusive trial
94 Lose it
98 Holiday quaff
99 Not worth ___
100 Singer of the 1958 #1 hit "It's Only Make Believe"
101 The first "H" in Hanukkah

by Alan Arbesfeld

105 Former TV judge
107 Suffix with cigar
108 Cousin of an ostrich
109 Back-to-sch. time
111 Growl
112 Sitting on one's hands

113 Simba's mate
115 ___ effort
116 Tactless
117 Mmes., over the border
120 Actor Alastair
121 Cambodia's Lon ___

ACROSS

1 Entourage, in slang
6 Hide pokers
10 *Patriot Caesar Rodney on horseback*
14 Person running the show
18 "___ Majesty's Secret Service"
19 *The Great Lakes*
20 Parallel, e.g.
21 "It's the Hard-Knock Life" musical
23 Some dabblers
24 Snake predators named for their calls
27 *Scissor-tailed flycatcher with wildflowers*
28 D-backs, e.g.
29 P.R. problem
30 Beach lotion abbr.
31 Ones getting away
34 Battery type
37 Zales rival
38 Reduce to a symbol
40 Hosiery shade
41 Irons, in Paris
42 "The Goodbye Kiss" author Massimo
44 Much-quoted line from Edgar in "King Lear"
48 Royal title that means "great house"
49 Common sweetener
50 Go by
53 Lacking rhyme or reason
54 Versatile delivery vehicles
55 Outlets in a chemistry lab
56 Island province of the Roman Empire
58 Nonauthoritarian
59 *Covered wagon next to Chimney Rock*
63 Concerning
64 United in purpose
66 *Rice stalks, a diamond and a mallard*
67 Old comic book cowboy
69 Eager reporter
71 Venture to postulate
72 Nassau residents
74 "Lose Yourself" rapper
79 The Perfesser's nephew in the comic strip "Shoe"
80 Party hat?
81 Beauty contest since 1952
82 Civil defense devices
84 Help in a bind
85 Simpson girl
87 Author Jorge
88 Sui ___
89 With 95-Down, "The Royal Family of Broadway" star, 1930
90 Postcard in a barrel, perhaps
91 Expose
94 Old French coin
97 Tennis's Stefan
99 Result of falling banks?
100 *Statehouse dome*
101 French Baroque artist who painted "The Fortune Teller"
106 "Get Smart" robot
107 Film composer Morricone
108 110-Across set in Egypt
109 *Abraham Lincoln*
110 See 108-Across
111 Fair sight
112 *Racehorse in front of the Federal Hill mansion*
113 "A madness most discreet," per Romeo
114 Not flabby

DOWN

1 "Wanderings: Chaim ___ Story of the Jews"
2 Quarter-mile, for many tracks
3 Noted exile of 1979
4 Home to the National Voting Rights Museum
5 Hosp. zones
6 "Thanks ___!"
7 Father of the Blues
8 Outgrowth from the base of a grass blade
9 Birth control pioneer Margaret
10 Handlers of brats
11 Stretched out
12 Designer Vera
13 Island protector
14 Islamic analogue of kosher
15 Like many music reissues
16 Military jacket with a furry hood
17 What a poor listener may have
22 Athletic awards since 1993
25 Some baseball scores: Abbr.
26 Salts
31 Inter
32 Neighbor of Poland: Abbr.
33 ET carrier
34 ___ belli (war-provoking act)
35 Transition point
36 Prefix with center
39 *Rocky Mountains*
40 Arctic ___ (pole-to-pole migrator)
41 Part of many a freight train
42 E.M.T. application
43 Bingo alternative?
44 Saint in a Sir Walter Scott title
45 "___ my garment and my mantle": Ezra 9:3
46 *"Commonwealth" statue and a keystone*
47 Too
49 Do dos, say
51 Goes across
52 "Cómo ___?"
54 Like the scent of many cleaners
55 Homo, for one
57 Area that's frequently swept?
58 "Lorna ___"
59 Uncool types
60 Spring ___
61 Severely parched
62 Part of Russia next to Finland
64 Like the eastern part of Russia
65 Herring varieties
68 Belgian river
69 *Old Man of the Mountain rock formation*
70 Winter solvent
72 Villain
73 "I ___ bored!"
75 *Lewis and Clark and the Gateway Arch*

by Byron Walden

76 Greenhouse workers
77 Sinuous character
78 ___ West
80 Fabulist
81 Word repeated before "tekel" in biblical writing on the wall
83 Billing fig.
84 Race, as an engine
85 Lord or vassal
86 Move toward the middle
88 "Boris ___"
90 Cereal killer?
91 Suffix with form
92 Kind of farming that doesn't disturb the soil
93 "Gangsta's Paradise" rapper
95 See 89-Across
96 Like zombies
98 Ireland
99 Unreliable
100 "I want my ___!" (old advertising catchphrase)
102 Benefit
103 Force
104 Cabinet dept. since 1979
105 Go up
106 Scorching

ACROSS

1 Pages (through)
6 Moon shots?
11 Lead-ins to many YouTube videos
14 Sunset color
19 Maker of Reynolds Wrap
20 Film composer Morricone
21 A fire sign
22 Saint Clare of Assisi's sister
23 WARNING: Suspension system prone to failure
26 Company that owns Lands' End
27 Tea flavoring
28 Gershwin title character
29 WARNING: May contain Greeks
31 High-precision rifle user
33 Its first car was the Model AA
35 Well-connected industrialists?
36 Generally preferred work shift
37 John
38 Raring to go
40 They get punched out
43 "The Ballad of ___," 1967 comedy/western
45 Part of L.A.P.D.
46 Litter member
49 Function
50 WARNING: Possible heart-related side effects
54 1966 Florentine flooder
55 Musandam Peninsula nation
56 Big-box store
57 Single-masted boat
58 Uncorks
59 Proves false
61 Crime film centerpiece
62 Very tame tom
63 Avoided bogey
64 Picket line?
65 Bordeaux grape
66 Silently says "So what?"
67 Furniture purchase
68 Rent
70 Newswoman Roberts
71 Source of the word "bandanna"
72 Saloon singer Sylvia
73 Pods often pickled
74 Foot, e.g.
75 WARNING: Cutting tool required
77 Tour de force
78 Entertainment center location
79 Unrefined
80 ___ United (English football club)
81 Perplex
82 Company whose ads have "Peanuts" characters
86 Not be entirely independent
87 Japanese kana character
88 Big name in suits
91 ___ Creed (statement of religious beliefs)
93 Gliding dance step
96 WARNING: Do not open
98 Nettle
100 Completely cover
102 "The Addams Family" actor John
103 WARNING: Effects on children unknown
106 Ending with farm or home
107 Nothing but
108 Olympic group?
109 "Rubber Duckie" singer
110 Thomas of stage and screen
111 Mens ___
112 Biofuel source
113 Supplement

DOWN

1 Old naval punishment
2 Actor Cary
3 Symbol used to mark England's National Trails
4 WARNING: May cause damnation if swallowed
5 Unfortunate
6 Consult, with "to"
7 Wraps up
8 1956 Ingrid Bergman/Yul Brynner film
9 Wheel part
10 Like used fire irons
11 Earmarks
12 Entertain a party, in a way
13 1998 home run race participant
14 Approach clubs
15 Antediluvian
16 Strip of weapons
17 Minister's reading
18 City that hosts the world's biggest annual game fair
24 Comply with
25 Seasonal yield
30 At all, in dialect
32 ___ de deux
34 "Ars Amatoria" writer
37 Canters leisurely
39 Sound heard at equestrian events
40 Critter with a lot of teeth
41 Cache for cash, say
42 Oscar winner for "Little Miss Sunshine"
43 Made a misleading move, in football
44 Required
46 Like Spam
47 Grotesque
48 Blog entry
50 Names
51 "It's the stupidest tea-party I ever was at in all my life!" speaker
52 Headed heavenward
53 Floorboard problem
54 WARNING: Improper use could lead to jealousy, treachery and/or war
58 They're sometimes seen in banks
60 Compulsion
61 Fictional friend of Peter the goatherd
62 Smallest
64 Charitable creation
65 Notes
66 Certain missile
67 Officer's title
68 "Bewitched" regular Paul
69 Home to many John Constable works, with "the"
71 Complain loudly
72 Really ridiculing
75 Gainesville athlete
76 Attention-getting sign

by Patrick Berry

79 ___ Beach (California surfing mecca)
81 "I suspected as much!"
82 Near the center
83 Shoe part
84 Part of a calf
85 Future C.P.A.'s study
87 Special creator?
88 Muscle woe
89 Food in many shapes
90 Cross the doorsill
92 Actor without lines
93 About to happen
94 Reliable
95 Grammy-winning Weird Al Yankovic song
97 In the distance
99 "Young Frankenstein" role
101 Kojak's first name
104 Afflict
105 Biblical "indeed"

GETTING AROUND

ACROSS

1 Benedictine monk who founded Scholasticism
7 Fire
11 Initial request?
15 One of three in Toyota's logo
19 Lunchtime errand
20 Have an ___ grind
21 What a koala really isn't
22 Horseplay?
23 *Ready for the present?
25 *Floatation device
27 Pennsylvania city or county
28 Blocks
30 Hockey feint
31 Call from a crow's nest
32 Sit on it
33 Chimera, e.g.
34 They're seen but not recognized
36 Bit of fallout
38 ___ populi
39 Grievances
40 Ring around the collar?
43 Vessel commanded by J.F.K.
47 *Brushback pitch
51 *All-in-one
53 Lot to take in
54 Soulful Baker
55 "Yeah, right"
56 Bub
58 ___ Martin Cognac
59 Pickup capacity, maybe
61 Bit to split
64 Wife of Uranus
66 *Animal that gives birth to identical quadruplets

72 Don't fess up to
73 Kind of counter
74 "Excalibur" role
75 Protest singer Phil
79 Comical Charlotte
80 South Pacific capital
82 Silent goodbyes
84 Cry of delight popularized by Homer Simpson
86 *Saturn and others
90 *Contents of a chest?
93 Heated patch
94 Broken off
95 Maker of watches and calculators
96 Signs off on
97 Unlock, poetically
98 "Jabberwocky" starter
99 Slack-jawed
102 Title acquired the moment someone is born?
106 $7x - 6 = 2x^2$ subj.
108 Five-spots
110 Salon supply
112 Curbside buys
113 *Surfaced, in a way
116 *Be repetitive . . . or what parts of the answers to the starred clues do?
118 Lipstick print, maybe
119 Co-worker of Clark
120 Alternatively
121 It's got chops
122 Like some praises
123 Start to matter?
124 Keeps the nest warm
125 Narcissus, e.g.

DOWN

1 Get riled up
2 Afrique ___
3 World capital that's also a girl's name
4 Embark (on)
5 "Ben-Hur" novelist Wallace
6 Styx song with some Japanese lyrics
7 Frank with the album "Sheik Yerbouti"
8 Nationals, before they were Nationals
9 Big blast, informally
10 Rock band composition?
11 Diamond stat
12 Party for departing parties
13 Redgrave of "Atonement"
14 Nursery school, briefly
15 Decide (to)
16 Deign
17 Duke of ___ (noble Spanish title since 1472)
18 Big name in cinemas
24 Tiptop
26 Lots and plots
29 Hush Puppies material
35 Oats, e.g.
37 ___-toothed
38 Cleared out
39 Recycling holder
41 Gentrification target, maybe
42 Nonsense word repeated before "oxen free"
43 Antidrug ad, e.g., briefly

44 Half a dovetail joint
45 Shrovetide pancakes
46 Repeatedly
47 "___ open!"
48 Greek water nymph
49 Searched (through)
50 Be a union buster?
52 Repeating part of "Hey Jude"
56 ___ Grand
57 TripTik, e.g.
60 "A Midsummer Night's Dream" fairy king
62 Uplifting piece
63 Spanish wine
65 High conflicts
67 TV scientist Bill
68 Gain maturity
69 Grassy plain
70 Add spring to, with "up"
71 "You're ___ talk!"
75 Boo-boo
76 Mass. neighbor
77 Cookout item
78 Ones you can count on?
81 Fingers
83 Job application fig.
85 No walk in the park
86 Parks with no intention of moving
87 Dander
88 South Vietnam's first president ___ Dinh Diem
89 Have a crush on, in middle school lingo
91 Responded to, as a tip
92 Something to try
96 Grp. that includes Ecuador and Venezuela

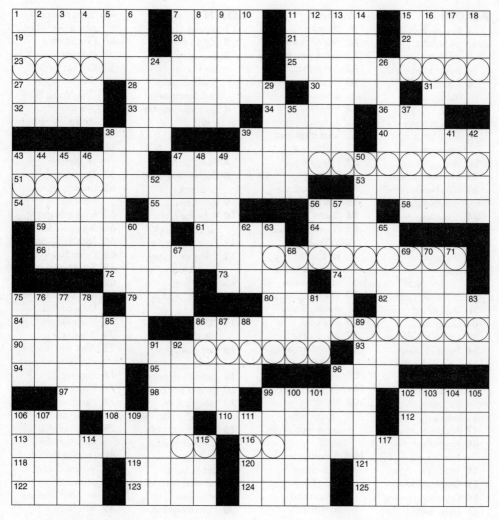

by Xan Vongsathorn

PLAYABLE

ACROSS

1 Grp. with an alphabet
5 Message from police HQ
8 It makes bubbly bubbly
13 Tar
17 Eastern nurse
18 Brooklyn, e.g., informally
20 Hoi ___
21 Mammy's place
22 Falter while imitating Jay-Z?
24 Something thrown in "West Side Story"?
26 Underworld deity
27 "Is that clear?"
29 Dickensian setting
30 Trick-taking game
31 Like pumice
33 Game-ending cry
34 See 107-Down
36 Sing high notes?
42 1970s exile
45 Noted 2011 TV retiree, popularly
47 Reduce marks?
48 Kind of column
49 Nesting site
50 Wall Street type
52 Develops slowly
54 Cry upon arriving at an earthquake site?
58 In a frenzy
59 Dines on
60 X, on campuses
61 Bridge locale
62 It may follow "forever and ever"
63 Didn't conceal one's smugness
67 Region of 70-Across for which a type of wool is named

69 Animal stomach
70 See 67-Across
72 Suffix with ball
73 "All systems go"
76 Tuition and others
77 What the turnover-prone football player had?
82 Fountain location
84 El Pacífico, e.g.
85 Ball-shaped part
86 "Hmm . . ."
87 Knock for ___
90 W.W. I battle locale
91 A bad one may contain holes
92 Shenanigans at the royal court?
95 Not a lot
97 Mil. leader
98 Points in the right direction
100 Ball partner
104 Begin a tour
108 He wrote "Knowledge is the food of the soul"
109 Senescence
110 Nickname for a hard-to-understand monarch?
114 Lens cover for a large telescope?
116 Classical bow wielder
117 Eats up
118 Outer: Prefix
119 Blood rival
120 Oxford profs
121 Feature of grocery purchases, often
122 Coral, e.g.
123 Numbers game

DOWN

1 Bigwig
2 Put a smile on
3 Source of the words "mulligatawny" and "catamaran"
4 "Are you kidding me?!"
5 Fives
6 ___ favor
7 Fort ___, N.C.
8 Source of a viral outbreak
9 American ___
10 Robe for one tending a flock
11 Fa-la connector
12 Telephone system connectors
13 Taser, say
14 Airport security item
15 "Giovanna d'___" (Verdi opera)
16 German train track
19 Dentist's directive
20 Record listing
23 Neighbor of Poland: Abbr.
25 The Atlantic, in a common phrase
28 Quick preview
31 Subject of Newton's first law of motion
32 Canon product, for short
33 "Have a look!"
35 Where pieces are put together?
37 Most holes in one
38 Nomad
39 Baseball's Justin or B. J.
40 Many a Silicon Valley hiree
41 Radical '60s org.
42 Genesis son
43 "Ver-r-ry funny!"

44 Some Monopoly properties: Abbr.
46 Exasperated outburst
51 Cry just before disaster strikes
53 "The Magic Flute" protagonist
55 Mercedes-Benz luxury line
56 ___ choy (Chinese vegetable)
57 Troop grp.
62 Lovingly, to a musician
63 Fairy tale girl
64 Big game fish
65 That, in Tijuana
66 Fiesta bowl?
68 Sex appeal
69 A tabloid keeps tabs on one
71 G.I.'s address
73 Genesis son
74 Promise, e.g.
75 Alter ego who carries a notepad
76 Burkina ___
77 Sorrow
78 Arctic waters, on historical maps
79 Mythical elixir of forgetfulness
80 Long-jawed fish
81 Where cheap seats are in a baseball stadium
82 Part of r.p.m.: Abbr.
83 Useful husband, say
88 Spanish bear
89 Befuddle
93 Nobel Prize subj.
94 "Frasier" character
96 Outdoor promenade
99 iPod ___
101 Brooch feature, maybe

by Kyle T. Dolan

ACROSS

1 Went easy on
7 Went 90, say
11 Pop's relative?
15 Nurse
18 18th-century Russian emperor
20 "___ homo"
21 Media executive Bob
22 Mobile info organizer
23 Every chemical element has one
25 Stalks in a soup kitchen
27 "Tough-actin'" medication
28 Ginger cookie
30 Eye salaciously
31 Bare
32 2012 Mark Wahlberg comedy
34 Load to bear
36 Present from birth
37 Antlered animal
38 Goggled
40 Worrisome Arctic and Antarctic developments
42 ___ anglais (English horn)
43 Congratulations indicator
45 Have loans
46 Sue Grafton's "___ for Outlaw"
47 Popular Caribbean destination, informally
51 "___ 1138" (1971 sci-fi film)
53 Search with a fine-tooth comb
55 Realm
56 Sommelier's pick
59 Drapery adornments
63 Backup procedure
64 Chorus line leader?
65 Seeing someone socially
67 Fan sound
68 Cost
69 Conservationist's catchphrase
71 Slope
73 Pose
74 Falls for married women?
76 Roker and Pacino
77 Supermarket datum
78 To date
80 Like puns among all forms of humor, it's said
82 In the arms of Morpheus
83 Place
85 ___ Diego
86 Harangues
88 Arm of the U.S. Cong.
89 Big tippler
91 Financial page abbr.
93 Some nods
94 Arborist's catchphrase
98 Gemini and Virgo
100 Exchange purchase: Abbr.
103 Dutch exports
104 Sight on an Alaskan cruise
106 Animal pouch
107 Transnational cash
109 Farm machines
110 N.Y.C. home of van Gogh
112 Cause panic in a theater, perhaps
114 Seltzer bottle capacity
117 Environmentalist's catchphrase
119 Hubbub
120 Neighbor of Sask.
121 Band with a juiced-up name?
122 Tokenish
123 Vacation acquisition, maybe
124 Edible root
125 ___ Hashana
126 Flirtatious lot

DOWN

1 Tiffs
2 Tiny
3 Like much avant-garde music
4 Comment
5 Dampier of the N.B.A.
6 Webster's ref.
7 Theological inst.
8 Potential landfill pollutants, for short
9 Car opener?
10 Presidential middle name
11 Signature piece?
12 Century, say
13 Nervous ___
14 Atmospheric worries
15 Pasta shapes
16 Brainstorm
17 Wallops
19 Question to a museum visitor
24 California's Santa ___ Mountains
26 "Girl With a Hoop" and "The Umbrellas"
29 "The Last Don" author
33 Bank statement abbr.
35 Farm females
38 45th American vice president
39 Processed material
41 Fruity drinks
42 Global warming calculation whose shape is suggested by connecting 14 squares in this puzzle in a closed loop based on the appropriate 23-Across
44 Kind of society that is careless of the environment
47 Éclat
48 1998 Alanis Morissette hit
49 Out of line?
50 Beanpole
52 Woman warrior
54 Nibble for Dobbin
55 Jack who's a picky eater
57 Montreal suburb
58 Farewells
60 Cleared
61 Soup servers
62 Followers
64 Like pre-1917 Russia
66 Shoulder muscles, in gym-speak
70 Love personified
72 Antagonize
75 ___ in igloo
79 Droopy-eared pet
81 Tolkien forest creatures
82 Scroll holders
84 One frequently being waved at
87 Worry
88 Part of the Spanish Armada
90 Semester, e.g.
92 Put down
94 Mosquito fleet vessel
95 Angola's capital
96 "Law & Order" figure: Abbr.
97 Green vehicle

by Elizabeth C. Gorski

99 Marvin who sang "Let's Get It On"
100 Follow-up letters?
101 Father, Son and Holy Spirit
102 Seoul soul
105 Old brand whose logo featured a torch
107 Varnish ingredient
108 Unloads
111 English connections
113 Ukrainian city, formerly
115 Bud holder
116 "King Kong" studio
118 Educ. facility

ACROSS

1 Plays a siren
7 Gold Coast, today
12 Meander
16 It's a plus in a bank acct.
19 Noted landing site
20 Player of the younger Cunningham on "Happy Days"
21 Mach3 predecessor
22 "Yes, I'm a Witch" singer, 1992
23 ___ Bay, 1898 battle site
24 Deliver
26 They push things
27 File folder, e.g.
28 President who was 65-Across (1872)
30 Heads up
33 Capital of Denmark?
34 Come to naught
35 Fermented honey drink
36 Where kips are cash
37 Observe, in the Bible
39 Presidential daughter who was 65-Across (1998)
41 First National Leaguer with 500 home runs
42 Act out
43 Staff
44 Some slippers
45 Novelist who was 65-Across (1804)
52 Early computer
53 Yevtushenko's "Babi ___"
54 Red Cross supply
55 Word with black or pack
58 "The Haj" author
61 Long way to go?

63 Bill provider
64 ___ Valley, 2002 Winter Olympics venue
65 See 28-, 39-, 45-, 83-, 95- and 107-Across
71 Plenty
72 Sri Lankan export
73 Film canine
74 "This is dedicated to the ___ love"
75 Wordsworth's "solitary Tree"
76 Interpret
78 Article in Der Spiegel
79 Sweater style
83 Team owner who was 65-Across (1930)
89 Have ___ one's words
92 Set-___
93 Sierra Nevada, e.g.
94 Building block, of sorts
95 Columnist who was 65-Across (1918)
99 Powerful blows
101 Attire usually worn with slippers
102 "Unfaithful" co-star, 2002
103 The final Mrs. Chaplin
104 Economic stat.
105 Initially
107 Literary critic who was 65-Across (1905)
111 Michigan college
112 When sung five times, an ABBA hit
113 Electrical impulse conductor in the body
114 Riffraff
117 D.C. player

118 Knightwear?
119 Maytag acquisition of 2001
120 And others, in a footnote
121 Most of a figure eight
122 Coolers
123 Water balloon sound
124 Out

DOWN

1 Tufted topper
2 Chapter
3 Some large tubes
4 They might be inflated
5 Part of Tennyson's "crooked hands"
6 Pinch-hits (for)
7 Former financing inits.
8 Wannabe surfers
9 Cove, e.g.
10 Sucker-like
11 Years at the Vatican
12 Wily sort
13 10th-century Holy Roman emperor
14 Iris part
15 Clayey deposit
16 Conclude negotiations successfully
17 Chess closing
18 Impersonated
25 Bundles of joy, so to speak
29 Infuse
30 "Home ___"
31 Lord of the Flies
32 Convoy component
38 Wide shoe spec
39 Wide-open mouth
40 Every, in an Rx

42 Lens used for close-ups
43 New World monkeys
46 Frequent
47 Singer Lovett
48 City on the slopes of Mount Carmel
49 What a thermometer measures
50 Garden chemical brand
51 One of the Estevez brothers
55 French game
56 Dish that may be smoked
57 Adjudge
59 Prelim
60 Range rover
62 Certain belly button
64 Magic lamp figure
65 Seabiscuit, for one
66 Crowd shout
67 Ticket datum
68 Den ___, Nederland
69 Eastern royal
70 What a thermometer may measure
77 Get off at a station
80 Like adversity, one hopes
81 Mint products
82 Sausage topper
83 Ancient Greek anatomist
84 Seventh chapter
85 "I'll send an ___ to the world" (Police lyric)
86 Bird's org.
87 Kind of test
88 Interstate sign

by Dan Schoenholz

89 "Good night, and good luck," e.g.
90 Six Nations tribe
91 Becomes established
96 Like some mutual funds
97 West of Nashville
98 Registers
99 Air show maneuver
100 Actress Ryder
101 Kettledrum
104 Opposite of break apart
106 High-heels alternatives
108 Anarchist Goldman
109 Meadowlands
110 Punkie
115 "The dog ate my homework," probably
116 Literary inits.

MAKE THE CHANGE

ACROSS

1 Hose shape
5 Building blocks
11 "The Office" woman
14 QB feats
17 Years in old Rome
18 Capital city formerly behind the Iron Curtain
19 Nephew of Cain
21 "Let's Get Lost" singer Baker
22 So happy you can't see straight?
25 Where to enter the theater, usually
26 Where "it's fun to stay" in a 1978 hit
27 Gleamed
28 Deserving praise
30 "Sk8er ___," 2002 top 10 hit
31 Acid
34 Argument about a fork-tailed bird?
36 Apt
39 Spend the night
40 Arizona senator Jon
41 It represents a 0 or 1
42 Trendy antioxidant berry
43 "Yeah, right"
45 Org. full of big shots?
47 Calpurnia's dream in "Julius Caesar" and others
49 Bear's cry
50 Circle above the airport?
55 Manager with four World Series titles
57 Very clumsy person, in slang
58 Subject of the 19th, 24th and 26th Amendments
62 Willing to do
65 TWA competitor
67 See 77-Across
69 Optima maker
70 Making one's way down the corporate ladder?
76 [This ticks me off]
77 With 67-Across, "That's not true!"
78 Relative of a harrumph
79 Not flat, say
80 One of two for four
82 Slalom obstacle
85 Passing
88 Breed hatred in?
91 It's seen on many roadside signs
95 When the witches in "Macbeth" say "Double, double toil and trouble"
98 "Sure thing"
99 ___ beetle
100 Eternally
101 Canterbury can
102 Org. trying to clear the air?
105 Ed Wood player in "Ed Wood"
108 Squad cars
110 Woman who's the very best at saying no?
114 Part of TBS: Abbr.
115 Pal of Pooh
116 Modern marketplace
117 Like the verbs "come" and "go": Abbr.
119 "Baseball Tonight" broadcaster
121 Bulldogs
122 Really enjoy giving specifics?
127 Art ___
128 Alexander Graham Bell, by birth
129 Get ready for a bomb, say
130 Corona garnish
131 Require (of)
132 "Your point being . . . ?"
133 Some close-ups
134 Take too much of, briefly

DOWN

1 It might be caught in the rain
2 Unrepeated
3 Hostile
4 Nickname for the Philadelphia Eagles' stadium, with "the"
5 Downed
6 Arranged, as the hair
7 Partners of scepters
8 Indiana political family
9 Gives support to
10 Spotted in the vicinity of
11 Eastern Canadian prov.
12 White, informally
13 Hair line?
14 Old Yankee nickname
15 Given a hand
16 Some are mean
20 Home office site
21 Curmudgeon
23 Painter portrayed by Adrien Brody in "Midnight in Paris"
24 Stanford of Stanford University
29 Actor Alain
30 Predilection
32 Marsh bird
33 It's a first
35 Zither cousins
37 "Get Low" rapper
38 Orange sign
44 Organ holder
46 Ancient royal symbol
48 Network with an annual awards show
51 German women
52 Fake
53 Not wavy, say
54 Basso Pinza
56 Hardly an exercise in restraint
59 "I get your point. Jeez!"
60 Pitchfork part
61 Unhurried
62 Fashionable boots
63 Read carefully
64 Like some offers
66 Van Gogh's "Starry Night Over the ___"
68 David Cameron's alma mater
71 ___ party
72 Red Scare grp.
73 Mild oaths
74 "I won't bore you with the rest"
75 What a Latino immigrant might learn
81 Sam Cooke's "That's ___ Quit—I'm Movin' On"
83 "Know ___ enemy"
84 Bit of music at a music conservatory
86 Old Russian line
87 One to consult for PC problems
89 Birthday party, e.g.
90 Words heard at a birthday party

by Joel Fagliano

92 Like pro athletes, some say
93 Jump accompanier?
94 +/−
95 War on terror target
96 Combines
97 Part of an ice skate
103 Combines
104 One of the five Olympic rings
106 Filled turnovers
107 "Steel Magnolias" actress
109 "Hmm . . ."
111 Petro-Canada competitor
112 English county
113 "Traffic Crossing ___ Bridge" (pioneering 1888 film footage)
118 Hit Fox show
120 W.W. II battle city
123 Airport approximation: Abbr.
124 Word before rip or slip
125 Infielder feats: Abbr.
126 "Dancing With the Stars" judge Goodman

18 "A" Trip Around the World

ACROSS

1 European spa site
6 Non-fiction
10 Clam (up)
14 French pronoun
17 Historic mission, with "the"
18 Borg rival
19 Words before may and might
21 They're often seen in banks
22 *Four stops on "A" trip around the world*
26 *Three more stops*
27 "___ be an honor"
28 Flashes quickly
29 Soft
31 Three Stooges specialty
34 John who is half of a popular singing duo
35 McIntosh alternatives
36 Bert, to Ernie
37 Lang. from which 8- and 24-Down come
39 Mag mogul with a mansion
40 Moneymaking concern
41 Bikini part
42 Like many an out-of-towner in Times Square
44 Sci-fi drug
46 Window-shopping purchase?
47 Manual contents
49 ___ Observatory
51 It comes and goes
53 Wander
54 Long-running PBS documentary film series
55 *Three more stops*
61 *Three more stops*
63 *Three more stops*

65 "That's yucky!"
66 Former senator Stevens
67 Speaks, informally
68 11-time N.B.A. All-Star Iverson
69 Bake, as an egg
72 Works on
74 Tostitos bowl?
76 Channel choker
77 Solo in the movies
78 Hacks
79 S.A. tin exporter
82 Sealing wax ingredient
84 Woman in Progressive Insurance commercials
85 "You're on!"
88 Punjabi princesses
90 Camel group?
92 Like a heckling crowd
93 Sight from Mount Olympus
94 Field fare, for short
95 *Three more stops*
100 *Three more stops*
102 River through Wroclaw
103 Wrapped (up)
104 Bubbly choice
105 O-O-O
106 Acid
107 Grammy winner born in Nigeria
108 Extrema, e.g.
109 Takeoff points for many test flights

DOWN

1 Meadow sound
2 Introduction for Romeo?
3 Flit
4 Designer Pucci
5 Ruling against a receiver
6 Eschew one's food?

7 Cheese choice
8 Braided bread
9 Home wrecker?
10 Gym wear
11 Traces
12 Singles grp.?
13 Love/hate separator, they say
14 Honoree in the arts
15 Some city sounds
16 "Patience ___ virtue"
20 Tab
21 Root in perfumery
23 "But despite it all . . ."
24 Thief, slangily
25 Highly rated
30 Six make a fl. oz.
31 Classic toothpaste brand
32 Early European visitor of India
33 Satirical Randy Newman song
35 Gain, as consent
38 "Don't play favorites"
40 French ladies
43 One clearing one's throat?
45 Piece of gold?
46 Name formerly on New York's MetLife Building
47 Handel bars?
48 The Fonz and Hannah Montana
50 "Ach du ___!"
52 Widens
53 Spoil
54 Campaign coffer fillers
56 Staff
57 Kay Jewelers competitor
58 Stored on board
59 Kind of nut

60 European event of 1948
62 Danny of "Do the Right Thing"
64 Olympian Apolo ___ Ohno
69 Branch of Islam
70 Fedora features
71 Put down
72 Warming periods
73 "I ___ you one"
75 Maze navigator
78 Ruinations
79 Score of zippo
80 What Madonna and Cher are each known by
81 Go-between
83 11-time M.L.B. All-Star Fisk
86 "___ Is Born"
87 Christian in France
88 Done over
89 Twisted and turned
91 Blow up, maybe
93 Like pop-ups
96 Electronics company bought by Sony
97 "Darn!"
98 Hollywood clashers
99 P. G. Wodehouse's ___ Agatha
100 E-mail inits.
101 Loser to D.D.E.

by Randolph Ross

19   A.A. MEETINGS

ACROSS

1 During which
7 Chooses
14 Unlike terra incognita, say
20 Olive oil alternative
21 Sexual drive
22 "Me! Me!"
23 Like the winner of the Miss Influenza pageant?
25 "Blast!"
26 Tiki bar order
27 Dons for the first time
29 Indulged in some capers?
30 Hovering falcon
33 Some cake slices
36 "I can see Mexico's southernmost state from this ship!"?
41 Tapas bar order
43 Quixote's pal
44 Art philanthropist Broad
45 Lend for a short while
47 Day during the dog days
50 When some coffee breaks begin
51 Bring in, as a big client
53 Like one who has gone green?
54 Rate setter, informally
55 Scoundrel
57 Place to get a learner's permit, for short
58 Fall guys
60 Some Kellogg grads
61 Literally, "fire bowl"
65 Stand sales
67 ___ dish
69 Before, to a poet
70 Article in Hoy
71 With 41-Down, Ford part
72 Like the Battle of Trafalgar
74 Kick oneself over
75 Kabayaki base
76 Entertainer with a Mandinka warrior haircut
77 French verb with a circumflex
79 Pro accompanier?
80 Guts
82 Danish Nobelist
84 Cousin to "Roger that"
86 Target of thieves who do card skimming
88 Some trailers
89 Vanidades magazine reader
91 Words before and after "what"
92 They vote first
94 "Look who's back!"
98 Brings out
99 "___ like a Maelstrom, with a notch" (Emily Dickinson poem)
101 Old Polly Holliday sitcom
102 Company with the slogan "At the heart of the image"
103 Is mannerly
105 Funding for a Spanish seafood dish?
108 Lucidness
110 "Babette's Feast" author
111 Gas pump abbr.
112 North by northwest, e.g.
115 For years on end
120 Game whose lowest card is the 7
123 Far Easterners signed to a St. Louis ball team?
127 Bleach
128 Top to bottom, say
129 Lick but good
130 Philosopher forced by Nero to commit suicide
131 Kids' summer activity center
132 Like mushroom heads

DOWN

1 Wee rooms, for short?
2 Onetime teen idol Corey
3 Their empire was the Land of the Four Quarters
4 "The Avengers" villain
5 Furniture piece
6 Tomoyuki ___, creator of Godzilla
7 Mel who was portrayed in "Field of Dreams"
8 N.L. East team, on scoreboards
9 Venice's La Fenice, for one
10 Fringed carriages
11 Easily injured
12 Double curve
13 Some M&M's
14 Steam bath enjoyed just before bedtime?
15 Nabokov novel
16 ___ ejemplo
17 Dos Equis-filled item at a birthday party?
18 Poet Sitwell
19 Is grandmotherly, in a way
24 Pump choice
28 Wine: Prefix
31 McDonald's offering since 1985
32 Dashiell Hammett's last novel, with "The"
34 "Rhoda" co-star David
35 "___ where it hurts"
36 Estate-planning pro
37 Place for a band
38 Gridiron stat.
39 Hyundai model
40 Style
41 See 71-Across
42 World ___
46 Pork-on-a-stick?
48 Came close to
49 Line in the 1950s
52 Scent coming from a Netflix envelope?
56 Answer to "Did you see which Greek goddess walked by?"?
59 Doughnuts, mathematically
61 Kind of pie
62 Foray
63 Filthy kid's laconic question?
64 Calvary initials
66 Actress ___ Marie Saint
68 Like some Facebook friend requests
73 Visa charge
78 1% group
81 Moving
83 Baby food preparation device
85 Ravens' cries

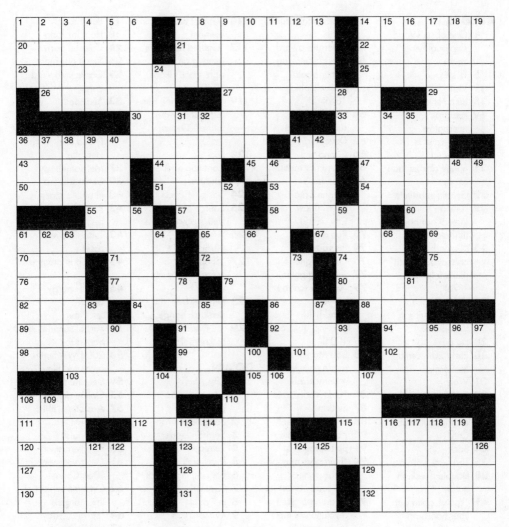

by Brendan Emmett Quigley

87 Store keepers?
90 Soda with a Blue Cream flavor
93 Sun, on the Riviera
95 Jamaican music
96 Jamaican fellow
97 Adenoidectomy specialist, for short
100 P.R. pro
104 Eustacia ___, "The Return of the Native" woman
106 Chest pain
107 Historical records
108 Rappers' posses
109 Café additive
110 Like some tricks
113 Many a prep sch.
114 Funny Carvey
116 "This is a priority!"
117 Copter's forerunner
118 Make
119 Tight
121 A U.P.S. driver may have one: Abbr.
122 Private eye
124 N.L. East team, on scoreboards
125 Stage item
126 Dangerous job

ACROSS

1 One of six World Cup qualifying zones
5 Tickles
11 Visit
15 Summer getaway
19 Pedigree alternative
20 Relative of a crow
21 Shade darker than azure
22 Gelatin substitute
23 "Get an inside look at our booth" (Buffalo, 1901)
25 "Come by and chat at our booth" (Philadelphia, 1876)
27 White Rabbit's song in "Alice in Wonderland"
28 Do a pit job
30 Early 20th-century Modernist
31 Whiz
32 Two-time world figure skating champ Slutskaya
33 Card
34 Back
35 Thruway warning
38 Double-check, in a way
41 "You've gotta get your hands on this" (Knoxville, 1982)
44 "Puts the keys of the future at your fingertips" (Philadelphia, 1876)
47 Inclusive pronoun
48 Russian city and oblast
49 Thompson of "Family"
50 Day spa treatment
52 Ones with natural curls?
56 Veteran's award
59 "Bring your dogs to our booth" (Philadelphia, 1876)
63 Queens neighborhood
65 Dove's sign
66 Grand __
67 Transcript meas.
69 "The fair's toughest man alive" (New York City, 1939)
73 Run into
74 Energizes
76 Ore. neighbor
77 Just for giggles
79 "Get the scoop on our new hand-held offering" (St. Louis, 1904)
83 Bob Marley tune made popular by Johnny Nash
86 "Quo Vadis" role
87 Swarm
88 Incredulous reply
90 It's unavoidable
91 Battalions, e.g.
94 "Fairgoers may be in for a shock" (St. Louis, 1904)
97 "Starting a giant revolution at the fairgrounds" (Chicago, 1893)
103 Winter reading, say
104 Pothook shape
105 Santa __
106 Muck
107 Fly without power
109 One that's hard to get ahold of?
111 It may receive a few pointers
113 Hullabaloo
114 Densest natural element
117 "Getting fairgoers moving on the right track" (Paris, 1900)
119 "Now showing our big vision of the future" (Osaka, 1970)
122 Pop __
123 Continue after landing
124 Designer Pucci
125 Source of the Hulk's power
126 Bull run participant?
127 "Shepherd Moons" Grammy winner
128 Remove from the stock exchange
129 __ Daddy (N.B.A. nickname)

DOWN

1 City where Cézanne was born
2 Bengalese wrap
3 Sermon leader
4 Retreats
5 Like hams
6 Eggnog ingredient
7 "Gross!"
8 Full of life
9 Mussorgski's "Bilder __ Ausstellung"
10 Judge to be suitable
11 Bistro dessert
12 First-year law student
13 'Fore
14 Faulkner's alma mater
15 "High Hopes" lyricist Sammy
16 Greek squares
17 Pull through
18 Hunt for food
24 Colorful parrot
26 Small garden
29 Game with Wild cards
33 Sea snail
35 Lay away
36 Neighbor of Draco and Hercules
37 Met somebody?
39 Sweet-talk, say
40 Firenze's place
42 Part of many a bistro's name
43 Tennis player's asset
45 Group in many a park
46 Small energy boost?
50 __ Piper
51 Part of summer in Santiago
53 2004 Will Smith animated film
54 Deer hunter
55 Online deluge
57 Aristotle's "fifth element"
58 Extinguish
60 Fiji alternative
61 Mezzo-soprano in "Don Carlos"
62 Onetime subject of the Mongols
64 "Have __ day"
67 Fightin'
68 Viva __
70 Lamar of the N.B.A.
71 Ready to move
72 Fight
75 Pore over
78 Divide
80 When some lunches end
81 Go well together
82 "Gross!"
84 See 115-Down

by Kevin G. Der

85 Some allergy sources
89 Nastygrams
92 Actor Bruce
93 Sequester
95 Single-issue publication
96 1972 Bill Withers hit

97 Act like an expert without being one
98 "Romanian Rhapsodies" composer
99 Bad blood
100 Female counselor

101 Antiquity, once
102 Like some ponds
108 Van ___ of "Timecop"
110 Ones with fictional accounts
112 "Small" prefix
113 Far from aerodynamic

114 Williams of the Temptations
115 With 84-Down, a Pac-12 team
116 "Big" prefix
118 Beach souvenir?
120 Year Claudius I became emperor
121 Course list abbr.

DOING WITHOUT

ACROSS

1 A person can take big strides with this
6 Hannibal's foil in "The Silence of the Lambs"
13 Museum piece
20 Forum fashions
21 Glade, e.g.
22 Hue akin to olive
23 ___-Itami International Airport
24 "Just do drills for now"?
26 Undo
28 Back to Brooklyn?
29 Slaughter
30 Disturb one's neighbors at night?
37 Comic strip "___ and Janis"
38 Inflation-fighting W.W. II org.
39 A pop
40 Former bill
42 Handful
44 Table saver
47 Don Quixote's love
52 Duffer's feeling toward a putting pro?
54 Meeting one's soul mate, perhaps?
56 Bogart's "High Sierra" role
57 Clive Cussler novel settings
59 Weight allowance
60 "Behold," to Brutus
61 Represent with a stick figure, say
63 Words on a Wonderland cake
65 Nonentities
67 Successfully perform a download?

71 Who wrote "A true German can't stand the French, / Yet willingly he drinks their wines"
75 Chamber exit
76 One who discriminates?
81 Naysayer
82 Fr. title
83 Fen-___ (former weight-loss drug)
86 Grow dark
87 Applied foil at the Hershey's factory?
91 One man's declaration to an upset party planner?
93 Sewing aids
94 Rider on a crowded bus, maybe
96 "I knew it!"
97 Relations
98 Shoppe modifier
99 Foreign football score
101 Blue shade
105 Drive by the United Nations?
113 Ponders
115 Upton Sinclair novel on which "There Will Be Blood" is based
116 Slum-clearing project, say
117 Impostor's excuse?
124 "Me, Myself & ___"
125 Tainted
126 Part of some Tin Pan Alley music
127 Went into la-la land, with "out"
128 Take control of
129 Original
130 Twisty curves

DOWN

1 Bundle bearer
2 "I'll have ___"
3 Response to a pledge drive request
4 Glen Canyon reservoir
5 Get a bit misty
6 Academy enrollee
7 Constellation whose brightest star is Regulus
8 Prince Valiant's eldest
9 Bunkum
10 EarthLink, e.g., for short
11 Actor Firth
12 Thrill
13 One may be overhead
14 "Little" singer of the '60s
15 Coll. elective
16 Capital city on the Atlantic
17 Comedian Bill
18 Model
19 Vodka drink, informally
25 "Definitely!"
27 Go into la-la land, with "out"
31 Strong cast
32 2010 Emma Stone comedy set in high school
33 Highway sign abbr.
34 Was audibly surprised, maybe
35 Shake
36 Holiday season event
41 Loos
42 Animal house, say
43 Creepy: Var.
45 Start
46 Hovel

47 Removal of restrictions, informally
48 Path of Caesar
49 One-named singer for the Velvet Underground
50 Suffix with depend
51 They might have it
52 Some appliances
53 Nag's call
55 ___-shanter
58 Tarot user, maybe
62 New York's Tappan ___ Bridge
64 Flat: Abbr.
65 Kill quickly
66 "South Pacific" hero
68 Diplomatic efforts
69 Hindu spring festival
70 French income
71 Exclaim breathlessly
72 Ready for service
73 Conseil d'___
74 Sports contest
77 Men of La Mancha
78 4-Down locale
79 Actress Sofer
80 Goal
82 Food in Exodus
84 Language from which "bungalow" and "jungle" come
85 Saxony seaport
88 Bad response upon first seeing one's new haircut?
89 Insomnia cause
90 Adaptable aircraft
92 From now on
95 Khan man?
100 Take charge?
101 Drivers of some slow-moving vehicles

by Tony Orbach

102 Allotment
103 Kind of nerve
104 One way to go, betting-wise
106 Word after an ampersand, maybe
107 Body cavity
108 Eccentric
109 What Oliver asked for more of
110 Berlin Olympics star
111 Rajah's partner
112 Malamutes' burdens
114 "Auld Lang ___"
118 Musician Montgomery
119 Things that may be 65-Downed
120 Cadge
121 Inventor Whitney
122 Itch
123 Motor finish?

ACROSS

1 DNA testing might reopen one
9 Uses a 13-Across on
13 "Star Trek" weapon
19 Person who's a zero?
20 What will the French think of next?
21 Troop group
22 Dream setting
24 After-dinner choices
25 PC key
26 Some online communications, for short
27 QB Tebow
28 Thérèse de Lisieux, for one
30 :D, e.g.
33 Battle-ax
37 Grp. that coordinates E.T.A. and E.T.D.
40 Letter-shaped girder
42 Basis of a lawsuit
43 "By ___!"
44 Slip-on
46 Places for rings, maybe
48 Humble response to praise
50 Organ repair sites, briefly
51 Polished
52 ___ B. Driftwood ("A Night at the Opera" role)
53 Org. that may assess violence levels
54 PBS flagship station
55 Part of a pinochle round
56 Former U.N. secretary general Kofi ___
58 Get ready to drive
59 x, y and z
60 Scot's "not"
61 Ousted from the ring, for short
62 TV station, e.g.
64 Cicely or tarragon
66 Weather comment represented visually by this puzzle's circled letters
72 Major artery through San Antonio
73 Plant tissue
74 Hunted
75 TV tavern keeper
76 Bud
78 Feel (for)
80 The Mediterranean has a warm one
82 Shade of a swan's bill in a Keats poem
83 Kindergarten stuff
84 Gravitate
85 Not cheating
86 Many wonks
88 Scat syllable
89 One of the Everly Brothers
90 Fate
91 Fictional Simon
92 Esteem
94 Rolling ___ (rich)
96 Kaput
98 Overseas Mr.
99 Austrian physician who lent his name to an English word ending in "-ize"
100 Propose
102 "True Colors" singer, 1986
104 Roam
105 Letters on some N.Y.C. luggage
108 Actress Tyler
111 Subject of a Vatican investigation
114 Artificial plot device
118 "The Conqueror," e.g.
119 "___ it" ("Understood")
120 Some bills have them
121 Dolls
122 Brit's teapot cover
123 Like some boards

DOWN

1 Chewed stimulant
2 Precious girl's name?
3 In the event that
4 2000 title role for Richard Gere
5 LL Cool J's "Going Back to ___"
6 "Lemme ___!"
7 "That is quite clear"
8 Directional suffix
9 "Shut your trap!"
10 Nudists
11 Nascar Hall of Fame architect
12 Part of a security system
13 It's lowered to hear music
14 Taft's partner in a 1947 act
15 Light reflection ratio
16 R.S.V.P. facilitator: Abbr.
17 Tolkien creature
18 Pharmacies fill them, in brief
21 Fourth letter after 49-Down
23 Leaf pores
29 You probably raise your arm for this
31 It's north of the South
32 Stock page listings: Abbr.
34 Big Apple team
35 Side (with)
36 Heroic deeds
37 ___ Hall (site on many a campus)
38 Attacked
39 Shows that can be racier than their network counterparts
40 Nest maker
41 Cheating
45 Angry Birds, e.g.
47 Manipulate to one's advantage
49 Fourth letter before 21-Down
53 Track ___
54 Prison unit
57 Security Council veto
58 Mine transport
61 ___ kwon do
63 Put away
65 Big name in frozen desserts
67 72-Across and others: Abbr.
68 "Cagney & Lacey" org.
69 Bazooka, e.g.
70 Yokel
71 Martial arts master
76 Lady
77 Villa, e.g.
79 Portuguese king
81 Tart drink
82 Doc's reading
85 Battle wear
87 Bond
89 Tediously didactic

by Finn Vigeland

90 North Korean leader or his father
93 White Rabbit's cry
95 Certain skiing competition
97 California beach town with a racetrack
101 Vicious
103 Doll
106 Player of golf
107 Climax
108 The euro replaced it
109 Signs
110 One with a neck and a lip
111 "I can't get excited about it"
112 Bit of investors' news, for short
113 ___ Tin Tin
115 I, to Tiberius
116 Struck
117 Laugh syllable

ACROSS
1 Colo. ___, Colo.
4 1040 preparer, for short
7 Heartbeat
13 Plied with spirits
18 Shakespeare
20 National Forensic League skill
22 Rare violin
23 Royal house until the early 20th century
24 Bad occupation for Sleepy?
26 One
27 Head of ancient Sparta?
28 Hardest to ship, say
29 Bad occupation for Happy?
31 Bit of wear for a fop
32 Hero who debuted in Weird Tales magazine in 1932
33 M.A. hopeful's ordeal
34 Like Oscar Wilde's humor
37 Ruler in a robe
41 Touch while running
42 Home of two M.L.B. teams
44 Villains in 1939's "Stagecoach"
48 Last ___
50 Ones running away with the game?
54 Mrs. Robinson's daughter
55 Having hands, maybe
57 Bad occupation for Sneezy?
59 More than a quarter of the earth's crust, by mass

61 Longtime Yankee nickname
62 Spot for a flame
63 Bad occupation for Grumpy?
69 2000 musical with the song "Fortune Favors the Brave"
70 Diplomatic, say
71 Some juices
73 Bad occupation for Dopey?
79 Grippers
80 Spanish dish
81 Classic figure in a top hat
83 It needs to be fed frequently
84 Best in the market
86 Last word of "Finnegans Wake"
87 ___ Canals
89 Gives a darn?
90 Bridge maker's deg.
91 Biblical mount
93 Singer John
95 Common tattoo spot
98 Bad occupation for Doc?
105 Hippocampus hippocampus, e.g.
108 Mishmashes
109 Employee of the month award, say
110 Bad occupation for Bashful?
112 Waldorf salad ingredients
113 Sports anchor Rich
114 Attacked ground units, in a way
115 Honchos
116 Lands in a puddle, maybe
117 Accent

118 ___-Magnon
119 ___-la-la

DOWN
1 Kerri ___, U.S. gymnastics star at the 1996 Olympics
2 45 player
3 Pay up
4 Cave ___
5 One going to market
6 Daily or weekly: Abbr.
7 "Friends" role
8 (0,0), on a graph
9 Eruption sight
10 "___ Frome"
11 A picky person may pick one
12 Trailer attachment
13 Bananas
14 "Somebody shot me!"
15 Questionnaire blank
16 Airport postings, for short
17 Force
19 Subject of dozens of Degas paintings
21 Vertigo symptom
25 Group with the 1995 #1 hit "Waterfalls"
27 Honor like a troubadour
30 Bar that shrinks
33 Miss
34 Like four U.S. presidents
35 Mathematician Descartes
36 River to the North Sea
37 Chapters in history
38 Half note
39 Novelist Calvino

40 Like lanterns at the start of evening
42 Log
43 Big bother
45 Degree of interest?
46 "Voilà!"
47 Fire
49 Convivial
51 Jai ___
52 Funeral song in Scotland
53 Cuts
56 Become a YouTube sensation
58 Finally edible
60 Zip
64 Duo with the 2003 hit "All the Things She Said"
65 Levi's alternative
66 Actors MacLachlan and Chandler
67 Serve up some ham?
68 Extend, in a way
72 Georgia and Moldova, once: Abbr.
73 Like two peas in ___
74 Hail
75 Is allowed (to)
76 Overhead transports
77 Tolkien's tree creatures
78 Some Jamaicans
82 "Switched-On Bach" instrument
85 Snares
88 Not a great hand for raising
92 Surgical inserts
93 Aristocracies
94 Big name in insurance

by Adam Fromm

95 [Give me the worm! Give me the worm!]
96 Hallmark of the Philadelphia sound
97 Sounds of hesitation
98 Relating to the palm of the hand
99 Apple software bundle that includes GarageBand
100 Volunteer's cry
101 "Shoot!"
102 Disgruntled worker's parting cry
103 External
104 "The Gondoliers" bride
105 Ballet bit
106 Malevolent
107 Lhasa ___
111 "Either plagiarism or revolution," per Paul Gauguin
112 Fighters' org.

ACROSS

1 Swivel on an axis
5 Cowboys' home, familiarly
9 Laughable
14 Marble, e.g.
17 One in Germany
18 Locale of St. Catherine's Monastery, said to be the world's oldest working monastery
19 Sources of many beads
21 Narrow inlet
22 Fancy footwear at a TV station?
24 Advertising department at a TV station?
26 Rugged transport, for short
27 ___ Levy, four-time Super Bowl coach for Buffalo
28 Visited
30 Western loop
31 Like some fortresses
33 Lose ground?
35 Classic toy company whose name is its founder's middle name
36 Slide show at a TV station?
41 "Puss in Boots" villain
42 "Barbarella" extras, for short
43 Person making waves?
44 "How ya doin', bro?"
47 Livid
50 River to Korea Bay
52 Insanity
53 Shave
54 Court recitation
55 Midpoints: Abbr.
56 Q&A at a TV station?
58 Lickety-split
60 Green-egg layers
61 Ruthless corporate type
62 Noted calendar makers
63 Underworld leader
64 Overflow
66 Skater Yamaguchi
68 Sort (out)
69 Instrument with a big bell
72 Expert at a TV station?
75 Cookie holders
76 Beginning of some temple names
77 Opéra part
78 Cockamamie
79 Carnal craving
80 European freshwater fish
81 Super ___
82 George nicknamed Mr. Basketball
83 "Tsk! Tsk!"
84 Baseball family surname
86 Enrollment at a TV station?
92 Shocked
95 How some stocks are bought
96 Hold fast
97 Seize
98 Playful response to a good insult
101 You might rub a knife across it
103 Country singer David Allan ___, writer of "Take This Job and Shove It"
104 Recruiters at a TV station?
106 Fish holder at a TV station?
109 It's picked in the Pacific
110 One taking the gold?
111 Meal with wine
112 Missouri relatives
113 It was dropped at Woodstock
114 "___ Got a Brand New Bag" (1965 James Brown hit)
115 Orange or olive
116 Await decision

DOWN

1 Opening word?
2 Tea merchant Sir Thomas
3 Early computer
4 Shout in a strip
5 Drink served with Brezeln
6 "What chutzpah!"
7 Miss at a hoedown
8 "The Simpsons" character with platform shoes
9 Old block deliverers
10 Gold rush town of 1899
11 Graceful horse
12 ___ a scratch
13 Utah's state animal
14 Mythical figure blinded by Oenopion
15 Do a certain dish duty
16 Zero, in slang
18 Beach umbrella, e.g.
20 Student involved in a prank, maybe
23 Appear on the scene
25 SpongeBob, e.g.
29 Sugary quaffs
32 Canine protector
34 Fishing gear
35 Blanket
37 "___ Place"
38 Continental prefix
39 Primo
40 Product from Mars
44 Sahara feature
45 Push
46 One of a group of 12, say
47 World org. based in Lausanne, Switzerland
48 Bowl call
49 Leucippus and Democritus, philosophically
51 Some Dadaist works
52 Go up
53 Oil producer?
55 It brings up many ticket holders
56 "Ta-ta!"
57 Place to live in Germany
59 Prefix with -plasm
60 Give lessons
64 Sheiks' garments
65 Sidecars might go on it
66 "Star Trek II" villain
67 Houston university
68 ___ Islam
70 Meadow call
71 "Ready!" follower
73 Joiner of a team
74 Gravy holder
75 Home of ancient Bethlehem
79 One of a secretive trio
80 Dairy brand
82 Get foggy
83 ___ decay

by Ian Livengood

85 One-point score, of a sort
86 It might be batted at a knockout
87 Clerics' homes
88 Half of a title role for John Barrymore or Spencer Tracy
89 Goddess associated with witchcraft
90 Like some T-shirt designs
91 Didn't wait until Christmas, say
92 Terrible
93 Savvies
94 Entranced
98 Other, in Oviedo
99 Crate
100 Lassie of Arg.
102 S-shaped molding
105 Quick drink
107 Gen __
108 Outdo

STATE ANNEXATION

ACROSS

1 Superfluous
6 Posed (for)
9 Follow persistently
12 Tiny blob
18 Charms
19 The Beatles' "All ___ Got to Do"
20 Old White House nickname
21 Badly beaten up
22 45-Down near Baton Rouge?
25 124-Across near Dover?
27 ___ contendere
28 Flower girl?
30 New Jersey town bordering Rahway
31 Photo ___
34 Swindle
35 Hindu title
36 ___ Brava
37 CD-___
38 117-Down near Salem?
42 When sung three times, part of a Beatles refrain
46 Bellyache
48 Seine summers
49 First name?
51 Starch-yielding palm
52 Old TV knob
54 How Shakespeare's Rosalind dresses
56 Sign by a theater ticket booth
57 Smithereens
58 1-Across near Hartford?
61 Blouse, e.g.
62 Still broken, say
65 Confirms
66 "Ancient Mariner" verse
68 Bad-mouthed
69 Bitchin'
70 Sun spots
73 Inter ___
74 Dante e Boccaccio
75 Rack for a rifle
76 Toss-up?
78 114-Down near Boise?
81 Santa ___ (desert winds)
82 Get it wrong
83 Certain implants
84 Role in "Nicholas and Alexandra"
87 TV police drama
89 Comics canine
90 11 or 12, but not 13
92 Paint choice
94 "___ teaches you when to be silent": Disraeli
95 76-Down near Springfield?
98 Mugful, maybe
99 Actor Quinn
102 Before, in verse
103 Pioneer in quadraphonic music
104 Caustic soda
105 Against
107 Badge earner
109 This and that: Abbr.
111 61-Across near Phoenix?
113 9-Across near Boston?
118 Critter whose name comes from Nahuatl
119 Cookout item
120 Roll of bills
121 Bring out
122 Assails
123 Staff ___: Abbr.
124 Whirlpool
125 Exorcism target

DOWN

1 Farm mother
2 Women's suffrage Amendment
3 Pampering, for short
4 Pull (in)
5 Regarding the price
6 Jazzy Nina
7 Boston's Mass ___
8 Lean
9 Doesn't budge
10 "Sure!"
11 E.U. member
12 "What ___!"
13 "Le Déjeuner sur l'herbe" artist
14 Expenditures
15 "The Time Machine" people
16 "___ your toes!"
17 B'nai B'rith grp.
23 Romeo or Juliet
24 French cup
26 Many a museum display
29 It might be blue, green or brown
31 Assn.
32 Like a sty denizen
33 6-Across near Indianapolis?
36 Some conifers
39 Do over, as a lawn
40 Abbr. before a colon
41 Prefix with -pod
43 119-Across near Albany?
44 Prefix with business
45 Basketball rim
47 Open
50 Housemother, e.g.
53 Passed easily
54 Weak
55 Armstrong and Sedaka
57 Pal
59 Light touch
60 Certain online request
63 Not quite right
64 Arrive at too quickly, in a way
67 "Hakuna ___"
69 In one's cups
70 Brewskis
71 How a fool acts
72 Spots
74 Bird wing
75 Knot
76 Spring time
77 Large-toothed whale
79 Paraded by
80 "Is she not down so late, ___ so early?": "Romeo and Juliet"
85 Number 2, e.g.
86 Still to be sampled
88 Shock
90 Sub
91 Site of a Greek tragedy
93 Big name in jeans
96 Respectable
97 Naval force
100 "___ the Sheriff"
101 Tidies up a bit
105 Number two
106 "Tu ___ mi amor"
107 Cozy
108 Drags
110 Give up
111 Weave's partner
112 Maternity ward workers, for short
114 Hip-hop
115 Deut.'s precede
116 Environmental prefix
117 Perfect rating

by Charles M. Deber

ACROSS

1 Bob Jones Award org.
5 "The straight path"
10 ___ cloud
13 Audacity
18 Stations
20 Girl's name meaning "night" in Arabic
21 Completely unthinking
23 Perfect job for Dustin?
25 Perfect job for Warren?
26 Better
27 Went scubaing
29 NaOH
30 Carter and Grant
31 Symbol of Communism
33 Kick-around pants
35 Is bound (to)
37 Sportage, for one
39 Woodworker's double boiler
41 Dr. Seuss's "___ Ran the Zoo"
44 Perfect job for Rowan?
51 Errs badly
53 Dove, for one
54 Lotto variation
55 Spam, say
57 Japanese gateway
58 Mischievous one
60 Manche department capital
61 Relative of the cha-cha-cha
65 Perfect job for Robin?
68 Steinway & ___
69 Target of core workouts
70 Child's cry of pain
71 Perfect job for Darren?
76 Excessively
80 "My bad"
81 One hanging out around shoppers
83 Stately
85 Pre-Civil War abolitionist
88 Deli spread
91 Dictionary info
92 "Just married" car decoration
93 Perfect job for Landon?
96 Letter after teth
97 Clean
99 Appetite
100 Band with the #1 album "Monster"
101 Refuse container
104 Nickname of the N.B.A.'s David Robinson, with "the"
110 Gin flavoring
113 CN Tower's home: Abbr.
115 Emperor son of Vespasian
117 Last, in León
118 Perfect job for Brandon?
121 Perfect job for Holden?
123 Half of a longtime comedy duo
124 New Year's month, overseas
125 Beast with twisted horns
126 Whatchamacallit: Var.
127 Early English playwright Thomas
128 98, e.g.
129 98, e.g.

DOWN

1 Concert hall employee
2 Backgammon playing piece
3 Common dried decoration
4 Orbital point
5 Québec's ___ de Montréal
6 Symbol of regeneration
7 Fat
8 Naproxen, commercially
9 Italian town where Napoleon won a historic 1800 battle
10 Big Blue
11 Ultimatum closer
12 Not
13 Little Rock-to-St. Louis dir.
14 Author Ferber and others
15 Stationery order
16 Diversify
17 "Slow Churned" brand
19 Shia, e.g.
22 Opening for winter fishing
24 Dull yellowish brown
28 Moral posers
32 "Casablanca" bistro owner
34 Some Egyptian pyramid art
36 Quantum mechanics model
38 Whiz-bang
40 Jim Lehrer presentation
41 Judas's question
42 "La ___ du Régiment" (Donizetti opera)
43 "___ no importance"
44 Birth month for most Libras: Abbr.
45 Be on the horizon
46 The olden days
47 Predecessor of Rabin
48 Confession receiver
49 Religious figure, to Pierre
50 Here-there connector
52 Scrub
56 Squash
59 Particle of a dwindling campfire
62 Assent
63 Writer of aphorisms
64 Typical
66 Shred
67 Shred
69 "Oh, yeah!"
71 Sentimentalist
72 "Road ___" (Hope/Crosby film)
73 Topple
74 Instant: Abbr.
75 Dims
76 Typesetter's choice: Abbr.
77 Arnaz of 1950s TV
78 The same to vous?
79 Steamed pudding ingredient
82 One could go up to 11 in "This Is Spinal Tap"
84 Tennis call
86 Nigerian-born singing star
87 Plea to a performer
89 "Wahoo!"
90 ___ Day
94 They're sometimes secret
95 Result
98 Bistro
100 Fix, as a skirt
102 In concord (with)
103 Prepared, as frozen foods, maybe
105 Lille girl: Abbr.

by Oliver Hill

106 ___-Turkish War, in which the first aerial bombs were used
107 Saudi Arabian currency
108 Fix
109 Royal court members
110 Heroin, slangily
111 Actress Anderson
112 Controls completely
114 Home of Theo. Roosevelt Natl. Park
116 Hospital fluids
119 Genre of Fall Out Boy
120 Supercool
122 Harry Potter pal

PERPETUAL MOTION

Note: When this puzzle is done, start at the end of 57-Across; then, beginning counterclockwise, connect the circles in one continuous line to identify a figure invented by 29-Down. The answers to the five starred clues will provide a hint to the figure.

ACROSS

1 Smart
5 Attention getters
10 Scot's exclamation
13 The fish in John McPhee's "The Founding Fish"
17 "I ___ sorry!"
18 "Same here"
19 By way of
20 "Here ___!"
21 *2007 Ken Follett novel
24 North of Virginia
25 *Bond film that's a real gem?
27 Relishes
30 Kisser, so to speak
31 Affluent
32 Literary ___
33 Bench presser's muscle, briefly
34 Newsman Peter and others
36 Where "thy will" will be done, partly
39 Big ray
42 Down Under critter
43 Buddhist school
44 Cookie store
45 England's first Stuart king
46 Craven
50 Teeming
52 "That's disgusting!"
53 "___ said!"
55 Wall St. deal
56 Legal org.
57 Own (up)
58 Turner autobiography
60 "Victory!"
61 Overhead light?
63 Descartes portraitist
64 Carriage driver's need
65 Kiln for hops
66 Knesset : Jerusalem :: Storting : ___
67 Roman ___
69 24 hrs. ago
70 Whatever
71 Mile High Center designer
72 Jazzy Laine
73 Plus
75 Real
78 In and of ___
80 They often come in threes
82 Clubber Lang portrayer in "Rocky III"
83 Term opener?
84 Greek consonants
85 A.T.M. button
86 Grace, basically
88 Fivesomes
90 ___ number
91 Gonitis locale
92 Set off
94 Classic Cremona family
98 "Perhaps . . ."
100 *Alexander Pope phrase appropriate to the start of a sports season
103 Be alive
104 *1974 Carl Carlton hit
108 "Exodus" actor
109 An original Star Alliance airline
110 Victorian home features
111 "Behold!," to Pilate
112 Brain tests, for short
113 Volatile stuff
114 Arthur ___, inventor of the crossword puzzle
115 Chocolate choice

DOWN

1 Cornfield sound
2 Med. care option
3 Country whose national anthem's title means "The Hope": Abbr.
4 Brewski
5 Take ___ view of
6 Baking need
7 Like some food
8 They can swing
9 The March King
10 Has thirds or fourths, say
11 Cannes subject
12 Lived it up
13 Computer switch
14 Turkish sweets
15 Sylvia Plath's last book of poetry
16 Caterpillar rival
18 "___ framed!"
20 Most in need of help
22 Handyman's letters
23 Price point?
26 Met regular, e.g.
27 "My Fair Lady" lady
28 Good "Dancing With the Stars" scores
29 See note
33 Corral
35 Wettest
37 Razor brand
38 Energy
39 OS X users
40 Film buff's channel
41 Certain pop
45 James or Jackson
47 *Song by Tejano singer Selena
48 Cousin of a stork
49 "Cut it out!"
51 Peek-___
52 Noticeably old, as paper
54 Platoon, e.g.
57 Makeup target
59 Nursery sights
60 Actress Skye
61 Southwest tribe
62 "Win ___ of . . ." (contest come-on)
63 C to C#, e.g.
68 Cut off all intake
69 River of Flanders
70 Tiny scurriers
72 Won't let go of
74 "Ain't ___ Sweet"
75 Temper
76 Trig ratios
77 Lips
79 Biblical interpretations
81 Most ready for commitment?
82 Six years before the Battle of Hastings
86 Common thing to count in
87 Thick-___
88 Slipcover trim
89 Stop
90 Conforms (with)
92 Composer's creation
93 "Chicago" song
95 Boss: Abbr.
96 Do ___ burn
97 About to cry
98 Quaint stopovers
99 [Awful!]
101 Tolstoy's "The Death of ___ Ilyich"
102 Vex
105 South American tuber
106 Clicker target
107 Animator's shriek

by Elizabeth C. Gorski

ODD ONE OUT

Note: Every letter in the answer to each starred clue appears an even number of times in that answer . . . except one. Altogether, those eight unpaired letters can be arranged to spell the answer to 68- and 70-Across.

ACROSS

1 End of a footrace
5 Creator of Princess Ozma
9 Satellite org.
13 State below Lower Saxony
18 "The Pearl of ___ Island" (Stowe novel)
19 Opposing
20 Technological debuts of 1998
22 Mountain, in Hawaiian
23 *Religious affiliation of John Adams and William Howard Taft
26 Cry from the bench
27 Foe
28 Ascension Day, e.g.: Abbr.
29 Sword material
31 Serve notice
32 Manila pact grp., 1954
33 *You raise your arms for these
36 Cultivate
38 Men of La Mancha
39 Big Apple subway line, with "the"
40 Do, re, mi
42 Sailor's realm
44 Business partner, sometimes
45 French word before and after "à"
46 Busch Stadium locale: Abbr.
49 *Physician's promise
55 "Gloria ___" (hymn)
57 Prefix with -naut
58 Primeval
59 Oregon city, with "The"
60 King of England, 946–55

61 Challenge for H.S. juniors
62 Film that lost the Best Picture Oscar to "Chariots of Fire"
64 Hogwarts professor Trelawney, e.g.
65 Montana Indians
66 Pilot's E
68 & 70 Some people are ___ crosswords
72 Paint choice
73 Illinois city
74 Ring
76 Form of acetylacetone
78 Corona
80 Scenic fabric
81 Narrow furrows
83 Maine coon, e.g.
84 You name it
85 Reduces to bits
86 *Hides out
89 Schooner's contents
90 Pack away
92 Travel plan: Abbr.
93 Trifling amount
94 Ocean's reflection
95 Boston's Liberty Tree, e.g.
96 Lack of faith
100 Jaw site
102 *Deficits
107 Jack Sprat's dietary restriction
110 Not too spicy
111 Comes out of one's skin
112 Quod ___ faciendum
113 ___ White, one of the girls in "Dreamgirls"
114 Given
116 *Ragged
119 Class
120 Bunches
121 Something to play
122 Raises the hackles of

123 Impressionist Degas
124 Scorched
125 ___' Pea
126 Peut-___ (maybe, in Marseille)

DOWN

1 Hitches
2 Golf's Palmer, to friends
3 *Not firm work?
4 Dead giveaway?
5 Honky-tonk
6 Hill of Hill hearings
7 The Osmonds, e.g.
8 Least
9 Fed. med. research agency
10 Jester, e.g.
11 Refuser of a 1964 Nobel Prize
12 Tap into
13 Managed care grp.
14 Swab's target
15 Nubian Desert locale
16 Comics canine
17 Pulls in
21 Common name for a working dog
24 Explorer ___ Álvarez de Pineda, first European to see the Mississippi
25 Sea lily, e.g.
30 "___ Marlene" (W.W. II love song)
34 Plains Indians
35 1967 #1 hit whose lyrics begin "What you want / Baby, I got it"
37 Style of furnishing
40 Fellow
41 Semi fill-up
43 Democrat Specter
45 Beta blocker?
46 *Real work
47 It may be tapped
48 Toppers
50 Driving hazard

51 Total
52 Nondairy product in the dairy section
53 Popular pain reliever
54 Ancient playwright who originated the phrase "While there's life, there's hope"
56 Italian Renaissance composer Banchieri
63 Firewood unit
67 Personal identity
69 Je ne ___ quoi
71 Laughs one's head off
73 Razor brand
75 Supermodel Hutton
77 State V.I.P.: Abbr.
79 Tennis's Roddick
81 Towser, e.g., in "Catch-22": Abbr.
82 Siren
87 Those with yens
88 Shot
91 ___ radio
95 Author Welty
96 Mercedes-Benz model
97 Whit
98 Prynne of "The Scarlet Letter"
99 Lark's home
101 Pushover
102 Persona
103 Canceled
104 Primitive weapon
105 Whit
106 Banal
108 Telecaster
109 Cliff-hanging
115 French 42-Across
117 She can be polled
118 Born overseas

by Kelsey Blakley

SHIFTY BUSINESS

ACROSS

1 As weird as they come
7 Where an M.I.A. might be
14 Parts of Fiji
20 "Beats me"
21 Biological rings
22 1950 University of Havana grad
23 Tightly stacked, as ice trays
24 Con artist
25 "Alrighty"
26 Like Tylenol PM: Abbr.
27 It might be dropped
29 Foot, to a zoologist
30 Crypt alternatives
32 Suffix with floor or roof
33 Teacher's question at the start of show-and-tell
35 Anticipate heading home
38 Endings for Shakespeare
40 ___ Reuters, media giant
42 New York tribe
44 Some early paintings
47 Prefix with ribonucleic
49 They're learning the ropes
53 Bless
54 Color Me ___, 1990s R&B group
55 "Friday the 13th" prop
56 Inning stretcher, maybe
58 Sequel to "Typee"
61 Audibly upset, as a bull
62 Norms: Abbr.
63 Long-snouted swimmer
64 Oil bigwig?

66 Thing absorbed by the ozone layer, for short
67 Doesn't care either way
70 Way to go on dates
74 Pet store category
75 Not big, in a small way
76 Diminish
80 Leaning, in a way
82 All-inclusive
83 Bruce Wayne and Batman, e.g.
85 Place for matches at home
87 "Calm down"
89 Drilling devices
90 Massage technique
91 Pole in sailing
93 Che Guevara's real first name
94 Big Apple daily, in brief
96 Verbally assaults
98 At once
101 Some summer feasts in the U.S.
103 Where to sign a credit card, e.g.
107 A bather may want one
108 Blind part
110 Grand ___ (wine designation)
111 Per diem worker
113 UPS option, briefly
114 Hopped up, in a way
116 Rashly
119 "Men in Black" figures
121 Negative influence
122 Gets fixed
123 Texas/Louisiana border river
124 You take it lying down
125 Views wide-eyed
126 It's bound to be used in a service

DOWN

1 Available for viewing
2 "A merry heart ___ good like a medicine": Proverbs
3 Boogie, Bee Gees-style
4 D.C. summer clock setting
5 Witnessed
6 "Brilliant, ain't I?!"
7 Bygone Toyotas
8 Frodo foe
9 Gave missiles to
10 Finish last on "Jeopardy!"
11 Donation receptacle
12 Oda ___ Brown (Oscar-winning role)
13 Look over
14 Clicked pic
15 It opened in Manhattan in 1924
16 W.W. II craft for getting troops ashore
17 Set of moral rules
18 Rock singer Reznor
19 Billboard listings
28 Corp. leadership
31 Isabella II, por ejemplo
34 Oktoberfest souvenirs
36 Currently
37 ___ minute
39 "Foundation" trilogy writer
41 Old El Paso competitor
43 E.R. folk
44 They get tired
45 Biol. subject
46 Empty
48 It freshens the air
50 Baker v. ___, landmark 1962 Supreme Court case
51 Spanish for "are"
52 Big name in vodka
54 Practice requirement?

55 As the center of attention
57 Summer camp locale
59 Other: Abbr.
60 Direction from Hannover to Berlin
64 Roman who declared "Carthage must be destroyed"
65 Taking care of business
67 TV advertising staple
68 Lush
69 Unclogs
70 Quarters, informally
71 Home of Rainbow Bridge National Monument
72 Suspense novelist ___ Hoag
73 Empties, with "out"
76 Fathers
77 A long time
78 Suit basis
79 Canadian station name
81 Sell for
83 Take ___ at (attempt)
84 Trick the defensive line, maybe
86 Kind of board
88 Double-deckers in the sky, maybe
91 Overseas seasoning
92 Energize
93 "Anything ___?"
95 Silencing
97 Brightness detector
98 Features of some 'Vettes
99 Former enemy capital
100 Sundance entry, often
102 Hardly commendable
104 Trap during winter, maybe
105 Title girl in a Ritchie Valens hit
106 Flop in a lot

by Jeremy Newton

109 Actress Olin
112 Reduce to a pulp
115 Org. in the 1946 film "Cloak and Dagger"
117 Class-based society?: Abbr.
118 La-la lead-in
120 Creator of the chess champion Deep Blue

30 D-Plus

ACROSS

1 1982 best seller subtitled "And Other Discoveries About Human Sexuality," with "The"
6 Team components
10 Diamond experts
14 Smartens (up)
19 Singer/songwriter Davis
20 Repetitive cry while waving a hand
21 Japan's first capital
22 Japanese import since 1986
23 Make necklace baubles?
25 Hip lineages?
27 Small detail?
28 Brian of experimental rock
29 "Great ___!"
31 Is a keynoter, e.g.
32 Shingles, say
35 "Dies ___"
36 Race segment
37 Tall, slender hound
39 Tonto's pep?
45 Many keys
47 Its natl. anthem is "Ja, vi elsker dette landet"
48 Black top
49 Stat for Gooden or Maddux
50 Gave Grey Poupon to the head of the table?
54 Drink made from a mix
57 De bene ___
58 Weight
59 Tiniest bit
61 Cut down
62 Hockey player's deceptive move
64 ___ the Orange (Syracuse University mascot)
65 Et ___
66 Greediest person in a Long Island locality?
71 Putts that might be conceded
73 "Desperate Housewives" role
74 Trans ___
75 Mrs. Ceausescu of Romania
76 Shortly
77 Mathematician Turing
79 Three-time A.L. M.V.P., informally
83 Way to the nave
85 Spotted feline's home?
89 HBO competitor
90 Jerry's uncle on "Seinfeld"
92 Latin law
93 Military strategist's plan
94 Like residential mail?
100 Like fourth-down yardage
101 Food pkg. abbr.
102 Remove, as text
103 Atlantic Division cagers
105 Confounds
108 Perform superbly
110 Rapper Kool ___ Dee
111 "Sexual Honesty" compiler
114 Certain Colorado headgear?
116 Bamboozle Eisenhower?
119 Cause of a stomachache
120 Five-star
121 Cone holder
122 Playground retort
123 Aquarium fish
124 Digital camera units
125 Red or Brave, for short
126 One of Us?

DOWN

1 Proceeds here and there
2 Undesirable serving
3 Unrealized hit taken on an investment
4 Short, as a meal
5 Like many lifeguards
6 Certain Bedouin
7 Some gas atoms
8 911 responder
9 1987 Costner role
10 Pop open?
11 Strong Chinese liquor
12 Ride shotgun for
13 "The best pal that I ever had" of song
14 Rabbit's home
15 When the Great Lakes were formed
16 Tallow source
17 One of the Planeten
18 Lip
24 Challenged
26 Slow dance with quick turns
30 Old Olds
33 Arkie neighbor
34 Infomercial cutter
37 Ex-Cleveland QB Brian
38 Actress Gardner and others
40 Classic pencil-and-paper game
41 One-named Brazilian soccer star in the 2008 Time 100
42 Parent or guardian
43 Actress Pam
44 When tripled, and so on
46 Having a low throaty quality
51 Irregular
52 Initiation, e.g.
53 Obsolete auxiliary
55 Paul Krugman pieces
56 After midnight, say
60 How cringe-making humor might go
62 1970s talk show
63 Hangar 18 contents, supposedly
64 Hooray, in Juárez
65 Monitor inits.
66 Quick look
67 One making lots of money
68 Revered figure
69 Unemployment office sight
70 Dad's rival
71 Tithe amount
72 National rival
76 Canned
77 Big lugs
78 Less strict
79 Suspected spy in a celebrated 1949 trial
80 They often start with "No"
81 "My treat"
82 Like some wool
84 Go by
86 O. Henry-winning author Tillie
87 Aslope
88 McFlurry flavor
91 Useless item in a closet
95 Bear, say
96 Curved high-back bench
97 Move, as a picture
98 Chosen groups
99 Vic who sang "On the Street Where You Live"
104 Motor-driven
105 Push up against
106 Hand (out)

by Brendan Emmett Quigley

107 Tube
109 "Around the Horn"
channel
112 Big chunk of moola
113 Cousin of -ule
115 Hit headfirst
117 Zero
118 Nintendo debut
of 2006

ACROSS

1 (With 13-Across) "My wallpaper and I are fighting a duel to the death. One or the other of us has to go"
6 "Pow!"
10 Cutup
13 See 1-Across
18 Kapa haka dancer
19 "I, Robot" extras
21 Fit, once
22 Cuba y Puerto Rico
23 Carpet store bargain bin
24 Get angry
25 Concern coming up?
27 "Die, my dear? Why, that's the last thing I'll do!"
29 Mineral suffix
30 Pair in an ellipse
31 Red ball?
32 "That was the best ice cream soda I ever tasted"
37 Way up
39 Actress Thurman
42 Huskies' org.
43 Cushion site
44 Mathematician ___ de Fermat
46 PC cores
47 Scottish hillsides
50 Words of disappointment
52 Character sets?
53 "Where is my clock?"
55 Adolescent admonishment
57 Fleischer and Onassis
58 Vocalist Yoko
59 Puts in a box, maybe
60 Kim Jong-il, e.g.
63 Yellowknife is its cap.
64 Madison or Monroe: Abbr.
65 Mild-mannered Mister
66 Taxpayer request
68 ___ American
69 Hose color
70 Ibsen title character
71 "Leave the shower curtain on the inside of the tub"
76 Others, in Andalusia
77 Building safety features
79 Pot grabber
80 Wii user, maybe
81 Rial spender
82 Ones sharing Durocher's astrological sign
84 Took sides?
85 Packed, in brief
86 Communal customs
87 "I've had 18 straight whiskies. I think that's the record"
91 Press
92 Some pitcherfuls
93 Dark time, for short
94 "Don't let it end like this. Tell them I said something"
98 Vatican rules
103 "You are not!" response
104 Raid targets
106 The Amazing ___ (magician)
107 Korean carmaker
108 Magnified
109 Yore-ic?
110 (With 113-Across) "I've had a hell of a lot of fun and I've enjoyed every minute of it"
111 Nine-digit ID
112 Supreme leader?
113 See 110-Across

DOWN

1 Strike out
2 Tiara go-with
3 Porter, for one
4 Like 1, not I
5 Meet
6 Voting area
7 Apricot and tangerine
8 Green machine?
9 Invader of Europe in 1241
10 McCain residence for 5½ years
11 U.S. island occupied by Japan during W.W. II
12 Not fem.
13 ___ Republic, toppled in 1933
14 Its literal translation is "submission"
15 Look like a wolf
16 French pair
17 Nero, e.g.: Abbr.
20 "I have not told half of what I saw"
21 1970 N.F.L. M.V.P. John
26 Capone's nemesis
28 Cheer
30 Hail
32 Bell ___
33 New Orleans staple
34 It has 10 branches: Abbr.
35 Minor errands
36 ___ effort
37 Date
38 Chief concerns?
39 Enlarge
40 [Grumble, grumble, grumble]
41 Weigh
45 Magician's name suffix
46 "I live!"
48 "Eva is leaving"
49 Some beachwear
51 Eugene ___, hero of "Look Homeward, Angel"
52 Fill with a crayon
54 Clueless
56 Exsiccate
59 Employers must meet them
60 Points on some lines
61 Academy town
62 Two-channel
63 "I'm late!"
64 2007 film that won the Academy Award for Best Original Screenplay
67 Ball of fire
68 "I'm going to heaven!"
69 Pelé's real first name
71 About 877,000 hrs.
72 Info in a real estate ad
73 Disneyland sight
74 Eight: Prefix
75 Con man's responses?
78 Hi-___
81 "Hello-o-o!"
83 Part of a program
86 Hipster's persona
88 First supersonic human
89 Learn by word of mouth
90 Like many hospital doctors
91 Cloven
92 Detective Pinkerton
94 Carson's predecessor
95 Part of O.A.S.: Abbr.
96 Stars
97 Contents of Pandora's box, except for hope

by Matt Ginsberg and Pete Muller

98 Anode indicator
99 Phobia of 100-Down
100 Ford role, familiarly
101 Xanadu
102 ___ Fein
103 Chemical suffix
105 Kerfuffle

ACROSS

1 Blade for blades
7 Pandemonium
13 1965 title role for Peter O'Toole
20 Rip into
21 Loose
22 Cow
23 Battle of Trafalgar hero
25 Last king of a united Israel, in the Bible
26 Chinese export
27 Sleep like ___
28 Kind of track
30 Proceed
31 "God's ___ heaven, all's right with the world"
33 Manhattan neighborhood
35 Two-time host of the Olympics
38 Oak or ash
43 Antique, say
46 Obama cabinet member Salazar
47 Silents star Renée
48 Platypus, e.g.
50 Hasty escape
53 Not so civil
56 Slate, e.g., informally
57 Computer letters
58 "She's ___ doll" (4 Seasons lyric)
60 Lucifer, notably
63 ESPN topic
64 It was flown by James Bond in "Dr. No"
66 Investor's concern
67 Mimic of a sort
69 Site of many a fountain
70 ___ Club
71 You may work on it
74 Container that's hoisted
77 Costume

79 Kid
80 Title girl of a 1964 Beach Boys song
81 Runner Zátopek
83 Suffer for acting unwisely
88 Spiny ___ (aquarium fish)
89 The Brady Bill is one
91 Elvis's middle name
92 "Me too"
94 Bar stock
95 German chancellor Merkel
96 1983 Peace Nobelist
98 Magazine department
100 Stop
101 New Jersey ecumenical institution
108 Daydreamer's doing
110 Biblical kingdom
111 Fifth-century pope
112 Medical suffix
114 Party to a financial transaction
118 Transaction option
120 Upper limit
121 Co-star of "Grumpy Old Men," 1993
124 Tiny friend of Dumbo
127 Amorphous
128 Like a yellow polka dot bikini in a 1961 #1 hit
129 The Father of Genetics
130 Eat away
131 Tumult
132 Lays low?

DOWN

1 Interference
2 Cesar ___, five-time Gold Glove winner, 1972–76
3 Kawasaki competitor
4 Numerical prefix
5 Tormentor
6 Abbr. after some names

7 City on the Penobscot
8 When école is not in session
9 Shoulder muscle
10 Perform high-tech surgery on
11 "And she shall bring forth ___": Matthew 1:21
12 It may be written on a blackboard
13 Finish behind
14 Egg: Prefix
15 Brother or brother-in-law: Abbr.
16 Be covered with, with "in"
17 "The World Is My Home" memoirist, 1991
18 Cry of glee
19 Heal
24 Time-consuming
29 Possible source of salmonella poisoning
32 Bug
34 Tulip-exporting city
36 Plain
37 Cheese town
39 Ample, informally
40 ___ in sight
41 Witty Bombeck
42 School appointment
44 Bash
45 Designer Schiaparelli
49 Sighting off the Florida coast
50 Dweller on the Arctic Circle
51 Uzbekistan's ___ Sea
52 Deadline maker
54 Place for a masseuse
55 "Dream Children" essayist
59 Swift runner
61 2002 British Open champ
62 Made introductions, say
65 Gymnast's need

68 Australian state: Abbr.
71 Equinox mo.
72 Buddy
73 Former Orr teammate, familiarly
75 Without purpose
76 It has 1,366 seats: Abbr.
78 To the stars
79 Principle
81 Old expletive
82 Bond type, briefly
84 Big bore
85 Gillette's ___ II
86 Argument weakness
87 Meander
90 Purina brand
93 Ones whose symbol is a harp
97 A person
99 Coyote's supply in Road Runner cartoons
102 Axis leader
103 Bag in a closet
104 Web site with the headings "Toys & Hobbies" and "Music"
105 Refer
106 Paul of "Mad About You"
107 Snack food made by Drake's
109 Blender brand
112 G4 or G5
113 ___-shanter
115 North Pacific island
116 Locale for Apfelstrudel and Sachertorte
117 Like 911: Abbr.
119 640 acres: Abbr.
122 "Curb Your Enthusiasm" airer
123 First ___
125 Poetic contraction
126 Home of Point Pelee Natl. Park

by Barry C. Silk

ACROSS

1 Wind source
7 Escalates
13 Watercolor technique
20 Annual event held at the Dolby Theatre, with "the"
21 Hero known for his nose
22 Intertwined
23 Give Axl and Pete a break?
25 Like the Twenties
26 Language that gave us "pajamas"
27 Saroyan's "My Name Is ___"
28 Elton John/Tim Rice musical
30 A bit more than never
31 ___ Palace
33 Tripping over a threshold, perhaps?
37 Bubbly place?
38 Carries, e.g.
39 BlackBerry and others, for short
40 Footwear that's hard to run in
43 Art school subj.
45 Pea farmers?
51 Summer apartment with no air-conditioning?
54 Home of the Blues: Abbr.
55 Powerful engine
56 Barkin of "Sea of Love"
57 English author Blyton
59 Co. bigwigs
62 "___ true?"
63 Solar ___
64 Swindler
67 Went long

69 Floral Technicolor dreamcoat?
73 Madrid newspaper
76 This-and-that preparation
77 Island near Naxos
80 Certain grains
81 Sets (on)
84 Fourier series function
85 Lively sonata movement
87 Pauline Kael's "___ It at the Movies"
89 Blow away
91 Strutting bird on an ice floe?
94 Residents at a Manhattan A.S.P.C.A.?
98 Yours, in Giverny
99 Nemeses
100 Actor Ventimiglia of "Heroes"
101 DC Comics superheroine
103 Genetic molecules
105 Move a movie camera around a community?
110 Some casino staff
113 Little or Short
114 Greenish-blue
115 Interlaken's river
117 Emmy-winning co-star of "Chicago Hope"
119 "Symphonie Fantastique" composer
122 Explanation for an interception?
125 One of the Andrews Sisters
126 Early anesthetics
127 Like some Swift writing
128 Electra's brother
129 Twos
130 ___ Falls, N.Y.

DOWN

1 "Yipe!"
2 Jelled dish
3 Extended operatic solo
4 Quarter back
5 Onetime HBO sitcom
6 Prime meridian std.
7 Deliverers of the unreturnable
8 Hess who was a dame
9 Cue
10 Airline to Stockholm
11 Digs up
12 Propose
13 Mustachioed TV muckraker
14 Plastic ___ Band
15 Suffix with form
16 Perennial N.L. leader of old
17 Sharing a memo with
18 For this reason
19 Lawn gadget
24 1980s street artist Keith
29 Spot
32 ___ impasse
34 Dobbin's nibble
35 "Dear old" guy
36 ___ mgr.
38 Batting coach's concern
40 One with a handle
41 "Damn Yankees" vamp
42 Too suave
44 Without ___ (quietly)
46 Series finale?
47 What a bee produces
48 "Superman II" villainess
49 Some
50 Favor cloyingly, with "on"
52 Just for laughs

53 Many a New Year's resolution
58 Pulls
60 1977 thriller co-starring Bo Derek
61 "The Odd Couple" director
65 Some legal scholars, for short
66 "The Time Machine" race
68 Co-founder of the Nonaligned Movement
69 Fastidious
70 Lane in Metropolis
71 Postrevolutionary councils
72 Language akin to Yupik
73 A Walton
74 Singer Lovett
75 "What's New Pussycat?" response?
77 Poop
78 Comics canine
79 End of some firm names
82 2005 Hoffman title role
83 Winter Olympics powerhouse: Abbr.
86 Summer at a ski resort, e.g.
88 Taj Mahal, e.g.
90 Bleach
92 One of the original Mouseketeers
93 ___ cloth (lingerie fabric)
95 1983 Duran Duran hit
96 China shop personae non gratae
97 Orlando-to-Ft. Myers dir.
102 Shortly
104 Attraction

by Tony Orbach and Amy Reynaldo

105 Literature Nobelist Neruda
106 ". . . in ___ tree"
107 Audacity
108 Bizet suite "The Girl From ___"
109 Attached, in a way
110 Chaff
111 River straddled by Basel, Switzerland
112 Impassive
116 Homeland plot?
118 Cuzco inhabitant
120 N.Y.C. subway line
121 A wee hour
123 Moo ___ pork
124 Hi-___

LINKS TO THE PAST

When this puzzle is done, interpret the answers to the seven starred clues literally, in order from top to bottom.

ACROSS

1 Figure in "Lost Horizon"
5 Intelligent, creative sort, supposedly
10 Fancy wheels
14 Pet protector, for short
19 Monthly bill: Abbr.
20 "___ Gold"
21 ___ Sea, 2,000-square-mile saltwater lake
22 Singer Collins and others
23 *Boondocks
26 Former presidential candidate in the Forbes 400
27 Standing by
28 Symbol of modesty
29 Away with an O.K.
31 PBS funder
32 Mobile-to-Birmingham dir.
34 *Ambulance destination
37 Group of genetically related organisms
40 "Buy ___ regular price, get . . ."
41 Directional suffix
42 It's within your grasp
44 With 51-Down, cry of sorrow
45 Specter in the Senate
48 Emulates AZ or T.I.
50 *Imam or priest
54 1986 Indy winner Bobby
57 Vacation itinerary
58 Literary heroine whose best friend is a goatherd
59 Copy
61 Looney Tunes nickname
62 San ___, Calif.

65 Straighten out
68 G or R issuer: Abbr.
69 *When the heavens and earth were created
72 Car driven by James Bond in "Octopussy," for short
75 Forward
76 "Sweet" stream in a Burns poem
77 Roadie's armful
80 Noisy but comfy chair
82 Wallop
84 First name in skin care
86 Material with a distinctive diagonal weave
87 *Deputy
92 Serving in the navy
94 Tweets, e.g.
95 Grandfathers of III's
96 Unpaid debt, e.g.
97 Let go
99 Strait-laced
101 Field for a fault-finder?
103 *Week after Christmas
108 G, musically
109 Lead-in to calculus
112 1, to a trucker
113 Love sign
115 Dog-___
117 Actor Jannings and others
118 *Lights out in New York City
122 Bathroom fixture
123 "Yeah, right!"
124 Children
125 Part of a French opera
126 Open stars?
127 Tops
128 Like mesh
129 Bartlett, e.g.

DOWN

1 A mechanic might see it a lot
2 Flared dress
3 Publicity push
4 Group with the 22x platinum album "Back in Black"
5 Saturn offering
6 P.S. in a Beatles song
7 Mortgage adjustment, for short
8 Subject of some modern maps
9 "___ Mio"
10 "Chicago Hope" actress
11 Choler
12 Nick, say
13 World Cup shout
14 Small, fruity dessert
15 Luster
16 Worrisome sight on the Spanish Main
17 Bee's target
18 Back on board
24 O'Brien's predecessor
25 Get together
30 Birthplace of James K. Polk and Andrew Johnson: Abbr.
33 Abbr. on a cereal box
35 Like most dorms nowadays
36 ___ Page, woman in "The Merry Wives of Windsor"
38 1950s Hungarian premier ___ Nagy
39 Birds with showy mates
42 "Hey there!"
43 Pacific capital
45 Foreman foe
46 Pleonastic

47 "The Divided Self" author R. D. ___
49 Former Swedish P.M. Olof ___
51 See 44-Across
52 Director Sergio
53 Bonnie in the Rock and Roll Hall of Fame
55 Wanted poster letters
56 Field of green
60 Sister of Erato
63 Indian tourist locale
64 Cover girl Cheryl
66 Cousin of a raccoon
67 Something to play
69 Forehead coverer
70 Desk tray
71 Memory: Prefix
72 They may be crunched
73 Wrangler rival
74 All over
77 No matter the cost
78 ___ items
79 Those hoofing it
81 Events that are barrels of fun?
83 '60s radical grp.
85 Eye irritant
88 Suffix with diet
89 Relinquish
90 Kind of saw
91 Peace Prize city
93 Verdi's "Celeste ___"
97 A-listers
98 Breakdown of social norms
100 Playful rodent
101 Payola, e.g.
102 Promise, for one
104 Gave the once-over
105 Exams for future docs
106 Uncooperative
107 Field Marshal Rommel
110 ___-car

by Alan Arbesfeld

111 Lawn tool
114 Method: Abbr.
116 "Hurry!"
119 Result of bringing someone home, for short
120 Etymologist's ref.
121 Science writer Willy

ACROSS

1 Where to spot a king or queen
5 ___-approved
9 Ridicule
13 Part of a college application
18 Socialite with a self-named perfume
20 Versatile body builders
22 Two-door
23 Lord's home
24 Corrupt financier's command?
26 Grocery store lineup
28 Trading post buys
29 Frequent figure in Renaissance art
30 Mama Bear at the stove?
32 Part of 5-Across: Abbr.
33 URL start
37 Starfish feature
38 "Catch-22" bomber pilot
39 Crowning point
42 View ruiner
44 Disputed
47 Pets with dewlaps
49 Like Larry King, repeatedly
50 Coaches
51 Word with beauty or pizza
52 Dumber than dumb
53 Heat
54 Alpo or Purina One?
56 Sanctioning assn. for pugilists
57 Like many a 21-Down
58 Percussion instrument in Off Broadway's "Stomp"

59 Topic in transcendentalism
60 Members of la familia
61 Familiar flight pattern
62 Painter Andrea ___ Sarto
63 Critical
64 Toxic spray
65 Give ___ shot
66 Droopy
67 In high esteem
69 U.S.S. Enterprise title: Abbr.
70 Certain power
71 Post-O.R. location
72 Greeting from Smokey the Bear?
74 Happy shouts
77 Good points
79 Pair of opposite electric charges
80 Best Actress nominee for "Indochine"
81 Singer John with the album "Bruised Orange"
82 Bacchus, notably
83 Agitated
84 "The Bald Soprano" dramatist
86 Schnauzer sounds
87 Poet Hughes
88 Cursor attachment?
89 Some food additives
90 Integral subj.
92 Pumpkin grower's cry of surprise?
95 "No problem!"
97 Something made in the still of the night?
100 Above: Lat.
101 Scheduled activity at a Vegas chapel?
106 Like "Have a nice day!"
108 Greek moralizer

109 What drives you to get better?
110 Fills to the gills
111 Waxes
112 Exam with 125 questions: Abbr.
113 Bygone depilatory
114 Douglas ___, first president of Ireland

DOWN

1 Unfavorable
2 Clears
3 Songbird at an eye drops factory?
4 Popular brand of bouillon
5 Kind of port for a PC
6 Daze
7 ___ Walcott, 1992 Literature Nobelist
8 ___ nitrite
9 Gets set
10 Unfavorable
11 Indifferent
12 Hatches, say
13 Capital subj.
14 From Polynesia and environs
15 Globe : Boston :: ___ : Baltimore
16 Inclined
17 Happy shout
19 Bohemian
21 Cool sort
25 Part of 85-Down
27 Searches high and low
30 Curator's selection
31 Some have a silver lining
32 Mean
34 Sodom or Gomorrah?
35 Snake with "lightning bolts" on its back
36 Baseball's Martínez and others
39 Culture medium

40 Triumphant spicy meal for the Three Little Pigs?
41 Affliction
43 Relatives of kites
45 Movie star with the most Oscar nominations (17)
46 Starter, perhaps
47 "___ a Spell on You" (classic 1956 Screamin' Jay Hawkins song)
48 King Minos' daughter who aided Theseus
52 Sch. or hosp.
54 Disagree strongly
55 Pioneer automaker
58 Fried rice ingredients
60 Some church income
61 Christopher Columbus, in the Indies
62 TiVo's, e.g.
63 Big-enough catch
66 Clear
68 First commercially successful computer
69 Sometime
70 Darling family pet
72 Early Coloradans
73 Draft picks
74 "Quality Is Our Recipe" franchise
75 Not as good as claimed
76 Worked on a shift, maybe
78 Held for later disbursement, as funds
80 Ngo Dinh ___, South Vietnam's first president
82 Plan of action

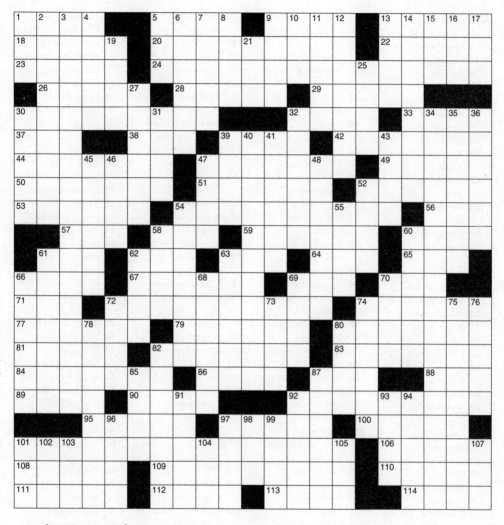

by Lynn Lempel

36 STORY CIRCLE

ACROSS

1 Do well in the Olympics
6 Choose to take part
11 Modern storage sites
16 Sky Chief company
17 Satisfactory
21 Low soccer score
23 Place in trust
24 Stabilizing track
25 Weaver's supply
26 Word with mail or letter
27 Actor Edward James ___
28 2001 headline maker
30 It's worth its weight in gold
31 PC linkup
32 Tweaks
33 Michael of "Juno" and "Superbad"
34 "Ixnay"
35 Bygone leaders
38 Fathers
40 Norse pantheon
41 Another name for 72-Across
45 Center
46 A Marx brother
48 Thither
50 Longtime Susan Lucci role
52 ___-Caps (candy)
53 Tulsa sch.
54 Largest moon of Saturn
55 Subject of a tipster's tip
56 Joe Montana or Jerry Rice, informally
57 Windsor's home: Abbr.
58 Additions to a musical staff
60 ___ but when
62 Blissful
64 Crackerjack
65 Expressed a welcome
68 Org. with spring playoffs
69 Dried seaweed popular in Japanese cuisine
72 Part of Canis Major
73 Boot camp affirmative
75 Fanatic
79 Be more than a dream
80 Lite
82 Clip, e.g.
83 Bring up, perhaps
84 Suffix with magnet
85 7'6" Ming
87 Green-eyed
89 ___ in Charlie
91 Wall-E's love in "Wall-E"
92 One side of an exchange
93 It may be bid
95 Big band instrument
96 It comes in volumes: Abbr.
98 Cartoon pooch
99 Slugger's stat
100 Tandoor flatbreads
101 Popular
103 Prefix with sphere
104 Galley figure
105 Bones may be found in it
107 Cousin of a clog
109 Oscar winner Patricia and others
111 It's found near the tongue
113 Achilles and Hector
115 Clothes rack abbr.
116 Gridiron scores: Abbr.
117 Scientologist ___ Hubbard
118 Crown covering
120 "Did you start without me?"
124 Rachmaninoff's "___-tableaux"
127 Island where Sundanese and Madurese are spoken
128 Take too much of, briefly
131 Windbag's output
132 Golfer Aoki
135 Certain infection
136 Operatic heroine wooed by Beckmesser
137 1963 animated film with the song "Higitus Figitus," with "The"
141 ___ Gold, character on "Entourage"
142 Stanford's Big Game rival
143 1998 animated film featuring the voice of Pierce Brosnan
144 Hollywood, with "the"
145 Notwithstanding that, for short
146 ___ jure (legal term)
147 "The Canterbury Tales" traveler
148 Gun for hire
149 Loser at Gettysburg
150 Heir, perhaps
151 Org. in Clancy's "Red Storm Rising"
152 Gives birth to a kid
153 Bit of cheer
154 Road twist

DOWN

1 Work together
2 1981 film in which Helen Mirren plays a sorceress
3 Onetime MTV animated title character and others
4 With 12-Down, 1889 Twain novel
5 Weathercast figure
6 Slothful
7 Underwater families
8 Japanese market: Abbr.
9 Memo header
10 Subtlety
11 Things first on the way up?
12 See 4-Down
13 Perceived to be
14 With 76-Down, 1953 Ava Gardner film . . . as depicted elsewhere in this puzzle?
15 ___-Japanese
16 Gumshoe
17 Relative of a grapefruit
18 Does some heavy lifting
19 Red alert?
20 Bilbao bloom
22 W.W. II vessel
27 Kind of inspection
29 ___ Gordimer, Literature Nobelist
35 Aid in finding a station
36 Magical glow
37 River that flows past more than 40 castles
39 Bishop's group
40 1973 Rolling Stones #1 hit
42 Davy Jones's locker
43 Years in old Rome
44 Drilling grp.
47 One of Iago's victims
49 Words of commitment
51 Five-carbon sugar
59 Culture areas?
60 Passover month
61 Arrive by air
63 "Winnie ___ Pu"
66 Pot-___ (French stew)
67 Overhang
69 Conductor Lockhart and others
70 Rustic transport
71 2001 Anjelica Huston miniseries, with "The"
72 Some steaks
74 Hot desert winds
76 See 14-Down
77 Magic trick's climax
78 Supreme Egyptian deity
81 Soap box?
82 One of Santa's reindeer
86 Drilling grp.
88 Chairman Arafat

by Kevin G. Der

90 ___ Rand, developer of Objectivism
94 Lou's "La Bamba" co-star
97 Rocker Lofgren
101 Temple structure?
102 Quick
106 Result of going out?
108 1971 Peace Nobelist from Germany
110 AARP concern
112 "Parlez-___ français?"
114 Delays
117 Heroine in Verdi's "Il Trovatore"
118 Gives the heave-ho
119 Arizona native
121 Not pick up
122 Highest worship in Catholicism
123 Antisub weapon
125 Cliff homes: Var.
126 Takes by force
129 ___ number on
130 About
133 What an inflectional ending is added to
134 Certain netizen
137 Area meas.
138 Up in the air
139 Canal sites
140 Emulate some of Goya's work

GROUP FORMATION

ACROSS

1 It's open for dinner
6 High ball, in pool
12 Pond organism
16 Sedaris of "Strangers With Candy"
19 Dish that may be served on a boat
20 Three-line poems
21 Put into piles
22 Traversing
23 Contents of four answers found in this puzzle
25 It covers a lot of leg
27 Good for nothing?: Var.
28 Alexander the Great conquered it
30 Rarely counterfeited bills
31 Fictional Plaza Hotel resident
33 Alexander the Great conquered it
34 Group formed at C.C.N.Y. in 1910
36 Weapon with many warheads
37 Roof of the World natives
40 Monaco is one
45 Given an eyeful, you might say
47 Accepting bribes
48 Brazil's ___ Alegre
49 "And all too soon, I fear, the king shall ___": "Richard II"
50 1971 album dedicated to Buddy Holly
52 Picasso's ___ Period, 1901–04
53 Surname of two British P.M.'s
54 Waterford purchase
55 Empties
57 Labor leader Chávez
58 Bridal wish list
62 Like some twisted ankles
63 Sam's Club rival
64 1992 Damon Wayans comedy
65 "Old MacDonald Had a Farm" sounds
67 Womanizers, slangily
68 Nitrogen compounds
69 Weenie roast needs
70 Cars that go toward other cars
72 Subjects of pneumography
73 Fended (off)
75 Something that's been clarified
76 Tavern orders
77 Old cracker brand
78 Co-organizer of the Montgomery bus boycott, 1955
84 Ill-looking
85 Renaissance painter Uccello
87 Bavaria and others, once
88 Bout of revelry
89 By and large
91 Engine attachment
92 Claw alternative
93 Group formed at Howard University in 1911
94 Sci-fi author's creation
96 Kentucky Derby drinks
98 Fire extinguisher's output
101 Mideast hub
103 Fill a box, say
106 Jason Bourne, in the Bourne series
108 Four groups found in this puzzle
112 Bounder
113 Umpire's wear
114 Retro headgear
115 Jay Silverheels role
116 Have a bite of
117 Quelques-___ (some: Fr.)
118 2000 Olympics locale
119 Golfer who said "Never concede a putt"

DOWN

1 "No ___"
2 First word in many church names
3 Pursue violent options
4 1980 double album by Springsteen
5 Raises
6 C&W singer Wooley
7 British art museum
8 Book of Hours entry
9 ___ & Tina Turner Revue
10 Determination
11 Ruhr industrial city
12 Gets several views
13 Actress Anderson
14 Social reformer Margaret Fuller, to Buckminster Fuller
15 "I already ___"
16 Skin So Soft seller
17 Lab test subjects
18 Asian bovines
24 Sheltered side
26 Meryl Streep title role
29 Most corrugated
31 Novel on which "Clueless" is based
32 Writer O'Flaherty
33 Like final contracts
35 Mexican-style fast-food chain
37 Comfortably warm
38 Personal, as thoughts
39 Group formed at Miami University in 1839
41 Furies
42 Antihistamine brand
43 Steals the show from, say
44 Urban railways
46 Figures out intuitively
51 Legal precedents
52 No longer on vacation
53 Oscar winner for "GoodFellas"
56 Remove the suds
57 Inducements
58 Pointy-eared "Star Trek" character
59 Highly respected
60 Round percussion instruments
61 Term for a judge
63 Enigma machine, e.g.
64 Nyasaland, nowadays
66 ___-European
67 New Journalism pioneer Gay
69 Areas of expertise
71 Choir attire
73 Liveryman's command
74 Celtic priest of old
79 Group formed at Trinity College in 1895
80 Wisconsin home of Lawrence University

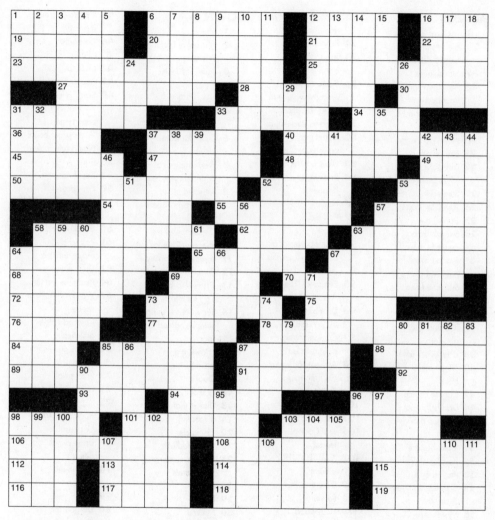

by Patrick Berry

81 Timberland limit
82 Villainous Uriah
83 Desires
85 Product with
a circular red,
white and
blue logo
86 Semiterrestrial
organism

87 The Who's
lead singer
90 Match played at
the local arena
95 Elizabethan
collars
96 Dean's 1960s
singing partner
97 Apartments, e.g.

98 Undisputed
point
99 W.W. II general
Bradley
100 Red's pal in
"The Shawshank
Redemption"
102 Slip (into)
103 English collar

104 French family
member
105 Speak up?
107 The Mustangs of
the N.C.A.A.
109 Get a total
110 J.F.K. board
info
111 Ground cover

ACROSS

1 Explorer who has a monetary unit named after him
7 Nasal tones
13 "Huddled" group inscribed on the Statue of Liberty
19 Chip in
20 Notre Dame cry
21 Like an ass
22 Dirt-dishing lass who's been cut off?
25 Summery
26 "Livin' la Vida ___"
27 Danish coin
28 Star of football, to most of the world
31 Jeanne d'Arc, for one: Abbr.
32 Seasoned rice dishes
36 Wayne ___ (Gotham City abode)
38 Entertainer Béla
40 "Right away, boss!"
42 Cheese choice
44 Dad is familiar with top Broadway star?
51 Block buster?
52 Peeples of "Fame"
53 Played again
54 Constellation near Scorpius
55 More raspy
57 "Finnegans Wake" wife
58 Epic poem in dactylic hexameter
60 Lhasa ___ (dog)
63 Fourth of September?
64 N.Y.C. subway syst.
65 See 114-Down
66 Actor Joel's crime scene analysis?

73 Printing on many a name tag
74 Ballpark figs.
75 Japanese band
76 Some depictions on a pyramid wall
77 It may be blind
78 Bygone stadium
80 Brand that's universally liked?
83 Used a tuffet
84 Backyard briquettes
86 Hack
87 Red head, once?
90 One-quarter of a mourning lacrosse team?
95 Emma of "The Avengers"
96 Dennis, to Mr. Wilson
97 Comparatively right-minded
98 Ancient Jordanian city with rock carvings
101 Landlord
103 O.E.D. filler
106 Jedi Council leader
107 "___ ELO" (1976 album)
108 Blow the whistle
110 Fervent
113 Hollywood hanky-panky?
121 Bad way to be caught
122 Bone receptacle
123 Lament
124 Tomoyuki ___, creator of Godzilla
125 Just followed Nancy Reagan's advice?
126 Some blackboard writing

DOWN

1 Tote
2 "Wheel of Fortune" purchase
3 Some U.S.N.A. grads
4 Beg
5 Some votes in Québec
6 Calendar data: Abbr.
7 When tripled, a W.W. II movie
8 Self-control
9 "Entourage" agent Gold
10 "Seduction of the Minotaur" author
11 Prime meridian std.
12 Continental ___
13 Grand Marquis, e.g., for short
14 Superhero with an octopus named Topo
15 "How's it goin', man?"
16 Quash
17 First of 12 abroad
18 Dinner that includes a reading
20 Cry uncle
23 "Skedaddle!"
24 Beverage brewed from petals
28 Kaput
29 Dash
30 Mikhail Baryshnikov, by birth
33 Clouseau title: Abbr.
34 Common setting in an Indiana Jones movie
35 Corroded
37 Pro-
39 Game played at the Mirage
41 "Encore!"
43 Accomplished

45 It's thrown from a horse
46 Carpenter of note
47 I.R.S. ID
48 Bob or weave
49 Said "Friends, Romans, countrymen . . ."
50 Waterproof boots
55 Noted rule maker
56 Briny
58 Set of hospital rms.
59 Fries order at McDonald's, maybe
60 Shocked and awed
61 Poli sci student's major, maybe
62 Do business with
64 Real-time e-notes
67 Word with milk or sauce
68 Colorado State, athletically
69 Future presenters of the past
70 In favor of
71 Summers
72 ___ Kundera, author of "The Unbearable Lightness of Being"
78 Bulb in the kitchen
79 "LOL!"
80 Do-gooder
81 One of the Baldwins
82 Goes back
84 B train?
85 ___ concern
87 Hombre's hand
88 Passed with flying colors
89 Southern staple
91 Financing fig.
92 One who loves pick-ups?

by Patrick Blindauer and Andrea Carla Michaels

93 Something you love to play with

94 What oviparous creatures do

98 Surmise

99 "Marcus Welby, M.D." actress Verdugo

100 Old TV western starring Rory Calhoun, with "The"

102 Character of a community

104 ___ Leppard

105 What traffic and dogs do

109 Greek theaters

111 "Wedding Bell Blues" singer Laura

112 Snick's partner

114 With 65-Across, like some orders

115 That, in Oaxaca

116 Hit TV show set in Las Vegas

117 Pill alternative, for short

118 Stumblers' sounds

119 One of 13 popes

120 Stop on a track: Abbr.

LET'S TALK ABOUT ME

ACROSS

1 Added (on)
7 Schisms
12 Says "Two 19-Across," e.g.
16 One of the Big Three, for short
19 See 12-Across
20 More than is required
21 Home of Rainbow Bridge National Monument
22 "Riddle-me-___"
23 "Pardon me"
25 Late 1920s to around 1950
27 North Carolina town that's home to Appalachian State University
28 Summer comfort stat
29 "Save me"
31 Seeding org.
32 Statement of fact
35 "My best soldiers," according to Douglas MacArthur
36 In shape
37 A.A.A. recommendation: Abbr.
38 "Feed me"
40 Physicist Bohr
41 Exactly right, in British lingo
43 "The Thorn Birds" and others
44 Stops on the road
45 Kind of column or committee
48 Put the kibosh on
49 It has strong jaws
51 Modern trivia competition locale
54 "For me?"
57 Irishman who was a Time magazine Person of the Year in 2005

58 ___ ligation
61 Ones entering rehab
62 Enters gradually
64 Snorkeling sites
66 Break off
67 Plug
68 Gets no answers wrong on the test
69 1993 TV western starring Kenny Rogers and Travis Tritt
71 Invites to one's apartment, say
73 Scott Turow's first book was about them
74 Nevada city
75 "Shoot me"
78 Mo. with Natl. Grandparents' Day
79 ___ Dubos, humanist who said "Think globally, act locally"
80 Old verb suffix
81 Superlative on "Top Chef"
85 Fearsome Foursome team
87 Like some grain
89 Rough shelter
90 N.C.A.A. women's basketball powerhouse
92 "Lean on me"
96 Herd of whales
97 Pickup place for pets
98 Airline mentioned in "Back in the U.S.S.R."
99 Former Miss America host
100 Al dente
101 "Make me"
104 Actress Hagen
105 Singing Simon
106 Bartender's announcement

107 "Kiss me"
111 Friend ___ friend
112 Draft status
113 Where Jean-Claude Killy practiced
114 Theater area
115 Lighting director's choice
116 Bank bailout acronym
117 Big success
118 Child often having special responsibilities

DOWN

1 Where many commuters live, informally
2 Balloon or blimp
3 Sweet potato nutrient
4 Icelandic money
5 To be abroad
6 British mil. decoration
7 Enter quickly
8 Won't take no for an answer
9 Org. overseeing trials
10 Port pusher
11 Come across as
12 Holders of body lubricating fluids
13 Lake ___, source of the Mississippi
14 Pops in the nursery
15 Send
16 "It's on me"
17 Go off track
18 What kings rule
24 Classical rebuke
26 Choose to participate
30 Cobblers' needs
32 Like some bonds
33 Stilt, e.g.
34 Eyes and ears

38 Arcangelo ___, Italian violin master
39 Sign of hunger
40 Tonga-to-Hawaii dir.
42 Daytime talk show starting in 1987
44 "___ little silhouette of a man" ("Bohemian Rhapsody" lyric)
46 Big word in German ads
47 Ballet set in the Rhineland
49 Word that led to the "Why a duck?" routine by the Marx brothers
50 Walk-___
52 Before
53 Cans
55 Nasty words
56 Housing arrangement
57 Congressional terms, e.g.
58 Scale weights
59 Functional
60 "Write me"
63 Child's wheels
65 Bank holdings?
67 Battle star
70 Hamper
71 Batsman
72 Mom-and-pop org.
76 Very, very tired
77 Singing brothers' surname
79 Presidential inits.
82 Wrap around
83 Hollywood hopefuls
84 Flapdoodle
86 "___ of robins . . ."
87 Ready for a drive?
88 Protest cry
90 Get moving again, in a way

by Randolph Ross

ACROSS

1 Shepherd
5 Logical beginning?
10 Regs.
14 Curio
19 Langston Hughes poem
20 Who said "No good movie is too long, and no bad movie is short enough"
21 House Republican V.I.P. Cantor
22 Windblown soil
23 Used a push-button toilet?
26 Difficult surface for high-heel shoes
27 The Jaguars, on scoreboards
28 "White trash," e.g.
29 Been in bed
30 Kind of school
31 Stop on ___
33 "Julius Caesar" role
36 12-time Pro Bowl player Junior
38 Super ___ (game console)
39 Neural network
40 "I can't drink beer this late"?
44 Operates
46 Flu symptom
47 Ovid's love poetry
48 Green
50 Largest city paper in the U.S.: Abbr.
51 Narrow estuary
54 Arg. neighbor
55 Dairy regulator?
61 Mil. unit
62 "Up and ___!"
63 It was destroyed by Godzilla in "Godzilla Raids Again"
64 Cans
66 "Zounds!"

68 Yeoman of the British guard
71 Sci-fi writer's creation
72 Like Rockefeller Center
73 Cantilevered window
74 "The Hallucinogenic Toreador" artist
76 Extinct relative of the emu
77 Baseball official gets revenge?
83 ___ Chinmoy (late spiritual leader)
84 Toon frame
85 Poetic dark period
86 "Concentrate!"
87 Govt.-issued securities
90 Pelé was its M.V.P. in '76
92 Shadow
93 "The bolt alone is sufficient"?
97 Stiff drink
101 Mil. address
102 Medicinal succulent
103 Native of Leipzig
104 One looking for a ticket, maybe
105 Spruce
108 Added value
110 Sons of, in Hebrew
112 Nashville-based awards org.
113 Pitcher Reynolds of the 1940s–'50s Yankees
114 Story of a small Communist barbarian?
118 Designer Geoffrey
119 Eric of "Munich"
120 Gettysburg general under Lee
121 Hammer part

122 "The East ___," song of the Chinese Cultural Revolution
123 Egyptian solar disk
124 Catch in a ring, maybe
125 Without much thought

DOWN

1 Bill collector?
2 Online brokerage
3 Sartre play set in hell
4 Fetes
5 Plastic surgeon's procedure
6 Shanghais
7 Colorful fish
8 Regal inits.
9 Native: Suffix
10 Emmy-winning Ward
11 Platitude
12 Miramax owner
13 P.T.A. meeting place: Abbr.
14 Sister in Chekhov's "Three Sisters"
15 Five-time Wimbledon champ
16 1960s sitcom title role
17 Prizes
18 Transmitter of nagana
24 Reno-to-L.A. dir.
25 News bulletin
30 Hawaiian attire
32 Basis of a Scouting badge
34 Neuters
35 Peyotes, e.g.
37 Litigators' org.
40 Chemically quiet
41 Mother ___
42 U.S. rebellion leader of 1842
43 Loyally following
45 Eye layers

48 McDonald's chicken bit
49 Affix
50 Having digits
52 "The wolf ___ the door"
53 Welcomed, as a visitor
55 Mated
56 Jazz genre
57 End-of-year numbers
58 P.M. between Netanyahu and Sharon
59 Aviator
60 Open
65 Neb. neighbor
67 Gets a C, say
69 Where Guinness originates
70 ___ pain
71 Words before may or might
75 The French state
78 Mantel pieces
79 Convenient meeting place?
80 Seed coat
81 "Put your feet up"
82 Tolkien hobbit
87 Overthrows
88 Oven option
89 Part of R.S.V.P.
91 Also, in Aries
92 Places for moles
93 Mustardy condiment
94 Cane accompanier, maybe
95 Curtis of cosmetics
96 Aristocrats
98 Fixed for all time
99 Gulliver of "Gulliver's Travels"
100 Gearshift mechanism, informally
104 Contend
106 "O.K. then"
107 Network signal

by Phil Ruzbarsky

ACROSS

1 Singer Lambert, runner-up on the 2009 "American Idol"
5 Talk to shrilly
10 Four-sided figure
15 Halloween purchase
19 "___ by me"
20 Slangy commercial suffix
21 Shelter org.
22 Scuba diver's worry
23 -IRC-MS-ANCES
26 Be a couch potato
27 Mystery writers' awards
28 Person with few possessions
29 Hymn whose second line is "Solvet saeclum in favilla"
31 Breeze
33 Pay stub?
35 Ninny
36 ANTI--VERNMENT UN--ST
45 Urge
46 Maker of Fosamax and Zocor
47 Moscow's home: Abbr.
48 Covered walkway
50 It's music to a musician's ears
52 AR--CL-
57 Size unit of an English soda bottle
58 Like 11-Down: Abbr.
59 Soon
60 "Is ___?"
61 Underground network
66 Shoe brand reputedly named after a Scottish golfer
70 P---ARY CARE PHY-ICIANS

76 Currency union since 1999
77 Together
78 PBS benefactor
79 Low clouds
82 Stranded messenger?
84 1991 Tony winner Daisy
86 FI-TH WH--L
92 Tips, e.g.
93 Heart lines: Abbr.
94 Where some people get tips: Abbr.
95 Like the Vietnamese language
97 Like some verbs: Abbr.
98 WHAT A -ANDA DOES IN -EIS-RELY FA-HION
104 Tiny tunneler
105 Tic-tac-toe loser
106 Box lightly
107 Hawaiian massage
112 Met, for one
115 Former home of the N.H.L.'s Thrashers
120 Modern home of the biblical Elam
121 W--THL-SS R-AD-TER
124 Stun
125 Take out
126 8½-pound statue
127 Regarding
128 Bob in the Olympics
129 Connection
130 Fresh
131 Favorite baby sitter, maybe

DOWN

1 Brut rival
2 TV screen meas.
3 "It's Time to Cry" singer, 1959
4 Hook up
5 Us
6 Gallery event
7 Kung ___ chicken

8 Alternative to satellite
9 Kind of shell
10 Stick in one's craw
11 Pres. when the C.I.A. was created
12 Piece of a newspaper?
13 1,111
14 French river craft
15 National monument site since 1965
16 Skis, boots, masks, etc.
17 Mideast tinderbox
18 ___-Ball
24 Very
25 "___ off?"
30 Bygone flier
32 Fresh
34 Company name that becomes another company name if you move its first letter to the end
36 Mackerellike fish
37 Kind of acid
38 Effluvium
39 Principal location?: Abbr.
40 TV exec's concern
41 Some E.R. cases
42 Chou En-___
43 ___ Chandler, longtime publisher of the Los Angeles Times
44 All's opposite
45 Icy
49 Dog breeders' org.
51 Send another way
53 Dangerous buildup in a mine
54 Preface online
55 "Excalibur" star Williamson
56 Knotted up
62 Senator Hatch
63 Spanish bear

64 Bygone flier
65 Word often following yes or no
67 Agreement abroad
68 Atlas abbr.
69 Wharton deg.
71 Like the face after a good bawl
72 A.C.C. athlete
73 It typically has lots of horses
74 Isn't inert
75 Less bananas
79 Toledo-to-Columbus dir.
80 N.J. or Pa. route
81 Music in Mysore
83 Architectural pier
85 Tel ___
87 Cry at a circus
88 W.W. II arena
89 Wii alternative
90 Male delivery
91 Some receivers
92 Dependent on chance
96 Sources of fleece
99 NBC inits. since 1975
100 Pirated
101 British weights
102 Cry after the rap of a hammer
103 Man's name that's an anagram of 108-Down
107 Caps
108 Exam format
109 Something to be threaded
110 Pure
111 Kind of screen
113 Psyche's love
114 Sub ___ (confidentially)
116 Similar

by Ashish Vengsarkar and Narayan Venkatasubramanyan

117 Ship that sailed "the ocean blue"
118 Shore flier
119 On the ocean
122 The Cowboys of the Big 12 Conference
123 They may be cloned

ACROSS

1 "This answer ends in a T," e.g.
5 Site of Daniel Webster College
11 Ninnies
16 ___ Vincent, former Major League Baseball commissioner
19 Jesús, for one
20 Internal settler?
21 Postgame discussion
22 "___ Maris Stella" (Latin hymn)
23 Pub quantity
24 Some skiing stars?
27 Tell ___ story
29 Bluesy James
30 Importune, informally
31 Make waves?
32 Teen leader?
33 Sault ___ Marie
34 Schools of thought
35 Charge up
36 Word of leave-taking
38 Far out?
41 Hampshire's home
42 Neptune, e.g.
43 French town in W.W. II fighting
44 Threnody
46 Defiant challenge to an order
47 To whom Mortimer declares "They were the footprints of a gigantic hound!"
50 Stuck
54 William Tell's canton
55 "Dies ___"
57 "___ expert, but . . ."
58 Winter hrs. in Winter Haven
59 ___-lacto-vegetarian
60 "Henry & June" author
62 Jiffy
64 Start of a German goodbye
65 Slung mud at
67 One of a pair of biblical nations
69 Unadulterated truth
72 Something of great interest?
73 Bartholomew, for one
75 Reprimand to a dog
76 "Norma ___"
77 Rapper ___ Jon
78 Person in a race
79 Laugh half
80 Speck
82 Transportation option
84 "Anytown, ___"
87 Volcanoes, e.g.
89 Result in
91 Brings with great difficulty
93 Rich people
95 Reykjavik's home: Abbr.
96 "Shadowland" singer, 1988
97 The Charioteer constellation
100 Big name in escapism?
103 Fictional village visited by Major Joppolo
104 Window cover
105 Hotel supply
106 Nascar event airer
108 Hall-of-Fame outfielder Roush
109 Light shade
110 Pro Football Hall-of-Famer Long
111 Blacken
112 Cambodian money
114 Departure call from a Spanish vessel?
118 Mideast sultanate
120 Contents of a stannary mine
121 Notes
122 Leaves at the base of a flower
123 Long-tailed moth
124 High-school subj.
125 Cameron who directed "Jerry Maguire"
126 Most sardonic
127 Stat

DOWN

1 W.W. II general ___ Arnold
2 Pelvic bones
3 Word signed for a deaf toreador?
4 Educational work after school
5 "Wagon Train" network, 1957–62
6 Buenos ___
7 Fish in a firth?
8 Reach in a hurry
9 "Superman" villainess
10 "Wagon Train" network, 1962–65
11 Obvious statement
12 Lost it
13 Metrical accent
14 Base protector
15 "Alias" type
16 Unlike the cards in a draw pile
17 Opposed
18 Toadies
25 River into which the Big Sandy flows
26 High point
28 Reaching 21?
35 What an unevenly milked cow might have?
36 Dentiform : tooth :: pyriform : ___
37 Singer/actress Linda
39 "___ Have to Do Is Dream"
40 Camouflage?
41 Simple writing
42 Dallas sch.
45 Cooler in the summer
48 Sufficient, informally
49 Until now
51 Mythical twin's bird tale?
52 Incessantly
53 Goodman of "Splash" and "Grease"
56 Sling mud at
61 One of the Cyclades
63 Power seekers, maybe
66 "Just ___ thought!"
67 Google service
68 Each
70 "Must've been something ___"
71 What the N.H.L.'s Hurricanes skate on?
74 Immature stage
81 Year the mathematician Pierre de Fermat was born
83 Chase in films
85 ___-Japanese War
86 Lee who directed "Brokeback Mountain"
88 Create quickly
90 Part of Christmas when lords a-leaping are given

by Robert H. Wolfe

92 Relative of an iris
94 Demonstrate
97 Carol starter
98 The Artful Dodger, e.g.
99 Eager
101 Lazy
102 ___-friendly
105 Hearst mag
107 Brings (out)
110 Garden worker
111 Novelist Caleb
113 Actress Turner
115 Cable station owned by Showtime
116 "Charlotte's Web" author's monogram
117 Onetime boom maker
119 Time out?

ACROSS

1 *Mark your card!*
7 Items in an ed.'s inbox
10 Covered, in a way
14 Briefly, after "in"
19 1960s–'70s Ford muscle car
20 On one's ___
21 Companion of Artemis whom Zeus changed into a spring
22 It comes after a "long time"
23 The Pequod, e.g.
24 Giggle syllable
25 *Mark your card!*
27 Slacken (off)
28 Sign off on
31 Emperor who married his stepsister
32 Child of the '70s, in brief
33 Third year in 31-Across's reign
34 Like any channel between 30 and 300 MHz
35 Plumbing or heating
37 Endangered Everglades mammal
39 Starbucks size bigger than grande
41 Diagram used for brainstorming
43 Other side
44 Manfred ___, 1967 Chemistry Nobelist
45 Classic Disney film that includes "The Nutcracker Suite"
47 Gravy holder
50 Hulu, e.g.
52 Enter
56 Pair

59 The Equality State: Abbr.
60 *Mark your card!*
61 See 54-Down
63 Parking lot mishap
64 Lose luster
65 State with the least populous capital
70 Raison d'___
72 Thrown off course
73 *Mark your card!*
77 Genetic stuff
78 Tailors
79 What "prn" on a prescription means
80 Muscular Charles
82 Any trump
83 Worry words
89 The "it" in the 1990s slogan "Gotta have it"
93 Writer Zora ___ Hurston
97 Opposite of charge
98 Exposed sandbar, maybe
99 Prodded
101 Pigs
102 Golfer Michelle
104 Org. headquartered in Detroit
105 Cover girl Carol
106 Placed
108 Vaughn's co-star in "The Break-Up," 2006
110 "This round's ___"
111 *Mark your card!*
114 Deuce, e.g.
115 Paris couturier Pierre
117 Occasional 1960s protest
118 Prefix with directional
119 What an aurilave cleans
120 Affirm, with "to"
121 Elates

122 Horse of a different color?
123 Genetic stuff
124 *Mark your card!*

DOWN

1 *Mark your card!*
2 "Me too"
3 Writing's opposite
4 Depraved
5 Chemical suffix
6 Singer Jones
7 Jay who once hosted "Last Comic Standing"
8 Better, as an offer
9 Mock
10 Places of worship
11 "___ Wiedersehen"
12 Monopoly token
13 Statement of self-confidence
14 "Who wants to go next?"
15 With 49-Down, order at a Chinese restaurant
16 *Mark your card!*
17 "Walk Away ___" (1966 hit by the Left Banke)
18 Combine that makes combines
26 Second-most common Vietnamese family name, after Nguyen
29 *Mark your card!*
30 Novelist Janowitz
34 Hollywood crosser
36 Prefix with center
38 Circuit
40 Bone attachment
42 World Economic Forum host city
46 Base's opposite
48 Put away
49 See 15-Down
51 Sick
53 *Mark your card!*

54 With 61-Across, prospectors' targets
55 The 13th item in a baker's dozen
56 Banned insecticide
57 Vote for
58 Mo. when the Civil War started
62 Number of wonders of el mundo antiguo
66 Department store department
67 Roar for a toreador
68 Untested
69 Football stat.
71 Within: Prefix
72 Soap opera, e.g.
73 Undergrad degs.
74 The A.C.C.'s Seminoles
75 *Mark your card!*
76 Celebrated in style
81 ". . . blackbirds baked in ___"
84 Baseball stat.
85 Skin colorer
86 School near Windsor Castle
87 Went around
88 German mercenary
90 Spoils
91 Sailor's vision obstructer
92 *Mark your card!*
94 Popular 1940s radio show "___ Alley"
95 Get ready to fall, maybe
96 Star employee
99 Does perfectly
100 ___ Janis, star of Broadway's "Puzzles of 1925"
103 Like some pyramids

BINGO

B	I	N	G	O
15	20	35	60	72
8	21	44	50	65
12	17	FREE	49	71
11	16	31	48	68
7	19	40	53	61

by Todd Gross

107 Try it out
109 Trillion: Prefix
110 "___ put it another way . . ."
112 YouTube clip, for short
113 Bambi's aunt
116 Agcy. regulating guns

ACROSS

1 Low-I.Q.
4 Slender amount
8 Letterman airer
13 Venerable
19 Gasteyer of stage and screen
20 He's less than a gentleman
21 Broadcast element
22 Carnival sight
23 Goal of Sun-Maid's marketing department?
26 You might give this a gun
27 Conclude by
28 Shower with force
29 Go back to square one
31 Office holder, of sorts
32 Willow twigs
35 Word with interface or option
36 Part of a brake
39 Salad bar activity?
45 Hot air
48 Composer Thomas
50 Beat poet Cassady
51 Actress Lotte
52 Book on how to repair rodent damage?
58 Immigrant's course, for short
59 Dwellers on the Strait of Hormuz
60 Overseas news source, in brief
61 Pays down incrementally
64 Murphy's "48 HRS." co-star
65 Seeped
68 "Drat!"
69 Reason that nothing's growing on the farm?

75 Peculiar: Prefix
76 Rugby play
77 Units of sweat
80 Subject for 48-Across
85 Athos, to Aramis
86 Dish served ranchero-style
87 Take a powder
88 Question from a campaign committee?
92 Old Apple laptop
95 Push
96 Company founded in 1940 as Standard Games
97 Bottom line
98 Exercise for beginning yoga students?
103 Hang around
105 Push too hard, maybe
106 Was gaping
108 Aloha Tower site
112 Porous kitchen utensils
117 Throws together
118 Eight-time Canadian skating champion
119 Repay
120 Tardy illustrator's assurance?
124 Be on the brink
125 Up time
126 Broadway columnist Wilson
127 Whiz
128 Position player's stat
129 Baron Cohen who created 25-Down
130 Cart for heavy loads
131 Lead character on "Pushing Daisies"

DOWN

1 Took a chance
2 For the birds
3 Ones who'll straighten you up?
4 Formal order
5 Cloud chamber particle
6 Form of 4-Down
7 P.M. preceded and succeeded by Shamir
8 Easy gallop
9 Chum
10 Reagan cause: Abbr.
11 Pantry array
12 Science fiction author A. E. van __
13 Against, with "to"
14 Well-bred
15 Cry before waving the hand
16 Ruler of the Aesir
17 Isolated
18 Had no play in crazy eights
24 Retailer beginning in 1867
25 Alter ego of Borat and Brüno
30 Start of a German goodbye
33 Two-time Haitian president Préval
34 In the public eye
37 Home south of the border
38 Gemstone sources
40 Zilch
41 Spare
42 Deadly 1966 hurricane
43 Closing bell place: Abbr.
44 Hoedown participants
45 Enter
46 Early Michael Jackson style
47 Petty

49 End of a ballade
53 Really engrossed
54 Something often thought of as impending
55 Lab challenges
56 Branching point
57 Diploma holder
62 Court of justice
63 Destitute
66 S.A.S.E., e.g.
67 Informal headwear
70 Actress Lollobrigida
71 Novelist Morrison
72 Sport of a rikishi
73 Sends out
74 California pol Newsom
78 Ready, in the kitchen
79 U.S. Army E-6
80 Naval lockup
81 Bumpkin
82 __ a secret
83 Pulitzer playwright of 1953
84 Heaps
86 Science fiction prize
89 Lots of moolah
90 Switch lines, say?
91 Mineral that crystallizes from magma
93 Town on the SE tip of Italy that's the title setting for a Horace Walpole novel
94 "M*A*S*H" corporal
99 Council members
100 One using a comb
101 Tokyo's airport
102 Meaning of the emoticon :-D
104 Whom a thane attended
107 Pushed, with "on"

by Michael Ashley

109 Broad style of cuisine
110 From this time
111 Pushed
112 Actress Blanchett
113 Much-repeated word in air traffic control
114 Creepy look
115 Vitamin bottle info, for short
116 Mex. miss
118 Right turn ___
121 Symbol of simplicity
122 When doubled, a musical effect
123 Prohibition, e.g.

45 THAT IS TWO SAY

ACROSS

1 Horrify
6 Get ready to go
10 Leopard's home?
14 Club
19 Excel
20 Jai ___
21 Baby carrier
22 Sierra ___
23 Resort region near Barcelona
25 Drug distributor
27 Famous Giant
28 Country singer Gibbs
29 Vein contents
30 Surface films: Var.
31 Dental problem
33 Key sequence in a chromosome
36 Chitchat
37 Very noticeable
39 Jacob who wrote "How the Other Half Lives"
40 Praiseworthy
42 Self-satisfied
44 Hospital bill items
46 Prefix with function
47 Chianti and Beaujolais
50 Big rush
52 ___ Cube
56 Authors' aids: Abbr.
58 ___-Japanese War
59 Brown v. Board of Education city
60 Music compilation marketer
63 Pro ___
65 Of the mouth's roof
68 Envision
70 1873 adventure novel that begins and ends in London
73 Less popular, as a restaurant
74 "Fer-de-Lance" mystery novelist
75 Certain palms
76 "WKRP in Cincinnati" role
77 Driving surface
79 Crown
81 Flicka, e.g.
82 Attacked
83 Republic once known as Dahomey
84 Surname of two signers of the Declaration of Independence
85 From ___ Z
87 Stop worrying
90 Take part in
93 Dipstick housing
97 Masters piece
99 Car make of the 1930s
102 No. on a check
103 American everyman
106 Unaccented syllable
108 It's not to be touched
110 Like some humor
111 Andrea known as the liberator of Genoa
113 "Patience ___ virtue"
114 Ethan Frome portrayer, 1993
116 Jealous
118 "Sesame Street" regular
119 It might be assumed
120 Opera set in ancient Egypt
121 Courtyards
122 Baby bottle tops
123 Tag in an antique store
124 Med. dose
125 "Sailing to Byzantium" writer

DOWN

1 Dressy tie
2 Life magazine staple
3 Something to draw
4 Queen's servant, maybe
5 Baseball coverage?
6 Catherine who survived Henry VIII
7 Screamer at a crime scene
8 Pricey appetizer
9 Maker of the Optima
10 Wow
11 "Real Time With Bill ___"
12 Antismoking org.
13 Latin catchphrase sometimes seen on sundials
14 Casual farewell
15 Numerical prefix
16 Passing
17 Closes tight
18 Doesn't bother
24 Post decorations on four-posters
26 "The ___ Love" (Gershwin song)
29 Depression-era migrant
32 Recommendation
34 Prestigious London hotel
35 Fill the tank
38 Yellow poplar
41 Some pop-ups
43 Singer Washington
45 Author of the Barsetshire novels
47 San ___ (San Francisco suburb)
48 Singer who played herself in "Ocean's Eleven"
49 Barbershop sights
51 Stomach
53 Suitable for
54 Venerated image: Var.
55 Units of fineness
57 Offensive lines?
59 Like vinaigrette
60 "Married . . . With Children" actress
61 Gloomy Milne character
62 Flat dweller
64 One of the Pointer Sisters
66 Full of fear
67 How drunks drink
69 Dutch export
71 Judge
72 Guitarist Eddy
78 One end of a digression, for short?
80 Go aboard
82 Flimflam
83 Chisel face
85 Large wardrobe
86 "From Russia With Love" Bond girl Romanova
88 Rejected as unworthy
89 Mug with a mug
91 Corrode
92 Density symbol
93 Pill that's easily swallowed
94 Driver of the Cannonball Special
95 Excellent
96 Flu symptom, with "the"
98 Leaf vein
100 "Peer Gynt" princess

by Patrick Berry

101 Bad connection,
    say
104 Carny booth prize
105 "Here Come the
    ___" (Abbott and
    Costello film set at
    a girls' school)
107 Sneaker material

109 Struck down,
    old-style
112 Harvest
115 The Great Lakes'
    ___ Locks
116 Slang for a
    3-Down
117 Suffix with favor

ACROSS

1 Political comedian with the 1973 album "Sing a Song of Watergate"
9 Breakfast dishware
16 Whispered message lead-in
20 Agreements
21 Major-league manager who won World Series in both leagues
22 Stat. for 1-Down
23 Article written by an early American patriot?
25 Line formed at a barbershop?
26 Ticked (off)
27 Active military conflicts
28 "No way, no how!"
29 Farm worker
32 Record label for Bill Haley and His Comets
34 Enemy in the 1980s arcade game Arabian
35 Alfred of "The Da Vinci Code"
36 Ditty, e.g.
38 Japanese drama
39 Dental problem for a boxing promoter?
42 When repeated, gleeful student's cry
44 Chinese dynasty of 1,000 years ago
46 Obstruct
47 Desire to be more like an actress of Greek descent?
52 Shrubby expanse

56 Godzilla contemporary that was a giant flying turtle
57 One rewarded for good behavior, perhaps
58 Like gymnasts' bodies
59 Saturate
61 Company that makes Styrofoam
62 Dance club V.I.P.'s
65 Silent signal
66 Adorable child of an edgy filmmaker?
73 Link letters
74 "___ to Joy"
75 Cut (off)
76 So-called art silk
77 Gulf of ___, modern pirates' realm
79 Become a sailor
82 Hidden
86 "D'Artagnan Romances" author
88 Tent used by a Latin musician?
90 Theme
92 Literary pen name
93 Attack tactic
94 Television award given to a Surrealist?
100 Alias indication
102 List
103 Inception
104 "___ note to follow . . ."
105 Asian film genre
107 Foxlike
108 Safari weapon
109 Oyster bed diver
112 R&B singer Hendryx
114 Noirish
115 Rodent named for a 20th-century novelist?

120 Name beside a harp on euro coins
121 Getting ready for a hand
122 Car air freshener shape
123 Brothers
124 Less lenient
125 Draws

DOWN

1 Range: Abbr.
2 3,600 secondi
3 "Stand" band
4 Stretched to the limit
5 The Black Stallion, e.g.
6 Actress Quinn
7 Cause of congestion
8 Deadhead's supply
9 Red-haired PBS star
10 Intestinal opening?
11 Slowly started pleasing
12 John of "High Fidelity"
13 "Back in the ___"
14 Smokey Bear spots, for short
15 Express
16 Looney Tunes lothario
17 Like much of the Danube's territory
18 First name at Wimbledon
19 Dish setting for watching satellite programs?
24 Brainstorming cry
28 "Ob-vi-ous-ly!"
29 Copying
30 Mobile phone giant
31 Latish wake-up time

33 Animal that leaves when it's cared for?
35 "Singin' in the Rain" studio
37 Get closer
39 Clue game board space
40 "If only ___ known . . ."
41 Parliament vote
43 Begin liking
45 Like
48 Overly enthusiastic
49 Crush, e.g.
50 Southern Conference school
51 Salamandridae family member
53 "___ Got No" ("Hair" song)
54 Empath on "Star Trek: T.N.G."
55 London's ___ Park
60 A, in Armentières
62 Forensic ID
63 Bloomsday honoree
64 Skedaddles
66 Campus space
67 Asian tongue
68 Something on a table: Abbr.
69 Heaps
70 ___-Rooter
71 Member of a modern theocracy
72 Debut
78 III, IV and V, maybe
79 Shower need
80 Chop ___
81 Electric ___
83 Modern pentathlon equipment
84 Imperial
85 Wee
87 More likely to snap
88 "America" contraction
89 Turning the other cheek

by Todd McClary

47

AUTHOR! AUTHOR!

ACROSS

1 Fish
6 Walk away with
9 ___ Wagner, player on an ultrarare baseball card
14 Fictional inspector Dalgliesh
18 Sounded soft and sweet
19 Name after "you"
20 Gulf Stater
21 Willing
22 Bret and Robert's treatise on acid reflux?
24 Nathanael and Jack's travel guide about Heathrow's environs?
26 Prove it
27 It includes the line "The True North strong and free!"
29 Maxima
30 To-do
31 Diminutive drum
32 Team on the Thames
34 Faux pas
37 Jonathan and Alice's account of a pedestrian in a hurry?
40 "___ hoppen?"
43 Prefix with metric
44 "Guys and Dolls" song
45 Old dancing duo
47 C. P. and E. B.'s essay on purity?
50 South Dakota, to Pierre
53 Admission of ineptitude
54 Apportion
55 "Come on, help me out"
57 Nightmare figure

58 ___ Treaty, establishing the 49th parallel as a U.S. border
59 Caleb and Robert B.'s novel about valet service?
62 Went undercover
63 Hunk's pride
64 Flag holder
65 Drop ___ (start to strip)
66 Small island
68 Six-footer from Australia
70 Richard and Thomas's book about a robot?
73 Golf ball feature
76 Advance
78 Very tense and excited
79 Went by Saturn, say
80 Make a commitment
82 British tax
83 Rex and Stephen's biography of Henry VIII?
85 Ally of the Cheyenne
87 Another ally of the Cheyenne
88 Ltd., in Paris
89 With 100-Across, Naples opera house Teatro di ___
90 Oscar and Isaac's profile of Little Richard?
94 Dells
96 Abbr. before a date
97 Hindu soul
98 He was born Lucius Domitius Ahenobarbus
100 See 89-Across
103 Big newspaper company, informally
105 Stuck
109 Dan and Virginia's story of a dark-colored predator?

111 Ezra and Irving's memoir of a stand-up comic?
113 Italian isle
114 ___ ligation
115 Breather
116 Plays the banjo, e.g.
117 Looking good
118 Coordinate geometry calculation
119 Sentence shortener, for short
120 Stations

DOWN

1 Berlin octet
2 Preparer for a flood
3 Colosseum spectacle
4 Freed
5 Gertrude ___, first woman to swim the English Channel
6 Declaration of 1941
7 Very quickly
8 Food brand name with an accent
9 Question to a brown cow
10 Golf champ Mark
11 Former stock regulating org.
12 Removes from a bulletin board
13 Part of R.S.V.P.
14 For whom Safire wrote the words "nattering nabobs of negativism"
15 Early vocabulary word
16 Madly
17 Department store department
19 One-piece outfit
23 Emmy-winning Arthur
25 They're on the Met schedule
28 Co. that dances at the Met
33 Go to bed

34 Gadget
35 "Fort Apache, The Bronx" actor
36 Horton and John's podiatry journal article?
38 Sweaty
39 In the future
40 Richard and Reynolds's bargain hunting manual?
41 Artist Rousseau
42 Posed
44 Keep away
46 Judge who presided over 1995's most celebrated trial
48 "And away ___!"
49 Some drivers
50 Sonnet ending
51 Typist's sound
52 Give ___ (care)
55 Holstein and Hereford
56 When repeated, a Thor Heyerdahl title
59 Browbeaten
60 Parisian walk
61 Grammy winner Bonnie
64 Javits Center architect
67 Response to "How are you?"
68 "___ Dream" from "Lohengrin"
69 Stiller and ___
71 Like a really good game for a pitcher
72 R&B and C&W: Abbr.
73 Very sweet, as Champagne
74 Big Red
75 Noses out
77 Temporary falloff
79 Sad time
81 Former capital of the Yukon
83 Leaves with notice

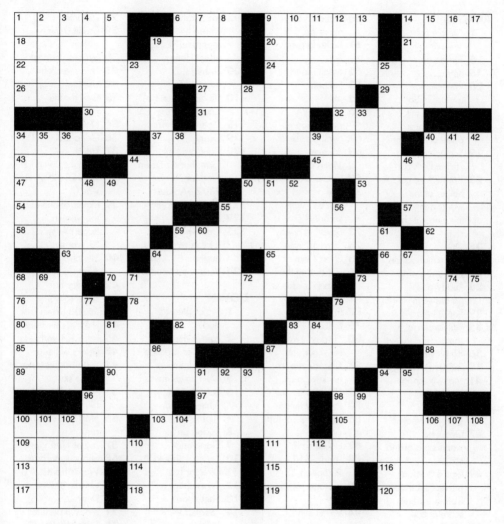

by Randolph Ross

84 ___ loop (skating move)
86 King Cole, e.g.
87 Brand that has "Real Facts" on its products
91 Bit of winter protection
92 Archie Bunker's plea to Edith
93 Baby-sitter's headache
94 Absorbs
95 Blew one's top
96 Stanford QB drafted #1 in 1983
99 Boundary
100 Semi conductor?
101 Janis's comics partner
102 Fleeces, perhaps
104 Detroit's ___ Center
106 Little, in La Scala
107 Cleaning up a mess, maybe
108 Mrs. Dick Tracy
110 Pkg. stats
112 A.C.C. school

ACROSS

1 *"Before the Mirror"*
6 Turned off
15 Bête ___
20 Westernmost avenue in Santa Monica, Calif.
21 Rewards of a political machine
22 Schindler of "Schindler's List"
23 With 29-Across, holder of the works named in the nine italicized clues
26 One at risk of excommunication
27 California wind
28 Ready-go go-between
29 See 23-Across
35 Philharmonic sect.
36 45 players
39 2000s TV family
41 Many a school fund-raiser
46 "What's going ___ there?"
47 One who works on a grand scale?
49 Game in which players subtract from a starting score of 501
50 "Big" number in college athletics
51 Station
52 Year Columbus died
53 Letter-shaped construction pieces
54 New Deal inits.
55 "___ party time!"
56 Legal org.
59 Horse and buggy

60 Needing a massage, say
61 Be hung over, e.g.
62 Small island
63 Enchant
65 Miff
66 1970s TV production co.
67 Symbols like @
68 *"Green Violinist"*
69 Gazes at
72 Like a bond you can buy with security?
73 Savor, in a way
74 "Frasier" role
75 Short swim
76 V.P. during the Cuban missile crisis
77 In order (to)
79 Lo-___
80 "Today" rival, for short
81 Canadian-born hockey great
82 "Eldorado" grp.
83 Perfectly timed
85 Like some YouTube videos
87 House call?
88 Landlocked European
90 Vintage Tonka toy
94 Water swirl
95 In need of blusher, say
97 *"Composition 8"*
98 Old credit-tracking corp.
99 Clytemnestra, to Agamemnon
102 Light planes
103 *"Peasant With Hoe"*
106 Subject of the Joni Mitchell song "Amelia"

108 Jazz standard whose title is repeatedly sung after "Honey . . ."
109 "May I ___ question?"
110 "Rebel Without a Cause" actress
118 Operatic prince
119 Grand
120 Controversial form that 43-Down used for 23-/29-Across
121 Like some traffic
122 Lummoxes
123 One who gets a lot of return business?
124 Verb with "vous"

DOWN

1 Lepidopterist's study
2 Pain in the neck
3 Poetic contraction
4 Enters leisurely
5 Govt. investments
6 Part of some Bibles: Abbr.
7 Flight
8 Midori on ice
9 North end?
10 ". . . ___ should I"
11 Director Lee
12 Cross shape
13 Shell food?
14 *"Seated Woman, Wiping Her Left Side"*
15 Like 43-Down's design for 23-/29-Across
16 Org. setting workplace rules
17 Swedish company with a catalog
18 Drops from the sky
19 Gospel singer Franklin
24 Flambé, say

25 ___'acte
29 Castle security system
30 Bygone channel
31 "No seats left"
32 Use (up), as time
33 One for the money?
34 *"Tableau 2"*
36 Good lookers
37 Fated
38 With 43-Down, what 23-/29-Across was
39 Player of one of the women in Robert Altman's "3 Women"
40 Site of Spain's Alamillo Bridge
42 Jewelry firm since 1842
43 See 38-Down
44 U.S.P.S. deliveries
45 Latin 101 verb
47 Drinks of liquor
48 Sixth-brightest star in the sky
51 *"Mandolin and Guitar"*
56 Start of a common run
57 Joy of "The View"
58 Showing surprise
64 Words from Charlie Brown
70 Dog-___
71 Many a perfume
75 Epps of "House"
78 Shrub that may cause a severe allergic reaction
80 Leaden, in London
84 Angela Merkel's one
85 Place for a stamp
86 Sorts
89 School popular in the 1920s
91 Autumn ESPN highlights

by Elizabeth C. Gorski

92 Sue Grafton's "___ for Ricochet"
93 Common middle name for a girl
94 Scholarly
96 Code-cracking grp.
98 "Time out!" signal
99 Old defense grp.
100 Turkish bigwig
101 *"The Antipope"*
103 Early spring feast
104 Just love
105 Life preserver, e.g.
107 Spanish tidbit
108 Skinny
111 B.O. purchases
112 *"Head and Shell"*
113 Roman household god
114 Paris's ___ Saint-Louis
115 Medium strength?
116 "Huh?"
117 Viking ship item

ACROSS

1 "My People" writer
9 Its motto is "Under God, the people rule": Abbr.
13 ___ Errol, main character in "Little Lord Fauntleroy"
19 Violent behavior due to excessive use of banned athletic substances
20 Humana competitor
22 Time's 1986 Woman of the Year
23 Start of a wish by 112-Across on 9/21/09
25 Big name in tires
26 ___ bark beetle (pest)
27 Nita of silents
28 Wish, part 2
30 ___ of the Guard
34 Actress Merrill
36 Like the best wallets?
37 Working hours
40 Lucy's guy
42 Big wheels
43 Wish, part 3
47 [Yuck . . . that's awful!]
50 Parliament output?
51 Toward the quiet side
52 It seemingly never ends
53 Page, e.g.
54 Malia's sister in the White House
57 Wish, part 4
63 Table scrap
65 Oxford, e.g.
66 Paragons
67 Garage container
71 Wish, part 5
73 ___ the Laborer, patron saint of farmers
74 Hell's Angels, e.g.
76 Aside from that
79 Prince ___ Khan, third husband of Rita Hayworth
80 Wish, part 6
84 Transition
88 Words of agreement
89 Musical sense
90 Not in operation
92 Christmas hours in N.Y.C.
93 Law, in Lima
94 Magazine for which 112-Across writes
101 Refuse
102 What can one do?
103 Actor who said "I'll make him an offer he can't refuse"
104 Tropical grassland
107 Astronomer's sighting
109 Minotaur feet
112 NBC football analyst/reporter and longtime writer
114 Flavor
117 Sudan neighbor: Abbr.
118 Kind of penguin
119 End of the wish
124 More massive
125 Magical symbol
126 Take for a spin
127 Infiltrates, say
128 Ballet jump
129 Soda bottle size

DOWN

1 Dick who was once House majority leader
2 Danny who directed "Slumdog Millionaire"
3 Windbags
4 Whirl
5 Long, long time
6 ___ Harbour (Miami suburb)
7 Sayin' no to
8 "99 Luftballons" pop group
9 Got hitched
10 Noah Webster, for one
11 "I already ___"
12 Pullover, e.g.
13 Middle-school Girl Scout
14 Draws a parallel between
15 Boneheads
16 Streamlets
17 Kind of tray
18 Hack it
21 Starting from
24 Obama's honorary deg. from Notre Dame
29 Creator of Oz
31 Dashboard stat
32 "L'heure d'___" (2008 Juliette Binoche film)
33 Historic ship whose real name was Santa Clara
35 Cockeyed
38 Nickname of the Spice Girls' Sporty Spice
39 Porcelain containers, maybe
41 Poem with the lines "Nobody'll dare / Say to me, / 'Eat in the kitchen'"
43 ___ in ice
44 Hush-hush org.
45 Michelle of "Crouching Tiger, Hidden Dragon"
46 Memo intro
47 Contraption
48 Freud disciple Alfred
49 Canada ___
53 Chemical coloring
55 Famous deerstalker wearer
56 Shady spot
58 "___ thought"
59 John Elway, for the Broncos
60 Printer resolution meas.
61 Piazza dei Miracoli town
62 Monthly expenditures: Abbr.
64 Battery, e.g.
67 Like most music
68 It has ray flowers
69 "Sheesh!"
70 Losing tic-tac-toe combo
72 Bridge expert Culbertson
75 Member of the Brew Crew, e.g.
77 Dirty
78 Land, eventually
81 "___ all!" ("Fini!")
82 Hot topic in insurance
83 ___ Schneider, villainess in "Indiana Jones and the Last Crusade"
85 "Stop your moping!"
86 Capitalize on
87 Flight board fig.
91 Impress permanently
94 More hairy
95 Some Warped Tour attendees
96 Big name in hotels
97 Lame excuse for missing homework
98 Endearing
99 2016 Olympics locale
100 It's got mayo
101 Thin
104 Alternative to a wagon
105 Secret event of '45
106 Harvesters, e.g.

by Brendan Emmett Quigley

ACROSS

1 Tops
5 Quilt filler
9 Detest
14 Some I.R.A.'s
17 Some extra books
19 Softly
20 Post a modern status update
22 Eyewear providing hindsight?
24 French town
25 Restrain
26 Game in which a player may be schneidered
27 Repeated a Benjamin Franklin electrical experiment
29 Peanut-loving ghost?
32 Intermittent revolutionary?
33 Afflicts
34 "___ Can Cook" (onetime PBS show)
35 Leader against the Aztecs
36 Hearing aids, briefly
37 Christianity, e.g.: Abbr.
38 Bluff bit
40 Desert stream
41 Emulate a grandparent, maybe
43 Rare mushroom?
47 "Uh-uh"
51 Backrub response
52 It comes before the carte
53 Put away
55 Some sushi bar orders
56 Give up smuggled goods?
62 Guards against chapping

64 Area code 801 area
65 Swamp thing
66 Use www.irs.gov, say
68 Not exciting
69 1989 Madonna hit
71 High-school athletic star at a casino?
74 ___ area
75 Indian government of 1858–1947
77 Word from Antony to Cleopatra
78 Parisian roll call response
79 Barack Obama, for one
81 Noble Les Paul?
88 "As ___ Dying"
90 Man's name meaning "young man"
91 Coward with a pen
92 ___ gratification
93 Boombox button
95 Hannibal of "The Silence of the Lambs"
97 Old TWA hub: Abbr.
98 Three or four
99 "Maybe" music?
101 Dreams that don't die?
104 1946 John Hersey book
105 Runner Budd
106 Simile words
107 Japanese financial center
108 Bug that never takes a ride?
113 Deux of these are better than one
114 "As You Like It" setting
115 Hustle
116 60 minuti

117 "This I Promise You" group, 2000
118 "Bill ___ History of the United States"
119 Détente

DOWN

1 Limo, e.g.
2 Form of the Egyptian god Thoth
3 Paunch
4 Gives up on
5 What "two" meant, historically
6 iPhone download
7 Broadway, say
8 Append
9 Give ___ on the back
10 Inexpensive pen
11 Greatly reduced
12 Trading unit
13 Fairy tale sister
14 Sporty Toyota
15 River areas named for their shape
16 Mettle or metal
18 "The Human Stain" novelist
20 Big Super Bowl expense
21 Like online medical advice for kids?
23 Pompom holder
28 Had as a base
29 One of three brothers in the Old West
30 White ones are little
31 Swimmer Diana
32 Fountain order
35 Kind of bean
38 Blacken
39 Go over and over
40 Director, writer and actor in "The Woman in Red," 1984

42 Age-old robbers' target
44 Vegetable that gives you an emotional release?
45 Eng. or Span.
46 "Lux et Veritas" collegian
48 Belief of about 1½ billion
49 Pause producer
50 City near Düsseldorf
54 Bias
56 New York politico Andrew
57 Follower of each or no
58 Source of a "giant sucking sound," according to Ross Perot
59 Common cause of a 3-Down
60 Not fun at all
61 Mad man?
63 Opposite of plus
67 "Dona ___ and Her Two Husbands"
70 Lever or level
72 "The Big Country," for one
73 Sci. specialty
76 Peachy-keen
80 "Happy Days" role
82 Poker star Phil
83 Like some stock market highs and lows
84 Lone
85 Strip, sand and stain
86 Tommie of the Amazins
87 Tugboat services
89 Sammy Davis Jr. autobiography
93 Hunt's "Mad About You" co-star
94 Slips

by Matt Ginsberg and Pete Muller

96 They've got promise
97 Like many an oath
98 Dormant Turkish volcano
99 Candid, maybe
100 Botanist Gray and others
101 Popinjay

102 Mings, e.g.
103 Job precursor: Abbr.
105 97.5% of a penny
109 X
110 Manage, with "out"
111 ___ premium
112 Mint

51

COLONIZATION

ACROSS

1 Oriole, e.g., briefly
5 "Still waters run deep," for example
10 Microwaves
14 Bygone Toyota model
19 Prefix with factor
20 Brand with a pyramid on the package
21 Verve
22 Person with a program
23 "O say can you see" or "Thru the perilous fight"?
25 Resident of a military installation?
27 Divine
28 Lace shade
30 Place on a bus
31 Business card abbr.
32 Boxful for Bowser
33 Miss in Monterrey: Abbr.
34 Bring in
35 Alarm
36 Architect Saarinen
37 Confronting boldly
39 Singer Simon
40 Tropical fruit seller?
44 Tape holder
47 Alley ___
48 Run down, in slang
49 Collectible disks
52 Singer India.___
53 Philadelphia's historic Gloria ___ Church
54 Singer Horne
55 Lacking serviceability
57 Poet Federico García ___
59 Hair net
61 Place to get drunk in the kitchen?
63 About to get
64 A as in Austria
65 Original nuclear regulatory grp.
66 Craggy ridge
67 What overuse of a credit card might result in?
70 "That's ___" ("It's done")
72 Seasons
73 Not so cool
74 Drains
76 Like, '60s-style
78 Old brand in the shaving aisle
79 Toledo-to-Columbus dir.
80 "Casablanca" role
81 Cool
82 Put back on the market
84 Gentleman's intransigent reply?
87 Means of identifying wood
90 Dry Champagne, e.g.
91 Horseshoer's tool
95 Columnist Barrett
96 &&&&
98 This one, in Acapulco
99 Against
101 Latin 101 verb
102 Redheaded kid of old TV
103 "The Time Machine" race
104 More than the immediate future
105 Where nitpickers walk on a street?
108 Online beauty contest?
110 Obliterate
111 Nabisco product
112 Group with the 2002 hit "Girlfriend"
113 Isn't straight
114 Cobbler's supply
115 Seizes
116 Drug agent's seizure
117 Handy ___

DOWN

1 Toward the stern
2 Poe poem
3 Beef Wellington, e.g.
4 Take up again, as a case
5 High points
6 Place for a rivulet
7 Porthos, to Aramis
8 Produce
9 Bygone Buick
10 Indian bovine
11 Part of many fancy dish names
12 Part of a book . . . or something to book
13 Scornful expression
14 Tallow ingredient
15 Blue Angels org.
16 Sci-fi weapon
17 Vacation place, often
18 Boulevard, e.g.
24 Impedes legally
26 Whip
29 Sent a message to shore, say
33 Guard
34 Heavy sheet inside a book's cover
35 Away's partner
37 ___ Motel
38 Home ___
39 Pauses during speech: Var.
41 Had the upper hand
42 Score just before winning
43 Bit of fluff
44 Back-room cigar smokers, say
45 United charge
46 Back up
49 Object of a scurrilous attack, maybe
50 Like surveyors' charts
51 Most withered
52 Makes flush
54 Cambodia's ___ Nol
56 54-Down, e.g.
58 Goldsmith, for one
60 Crude transports
62 College world
65 Utterances around baby pictures
68 Moccasin decoration
69 Diner manager/waitress in "Garfield"
70 Shirts and blouses
71 Rice ___
75 "Je vous ___"
77 Gibson necessity
82 Most dilapidated
83 Muscly
84 Cara ___ (term of endearment)
85 Sherry-like wine
86 Takes out of the will, say
87 Basis of 85-Down
88 "Night of the Living Dead" director, 1968
89 From one end of a battery
92 Cartwright of "Make Room for Daddy"

by Robert W. Harris

93 Group of viruses
94 Trimmed
96 Quick
97 Subject of a museum in Yorba Linda, Calif.
99 One way to fly
100 Fidgety
102 Till compartment
103 Cause of star wars?
104 Hosp. staffers
106 Enzyme suffix
107 Wyo. neighbor
109 ___ hair

52

MAN OF MANY WORDS

Note: When this puzzle has been completed, connect the circled letters in order from A to N to get an appropriate image.

ACROSS

1 Pair of pears
7 Young socialites
11 "___ Nagila" (song title that means "Let us rejoice")
15 Move from Los Angeles to New York, say
16 Ply with liquor
17 Helped settle an argument
21 *Tony Parsons novel [1943 song]
23 Source of black diamonds
24 Workout count
25 Like some valves
26 *Mandarin variety [1942]
27 Had brunch
28 Some dogs
29 Aminos, e.g.
31 Robert of "The Sopranos"
32 No-good
34 Lost
35 Thrice daily, on an Rx
37 Molokai and Maui: Abbr.
38 Left-wingers
40 Bread box?
41 Last non-A.D. year
44 One way to put out an album
45 "Blah, blah, blah"
47 William ___, the Father of Modern Medicine
49 Seeds might be planted in it
51 Greek god of the north wind
53 Late Saudi king
55 2001 World Series winner
57 Uranium source, e.g.
58 "Mad Men" extra
61 Stylish filmmaker

64 Pink-slip
65 Mental flashes
67 *It flows into Ontario's Georgian Bay [1961]
69 Soup server
70 9/
71 "Pretty please?"
72 Glide (over)
74 Weak-looking
75 Girl Scout symbol
77 Revise
79 Nanny's warning
81 Orch. section
82 Attack fiercely
85 Curvy-horned animals
88 Took a gander at
89 Of element #76
91 Strong joe
93 ". . . ___ saw Elba"
94 Copy job delayers
95 Hubbub
96 "Are you in ___?"
98 Faux gold
100 Billing no.
103 Beachgoer's hair lightener
104 Get 100 on a test
105 Ungodliness
108 *Laurel and Hardy flick [1949]
111 Oil source
113 Suffix with billion
114 Move from New York to Los Angeles, say
115 Lyricist who wrote the words to the 10 songs with starred clues
117 Whenever
118 Dr. Alzheimer
119 Off the coast
120 Suffix with tip
121 "What's Going On" singer
122 Some wraps

DOWN

1 Greek market
2 Three trios
3 *"Omigosh!" [1938]
4 Dummkopfs
5 Show grp.
6 Narrow way
7 Shopaholic's accumulation
8 Morales in movies
9 Texas State athlete
10 It's a mess
11 *Rural jaunt [1945]
12 "Garfield: ___ of Two Kitties" (2006 film)
13 "Les Voyages Extraordinaires" writer
14 Abacus user
16 Like "Don Juan"
17 Rachel of "Mean Girls"
18 Ages and ages
19 Nobelist Hammarskjöld
20 Suffix with duct
22 Vintage Ford
26 Associate with
28 Knox and others: Abbr.
30 See 110-Down
33 Vintage sign word
34 Hollywood pooch
35 Start of an adage about forgiveness
36 Cross inscription
37 So that one can
39 Hoodwink
42 Many a 115-Across collaboration
43 Assemblies
44 Some Juilliard students
45 Maximal ending
46 *Total sham [1963]
48 *Former first lady [1945]
50 Came alive

52 Stubborn sort
54 Hwy. offense
56 Hungarian half sister?
59 *One of the Brontës [1964]
60 Cambodia's Lon ___
62 Emmy winner, e.g.
63 Hair-raising shriek
66 Div. of Justice
68 Nevada's largest county
69 See 110-Down
71 Ham radio catchword
73 Cable inits.
76 "The Wizard ___"
78 "Why did ___ this happen?"
80 Get better
83 Comes (to)
84 Swings
86 Former 38-Across
87 With desperation
90 *Toro's target [1956]
92 "Where ___ sign?"
94 Tittle
97 7-Up, with "the"
99 Indiana/Michigan natives
100 Eastern titles
101 Cardinal's topper
102 Knock it off
103 City rebuilt by Darius I
104 Photographer Leibovitz
106 Peace goddess
107 Studious crowd
109 Tandem's capacity
110 With 69-Down, V.I.P. in the 30-Down
112 Cry from a deck
113 Janis's comic strip hubby
115 Sporty wheels
116 Med. specialty

by Elizabeth C. Gorski

ACROSS

1 White-tailed movie star
6 Barbecue byproduct
11 "Many good nights, my lord; ___ your servant": Shak.
16 N.Y.C. airport
19 Literary work in which Paris is featured
20 County abutting London
21 Candy wafer company
22 Hosp. workplaces
23 Career Day Speaker #1: Meter maid?
25 Unwrinkle
27 Talk up
28 #2: Tea server?
30 Blues musician Baker
33 Chocolate-and-caramel brand
36 Filmmaker Martin
37 Big bin
38 #3: Golf pro?
44 Swan's shape
45 Many four-doors
46 1985–88 attorney general
47 Toast starter
49 Mendes of "2 Fast 2 Furious"
50 Growing-friendly
52 Perturb
56 Rap's ___ Wayne
57 Suffix with pant or aunt
58 #4: Tree surgeon?
63 Sex symbol once married to Vadim
66 Flightless bird
67 Button materials
68 First landfall north of Oman
70 #5: Manicurist?

74 Reeve or Reeves role
75 Gambler's holy grail
78 They take the bait
79 Warranty invalidator
82 #6: Justice of the peace?
86 Long. partner
87 ___-wolf
90 Literary creation
91 Skywalker's cohort
93 "No ___!"
94 "Aunt ___ Cope Book"
96 Play byplay
98 ___ Chao, only cabinet member to serve through George W. Bush's entire administration
100 Dillinger's derringer, e.g.
103 #7: Grocery store owner?
106 2007 Steve Carell title role
108 I's
109 Job bidding figs.
110 First of two choices
111 #8: Disc jockey?
116 "___-A-Lympics" (old TV cartoon series)
118 Bullies
119 Career of the parent who typed up the Career Day schedule?
125 Conclusion for many believers?
126 Bay, for one
127 Sideways up
128 Of interest to ornithologists
129 Grazing ground
130 Dump and road endings

131 "Midnight Cowboy" nickname
132 College classes

DOWN

1 Iota
2 Larter of "Heroes"
3 Amp plug-in
4 Honeyed pastry
5 Start of a plan
6 Old salt
7 Bouillon cube ingredient, usually
8 Sugar suffix
9 Boy toys?
10 Shakes down
11 Untouched
12 The Thrilla in Manila, for one
13 Reforestation subj.
14 Garbage hauler
15 Emerald City visitor
16 "Hey, see what I got!"
17 Meager bowlfuls
18 Club that began as the Colt .45s
24 Blushes
26 Over-the-wall wallops: Abbr.
29 Glazed fabric
30 It debuted on "E Day"
31 Fountain in front of the Palazzo Poli
32 Large body in Washington, D.C.
34 Appendage
35 16 oz.
39 Where Key's bombs burst
40 Reader of signs
41 Wagon puller, often
42 It's often played on Sunday
43 Madrid's ___ Sofía Art Center
48 Library section

51 From
53 Seconds
54 Many a bar mitzvah attendee
55 First, in Frankfurt
59 Prefix with -tect
60 Goal-oriented org.
61 Middle grade
62 Impair
64 San ___, Lone Star State city
65 Slight fight
68 Leads (by)
69 Hall-of-Famer Sandberg
71 A little over half a century in old Rome
72 "Help!" key
73 Unit of contraband
76 Equip with weapons, old-style
77 Mell Lazarus comic strip
80 Hand-held cutter
81 Functional
83 Cause of quailing
84 Comparable (to)
85 Break in a building's facade
88 World capital once under French rule
89 Spectators
92 Beatty and Sparks
95 Pesky biter
96 Mounted on
97 Approval for Juan Valdez
99 When Juliet says "O happy dagger!"
100 Animal in an exercise wheel
101 Unwilling
102 City in Mount Rainier's shadow
104 Disgorges
105 "I can get by with that"

by Patrick Merrell

107 Parental imperative
112 Result of 26-Down, often
113 Lot "souvenir"
114 Leafy vegetable
115 Author Jaffe
117 Skirmish

120 One likely to have pet peeves?
121 Dash lengths
122 ___ Maria
123 Human body part with vestigial muscles
124 Hosp. V.I.P.'s

54 CUED UP

ACROSS

1 Government pubs., say
5 Twine holder
10 Amateur publication, for short
14 What a migraine might feel like
18 Moonfish
19 Primary stratagem
20 Like much music
21 Old alpaca wool gatherer
22 Delighted exclamation?
25 Cough cause
26 Sail extender
27 Inventive type
28 Bit of attire for a carriage ride
29 Pitcher's feat
32 One all, say
33 Tame
34 "Tamerlane" dramatist Nicholas
35 V-chip target
36 Part of an Irish playwright's will?
38 Museum worker
40 Bank statement entry
42 It came up from Down Under
43 Tom of "The Tomorrow Show"
45 Fish-and-chips fish
46 Sultan's land
49 Aquafina competitor
54 Impertinent sort
56 TV character often seen in a Metallica T-shirt
58 Pipe attachment
59 Needle problem
62 Tests the water?
64 "Don't fight"
66 Game grp.
67 Many curves, in math
68 Carsick passenger?
70 Bon mot
71 Babylon's site, today
72 Conventions
73 Starting point
74 Some pieces in an archaeological museum
75 Bratislava's river
77 "Come on, guys!"
79 "Jour de Fête" star, director and writer, 1949
81 Neighbor of a shift key
82 "Little Women" woman
83 Iranian supreme leader ___ Khamenei
85 New Zealand's discoverer
89 49-Across, e.g.
91 Red leader?
93 Spanish girl
94 Causing uneasiness?
101 Not safe
103 Schools of thought
104 Drawers, e.g.
105 Plain and simple
106 Darjeeling, e.g.
108 White as a sheet
109 Germane
111 Last stage of insect development
112 Believe
113 Carryin' on, in olden times?
117 Gambling game enjoyed by Wyatt Earp
118 Paunch
119 Wake Island, e.g.
120 Turn over
121 Irish ___
122 Put in stitches
123 Poet who wrote "An' the Gobble-uns 'at gits you / Ef you / Don't / Watch / Out!"
124 Walked

DOWN

1 Bobs and such
2 Alphabetic trio
3 Florida Keys connector
4 Anger at losing one's flock?
5 Gymnastic feat
6 Conspired
7 Unlikely ballet dancer
8 Sign warning people to be quiet
9 Columbo's employer, for short
10 Whizzed along
11 Maraud
12 Tandoor-baked bread
13 Head of lettuce?
14 Krishna is one of his avatars
15 One surrounded by cell walls
16 Looks sore
17 Bald baby?
20 Bring up the rear
23 N.L. West team, on scoreboards
24 ___ four
28 "The Dark Knight," for one
29 Assns.
30 It may be declined
31 Suit
33 Absolute beauty
36 Call on a pitch
37 Nebraska senator Nelson
39 Easy chair site
41 Narrator of "How I Met Your Mother"
44 Blue
46 Superior to
47 It may feature a windmill
48 "Don't Be Cruel" vis-à-vis "Hound Dog"
50 Subjugation?
51 Bring about
52 Time's partner
53 Some tides
55 Name shared by 12 popes
57 Big gulf
58 French mathematician who pioneered in the theory of probability
59 Water park feature
60 Sura source
61 "Impossible!"
63 Positive thinking proponent
65 Legal writ, in brief
69 Clockmaker Thomas
76 German city where Beck's beer is brewed
78 "Our ___"
80 Certain X or O
82 Programming problem
84 Wood alternative
86 Get fogged up
87 Greatest flowering
88 Astronaut's insignia
90 Dolt
91 Like a butterfingers
92 Within earshot
94 Hearty drafts
95 Prevent from being reelected
96 Cleave
97 Try to avoid detection
98 Chevy model
99 Forsooth

by Will Nediger

100 It may be dramatic
102 Opportune
106 Matthew 26 question
107 Sound at a spa
109 "The Clan of the Cave Bear" author
110 Baseball G.M. Minaya
113 Montana and others, for short
114 Helios' counterpart
115 It may be said before a kiss
116 ___ Land of "Twenty Thousand Leagues Under the Sea"

55

DOUBLE BREAK POINT

ACROSS

1 Like mountains and maps
7 "The Lord of the Rings" dwarf
12 Attack helicopter
17 1930s heavyweight champ known as the Ambling Alp
18 Choose not to cook, say
19 Plays at maximum volume
20 Deciding the best man is better, perhaps?
22 As yet unactualized
23 Where Caleb was sent as a spy
24 Seaside bird
25 Memento of an old athletic injury?
27 Suave competitor
28 Many a shipment to Detroit
30 Air play?
31 Med. care provider
32 Nitpick?
36 Uses as a source
38 Like a foreboding sky
39 What white flour lacks
40 West Bank grp.
41 Majestic
45 Professorial material?
47 Bottom line?
50 Sorters' formations
51 Architect of the Guggenheim Museum in Bilbao
52 Double or nothing, say?
54 Gambler's declaration
55 Hymn starter
57 Like many rugs

58 Keats's "___ on Indolence"
59 Pickett's Charge participant
60 Begging soldiers?
62 Co. of which Howard Hughes became the principal shareholder in 1939
63 ___ rigueur (literally)
64 Call before a football game
65 Manchester moms
66 Handle
67 Young scientists who are impossible to work with?
69 Tips
70 View from the Quai d'Orsay
71 Sir ___, nephew of King Arthur
72 X-ray view
73 Gave birth to a litter
75 Triumphant cry
76 Kick in the rear, maybe
77 Senate tie breaker
78 Country whose name means "warrior king"
81 Things heard after thumbs are hit with hammers?
87 Languish
88 Water carrier
90 Maker of "the plow that broke the Plains"
91 Prostitute who protected Israelite spies, in Joshua
93 Holder of pet electrons, protons and neutrons?
97 Windup

98 Pro ___ (for one's country)
99 Get by somehow
100 Reductions in rank that aren't entirely bad?
103 Key holders
104 Spectacular autumn trees
105 Up
106 Setting of van Gogh's "Cafe Terrace at Night"
107 Shy
108 Adjusts for daylight saving, e.g.

DOWN

1 Large hot spot
2 Heavy lifters
3 Archival material
4 They're set for drinking and smoking
5 John-Boy Walton's sister
6 Brown who wrote "The Lost Symbol"
7 Earn
8 Skater Midori
9 Farmyard chorus
10 Mattress problem
11 "Come on in!"
12 School cards
13 Muesli ingredients
14 "Mother Courage and Her Children" playwright
15 Call again?
16 Minute Maid Park players
17 Letters on old rubles
18 Great white ___
19 Lunch orders that are typically sliced in half
21 Los Angeles museum, with "the"

26 Coll. dorm overseers
28 Off
29 Tolerant of other opinions
33 It might have an extension: Abbr.
34 James who wrote "A Million Little Pieces"
35 Boyo
37 Trace
40 Superheroes have them
41 Galaxy shape
42 Delay
43 "Arabian Nights" opener?
44 Olympics ideal
45 Competitors of Wahoos and Tar Heels
46 It's most useful when it's cracked
47 Peggy Lee's signature song
48 Vanity case?
49 Médoc, for one
51 Stock in trade
52 Stem joints
53 Brought in
55 Hall-of-Famers
56 Reluctant
57 South Los Angeles district
60 1986 film featuring Chevy Chase as Dusty Bottoms
61 Affluence
66 Cream alternative
68 ___ Mawr College
69 Ankh's top
70 Becomes layered while settling
72 Shaker's sound
73 "___ here!"
74 "Away From ___" (Julie Christie film)
76 Headwear also known as jipijapas

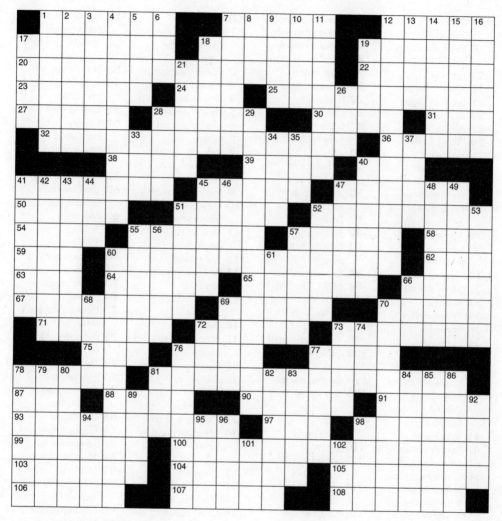

by Patrick Berry

77 Colorado's Mesa __

78 Rocking chair storyteller

79 Empty words

80 Keyless

81 Pres. title

82 "You __ bother"

83 Looks after

84 Best guide around town, probably

85 Dewlap's place

86 They're all good

89 Bullets, in Texas hold'em

92 Dishonorable

94 Horsehair source

95 "Intolerance" actress Lillian

96 Fair

98 Subway car feature

101 Suffix with slogan

102 France's Belle-Île-en-__

56

SOMETIMES A GREAT NOTION

Note: The words in the shaded spaces will spell a quotation from Linus Pauling.

ACROSS

1 Intrinsically
8 Purple-flowering tree
13 Intensify
19 Rows of buttons
21 Superior group
22 ___ Nehru Gandhi
23 Setting setting
24 "That's patently ridiculous!"
26 The Beatles' "___ Loser"
27 He played Dr. Kildare in 1930s–'40s films
29 Apartment manager, familiarly
30 Leviathan's home
31 Atkins diet no-no
33 Artoo-___
34 TV networks, e.g.
36 Caper
38 Cariou of Broadway's "Sweeney Todd"
39 Victim of Achilles
41 Muppet with a goldfish named Dorothy
45 Swabbies
47 Remote possibility?
48 Kind of butterfly
50 Giovanni of "Lost in Translation"
53 It borders the Brooklyn Botanic Garden
56 Unstressed
57 Olive in the funny pages
58 Wishful thinker of story
59 Band with the 1998 #1 hit "Iris"
62 Set the price at
64 Where a flock flocks
65 300-cubit-long craft

66 Activity for good-looking people?
69 Femur terminus
72 Carol contraction
75 Muttonhead
76 Rich blue stone
79 Hold back
82 Carry the day
83 Easily identifiable
84 All out
89 Birthplace of Jules Verne
90 White Rabbit's lament
91 Spring site
92 Piddling
93 College freshman, usually
94 Turned informer
96 Night "The Wild Wild West" was shown in 1960s TV: Abbr.
98 Pulitzer category
102 Seeks water, in a way
104 Related groups
106 Dry cleaner's challenge
107 Sculpting medium
110 Junket
111 Western accessories
114 Wrecking ball alternative
115 Cause of Irish emigration in the 1840s–'50s
118 Churlish
120 Dish often served folded over
121 Mouth feature
122 Is around longer than
123 Yen
124 Business that makes the cut?
125 Frequent Security Council topic

DOWN

1 Region of Greece containing the capital
2 Without exception
3 Tasmania's capital
4 Perpendicular wing
5 Early shepherd
6 Like bonds and movies
7 Helps in planting
8 Director Almodóvar
9 Sunscreen additive
10 They may be bowled over
11 Brief writer, in brief
12 Net assets?
13 Riot police goal
14 Key in
15 Part of a dean's address
16 Deck spots
17 Niagara River's source
18 Squat
20 Sudden rush
25 100 cents
28 Over there
32 Heavily satirical
34 "Because Freedom Can't Protect Itself" org.
35 Break off
37 Digital watch brand
39 Skimmer, e.g.
40 Lose intensity
42 She won her Best Supporting Actress Oscar for playing a man
43 Haleakala National Park setting
44 Author Robert ___ Butler
46 Big name in copiers
47 Lily variety
49 Amphitheater shape

50 Ravi Shankar performance
51 "Believe ___ Not!"
52 Spine feature
53 Nutritionists' topics
54 Actor Waggoner and others
55 Codlike fishes
60 Lane in Hollywood
61 Long-running NBC show, for short
62 Meat-stock jelly
63 The Pont Neuf spans it
67 Begins
68 "In & Out" star, 1997
70 Netman Nastase
71 Snaps
73 Under control
74 "Now!"
77 Have ___ up one's sleeve
78 Members of some city commissions
79 "M*A*S*H" co-star
80 Proctor's call
81 Replaced, on a hard drive
85 List holders
86 G-men's weapons
87 Jargon ender
88 Support
92 Low point
95 "Like that'll ever happen!"
96 Sitcom waitress
97 Numerical comparison
99 I.B.M. computer of the 1990s
100 Peaks, to Pedro
101 Bear witness
103 Web-footed mammal
104 All washed up?
105 Three more than quadri-
107 It can carry a tune
108 Turn up

by Mike Shenk

109 Busy times on the French Riviera
111 Platypus part
112 Aboard
113 Cry accompanied by a gavel rap
116 2001 biopic
117 ___ culpa
119 Creative story

ACROSS

1 Crib cry
5 N.B.A. Hall-of-Famer Thomas
10 Like some waves
15 Pillow cover
19 Jessica of "Fantastic Four"
20 Where to go for the big bucks?
21 Item on a toothpick
22 La ___, Calif.
23 It has a large canopy
25 Average Joes
27 Connected with
28 Rugby action
30 Where 7-Eleven is headquartered
31 Counter view?
33 Christmas sounds
34 "Finished!"
35 Republicans in 2008
40 See 104-Across
41 William ___, longtime editor of The New Yorker
42 Increase
43 Mastroianni's co-star in "La Dolce Vita"
45 V.I.P. locale
46 Six-Day War hero
48 "Me too"
50 Battery option
53 Bruin great
54 Lap inspector?
55 Busboy's assignment
59 Lincoln trademark
62 One who might be left holding the bag?
63 Sesame Street resident
64 Lay to rest
65 N, E, W and S
66 Title role for Arnold Schwarzenegger
69 French seaport
72 Not orig.
74 "You bet"
78 Stop a trip?
82 Avenue ___ Champs-Élysées
83 Charlotte of "Diff'rent Strokes"
84 Big name in kitchen utensils
85 Boy's name that means "the king"
86 Horace, e.g.
88 Goes to hell
89 Attack, bear-style
92 British gun
93 ___ Vivien, British poet known as the Muse of the Violets
94 Makeup boo-boo
96 Rafael Nadal specialty
101 Associate
103 "Gotcha!"
104 With 40-Across, some Election Day prizes
105 Wild
106 Lead-in to phobia
108 "Fa la la la la la la la" and others
112 Expect, everything considered
114 Unite
116 Whitaker's Oscar-winning role
117 Army of the Potomac commander during the Civil War
118 Seething
119 Put in the ground, in a way
120 Director Vittorio De ___
121 Prize for Paganini
122 Country singer Travis
123 Tolkien tree creatures

DOWN

1 Target of salicylic acid
2 Jai ___
3 Title fellow in a 1922 Broadway hit
4 Shop tools
5 Like some transfers
6 In a way
7 Communism, for one
8 Two-time loser to D.D.E.
9 Intense attraction, with "the"
10 1, 2, 3, 4, 5, etc., on a standard keyboard
11 Mistreatment
12 Geom. measure
13 Prefix with fauna
14 Three-time U.S. Open champion
15 Barely contain one's anger
16 "Oh, you're back"
17 Obliquely
18 Hoi polloi, with "the"
24 Belong
26 Like some starts
29 Dice
32 Everett of "Citizen Kane"
34 Request from
35 Windows precursor
36 Patient record
37 Home of the mask of King Tutankhamen
38 Old Coney Island's ___ Park
39 Frequent Borat target
44 Library section, for short
46 State, e.g.: Abbr.
47 Play to ___
48 Takes to the hills?
49 Meteor trailer?
51 "Wheel of Fortune" request
52 Obituary datum
54 20-ounce coffee size
56 Page of music
57 Does Rudolph's job
58 1962 film set partly on Crab Key
60 Discover alternative
61 Before
65 "A woman's ___ often opens the door to love": Henry Ward Beecher
67 Lib. references
68 Dmitri's denial
69 Good pal
70 Reagan White House dog
71 Having I trouble?
73 Jersey call
74 Nash and others
75 Money in Malmö
76 Put away
77 Was sycophantic to
79 Just out
80 Scruggs's partner in bluegrass
81 "Don't look at me!"
87 Second-rate
88 Run through
90 Trattoria offering
91 Kitchen draw
92 Lock horns (with)
93 Back in
94 Explores with a tank

by Alan Arbesfeld

95 French term of address
97 Taoists' locate
98 Held (up)
99 Low soccer score
100 Fund-raising option
102 Old French coronation city
106 Miles off

107 Stuck, after "in"
109 Che Guevara, e.g.
110 House speaker between Tom and Dennis
111 Some employment records: Abbr.
113 It's not gross
115 U.K. award

58

TOASTING THE NEW YEAR

ACROSS

1 Common toast
7 Be ___ (constantly complain)
12 Sounds accompanying toasts
18 Make sacred
19 Actress Tierney
20 Neighborhood in Queens
21 Store
23 Cousins of Drama Desk Awards
24 Most hopeful
25 Purported cry from 100-Across upon discovering this puzzle's subject
28 Bygone Dodge
29 Vietnamese leader ___ Dinh Diem
30 Help out in a bad way
31 Tries
35 "Livin' Thing" band, for short
37 Honor society character
38 Prepare for a bodybuilding competition
43 Actress Skye
44 11:59 p.m., e.g.
46 ___ double life
48 Summer shades
49 Later
51 Cream puffs
53 Joint seal
55 Sutherland of "24"
57 Titleholder
58 Beverage brewed naturally
59 Hoity-toity
61 Once more: Abbr.
62 Follows the path of 19th-century pioneers
64 Nail the test
65 Sweet talk

67 Sine ___ non
68 Lodge of the Fraternal Order of Eagles
69 Person on the alert for snow?
70 Late choreographer Cunningham
72 Swindle
74 Mechanic's ___
75 Alternative to 1-Across
77 Connoisseur of this puzzle's subject
79 Dressed up, maybe
80 C
81 Name of seven Norwegian kings
84 Thai's neighbor
85 Beatty of "Superman"
86 Ex-lib, perhaps
90 "___ can survive everything but a misprint": Oscar Wilde
91 Al dente
92 Terriers' warnings
94 ___ Lodge
95 Bad end
96 Symbol of strength
97 Pay back?
99 Scientologist ___ Hubbard
100 See 25-Across
108 Fakes
110 Restrained
111 Italian dumplings
114 Genetic material with no known function
115 Japanese porcelain
116 Become enraged, as a comic book figure
117 Miss, e.g.
118 Alcatraz, for one: Abbr.

119 Common overseas toast
120 General name on menus
121 Jump into a pool?

DOWN

1 When said three times, a dance
2 Spy Mata ___
3 Mrs. Albert Einstein
4 Na, Ne, Ni or No
5 Some Mozart works
6 Hive mentality?
7 Berserk
8 Part of a plane
9 Having certain misgivings
10 "All systems ___"
11 Rope fiber
12 Went with
13 Was beaten by
14 1998 Olympic figure skating gold medalist ___ Kulik
15 D-back, e.g.
16 New Year's Eve action
17 Grounded flier
22 Napkins and such
24 Up an offer, e.g.
26 "Frasier" role
27 What the Laugh Factory produces
31 Do bad
32 Skipped the subway, say
33 Raskolnikov in "Crime and Punishment," e.g.
34 100-Across, for one
36 Of the ears
37 Slightest protest
39 Cry before "Happy New Year!"
40 Discovery of the explorer Louis Joliet

41 More restless
42 LAX setting
44 Due
45 Workplace watchdog grp.
46 Describe
47 The chills
50 The wonder ___ all
52 Wise
54 Looped handle, in archaeology
56 Flower arrangement
58 Super ___ (water shooter)
59 Office PC hookup
60 Equine
62 Pursued tenaciously
63 Big ___
66 Of the eyes
67 It may be taken with a bow
70 ___ scale
71 English Derby site
72 Swahili honorific
73 "The Good Earth" wife
76 Carpentry fastener
78 S-shaped molding
81 "Are you ___?"
82 Mil. address part
83 "Funny!"
87 Biodegradable pipe material
88 Lennon's lady
89 French vote
91 Former Saudi king
93 Cold-shoulder
96 Taps, in a way
98 "___ Dei"
101 Skirt length
102 Diamond stats
103 "___ Lama Ding Dong" (1961 hit)
104 Series ender: Abbr.
105 Arequipa is its second-largest city

by Elizabeth C. Gorski

106 Make a long story short?
107 Start of a plea
108 Comfy evening wear
109 "You talkin' to me?"
112 Shade
113 Cousin ___ of "The Addams Family"

59

ANTIQUE FINISH

ACROSS

1 Singer with the compilation "A Box of Dreams"
5 Well-running group?: Abbr.
9 Boom box setting
13 Charmer's subject?
18 Drop anchor
19 Block in Washington
20 Run in "The Alphabet Song"
22 "Power corrupts," e.g.
23 Wins a bridge hand?
26 iPod sound?
27 Salon appliance
28 Fertility goddess
29 Object of many 1950s jokes
31 Whirlpool alternatives
32 Car with "three deuces and a four-speed," in a 1964 song
33 Fame fades?
36 Like cases on "The X-Files"
40 Western capital: Abbr.
41 A in German class
42 Modern home of ancient Persepolis
43 It ends in septembre
45 ___ of Attalos (Greek museum site)
47 Exquisite curio
51 Stuns experts after new findings?
57 Let go
58 Inventor of alternating current
59 Resistance units
60 Cry on game day
61 Mex. title
62 "S.N.L." veteran Gasteyer
64 Newborn puppies enjoy the sun?
68 Not moving smoothly
72 Rejuvenation site
73 Local fan of the N.H.L.'s Senators
74 Recruits people to sell stolen goods?
76 General on Chinese menus
77 H. G. Wells people
78 Talk as lovers do
79 They're dedicated
81 Winter coats?
85 Setting in the film "Tropic Thunder"
86 A lace starts to come undone?
91 Real downer, for short?
93 "All righty ___!"
94 Spray-can art
95 Airborne irritant
96 Ship-to-shore aid
98 Agent Gold of "Entourage"
99 Exchange of spies, maybe
101 Words escape President Karzai?
109 Slip behind
110 Not, to Scots
111 Words before a deadline
112 His twin duped him
113 Never-before-seen
115 Viking garment
117 Rebels against military forces?
121 Fictional Doolittle
122 Questionnaire line
123 It has an expiration date
124 Shot, as a photo
125 Turn left or right, say
126 Govt. bodies may issue them
127 Place where leaves are collected
128 "As rust corrupts iron, so ___ corrupts man": Antisthenes

DOWN

1 Mouth-to-mouth pro, briefly
2 N, on a French map
3 What to call an archbishop
4 Periscope users
5 Just a memory now
6 Prized
7 Set of morals
8 Thicket of trees
9 Been-there-done-that
10 Grant with Grammys
11 Pooh-poohs
12 Seamy
13 Stake a claim
14 Tic-tac-toe line
15 Opposite of fast
16 Reference volume, informally
17 People without power, often
21 [Nudge]
24 Lowly sort
25 Short; for short
30 Size up
34 "___ appetito!"
35 Pasta suffix
36 U2's Bono, since 2007
37 Bring (out)
38 Start hankering
39 Neighbor of Sudan: Abbr.
44 Anka's "___ Beso"
45 Like chimpanzees
46 Datum in a college application
48 National clothing chain based in New York's Greenwich Village
49 "Get ___ here!"
50 Many a Mormon
52 Tickle to pieces
53 Actress Webb or Sevigny
54 Half-price bin abbr.
55 Footwear that's hard to run in
56 "Wow, congrats!"
61 Reggae relative
63 Allergic response
65 Linked
66 City SSW of Münster
67 Endured
68 Wiped out
69 Pertaining to hair
70 In ___ (unconscious)
71 Sea's partner, commercially
75 Bizarro, to Superman
80 "Ten-hut!" yeller: Abbr.
82 Worsen
83 Broke, as a promise
84 "Like, now!"
86 Black-and-white
87 Pound escapee, maybe
88 Weak, as a plot
89 Degrees in hist. or social sci.
90 Brooklyn ___, N.Y.
92 Ridiculous degree
97 White-bearded Kenyan
98 Photo groups on Facebook
100 Cousin of a 55-Down
101 Gets in the game
102 Wimbledon no-no
103 Coming-out party?
104 Tiny addition to la familia
105 Topples
106 E, on a French map
107 Chevy S.U.V.
108 When repeated, a luster's cry
113 When the stars come out, in ads

by Jeremy Newton

60 CROSS WORDS

ACROSS

1 Super Bowl XIII and XIV winning player
8 Turkish honchos
13 Some beachwear
19 Love, in a way
20 River at Avignon
21 Posts on a wall, say
23 Penn State campus site
24 With 10-Down, stopover
25 Hyundai model
26 With 4-Down, alternative to free enterprise
27 Paris's ___ Rivoli
28 With 16-Down, certain plate
29 Canadian gas brand
30 Picking up, as perfume
33 Unfermented grape juice
34 Subway posting
37 Magazine no.
38 Complete bomb on a test
40 Telephoned
43 "Help yourself!"
47 President who took office in 1946
48 Wyoming peak
49 D.D.E.'s 1942 command
50 PIN requesters
51 Imminent alumni: Abbr.
52 Thunderbird enthusiast?
54 ___ particle (electrically neutral meson)
55 With 45-Down, about 29½ days
57 Calvino who wrote "Mr. Palomar"
59 Sped up, and how!
61 Baltic land: Abbr.
62 Passed without effect
64 Rocket head
65 How something might be washed
67 With 47-Down, Manitoba, Saskatchewan and Alberta
69 Angry with
73 Pro follower
75 "That Girl" girl
77 "Othello" provocateur
78 Dulciana, for one
82 "Gigi" star
83 With 70-Down, skilled lawyer
84 Conductance unit
85 Easter rabbits' needs?
86 ___ Plaines, Ill.
87 Sucker
89 Tell tales
90 Save for the future
92 Nebraska natives
94 Portray
96 Leader of a musical "gang"
97 Is snug
98 Relaxation site
99 Certain therapy, commonly
100 Covers, as the earth
103 Epicurus and Democritus, philosophically
106 German exclamations
110 With 91-Down, hypertension control option
113 Old car similar to a Malibu
114 With 95-Down, meteorological post
117 Record label of the Cars and the Doors
118 With 104-Down, utility gauge
119 Much Marcel Duchamp work
120 In a smooth manner
121 Bikini blast, briefly
122 Ship out
123 Many perfumes
124 "Darn it!"
125 Craft

DOWN

1 Potter professor Severus ___
2 Causeway fees
3 These, in Madrid
4 See 26-Across
5 Fruitcake
6 Fish-loving bird
7 Interprets
8 Place for a cup holder
9 Grave robbers
10 See 24-Across
11 Coats with a protective oxide
12 Less flustered
13 Challenge for the wheelchair-bound
14 Chicago Bears coaching legend George
15 Split
16 See 28-Across
17 In round figures
18 Koran chapter
22 Close one
31 Boo-boo
32 Stomach sound
35 Gel made from seaweed
36 "___ 'er there!"
39 Pizza topping
41 Reply in "The Little Red Hen"
42 Annoying buzzer
43 Woman's name meaning "beautiful"
44 Pin holders
45 See 55-Across
46 Jannings of "The Last Command"
47 See 67-Across
48 The Belvedere ___ (Vatican sculpture)
51 "McSorley's Bar" artist
53 The loop it's best to be out of
56 Nogales "now"
58 "That's ___!"
59 Monastery resident
60 Unnerving, perhaps
62 ___ Bobbin of the Oz books
63 "Aunt ___ Cope Book"
66 Lustful
68 Tending to wash out
70 See 83-Across
71 "From the top!"
72 Landlord's sign
74 Tasted, biblically
76 ___ to one's neck
78 Trans-Siberian Railroad stop
79 -stat starter
80 Nod off
81 Ancient Rome's port
83 "The jeans that built America"
86 Uninhabited
88 Post- opposite
91 See 110-Across
93 Paul Anka or Dan Aykroyd, by birth
94 They might have springs
95 See 114-Across
98 Most urgent
101 Chicago Bears coaching legend Mike
102 Crabbed
104 See 118-Across
105 Festoons
107 Action film staple
108 Old "Tonight Show" starter

by Mel Rosen

109 Some Madrileñas: Abbr.
110 These, in Oise
111 Ending with over or cover
112 Baseball great who's Bonds's godfather
115 Organic compound
116 Advocate: Abbr.

61 SUBTLETIES

ACROSS

1 Blubber
4 Updates electrically
11 Liturgical reference
17 Ivanhoe's lady
20 Spiritedly, in scores
21 Santiago is its patron saint
22 Slip hider
23 Dr. Westheimer telling it like it is?
25 Grammar class exercise
27 Chief Ouray's tribe
28 Fourth word in the "Star Wars" opening crawl
29 Angel, e.g., for short
30 Something an office worker might file
31 All you need to brew a lot of coffee?
36 Huge opponents
38 Aging vessels?
39 Whence the phrase "sour grapes"
43 Healthful husks
45 Educ. group
46 Kind of talk
47 Male symbol components
48 What you might bow your head to get
49 Result of a plumbing disaster in the apartment above?
54 Pitcher plant victim
55 Viscera
57 Playmate of Piglet
58 ___ Gillis of 1960s TV
59 Spade, e.g., for short
60 Rapper's retinue
61 Father of Ariadne
63 Abbr. after many a capt.'s name
64 Essence
65 Tome that makes a pub owner feel nostalgic?
70 "Hard ___!"
72 Pol Paul
73 Cel
74 Great trait
77 Eighth or ninth word in the "Star Wars" opening crawl
78 Law school course
80 1977 Sex Pistols song . . . or their first record label
81 Longtime Buick model
83 Scottish seaport
84 Where to find a best-selling CD?
87 "Ghost Whisperer" skill
88 Bleach brand
90 Cabbage batch?
91 Julio to julio
92 Sacrament, e.g.
93 Tea leaves alternative
94 Help, wrongly
96 "The Office" city
99 Something kids might very well tune out?
102 Orange-roofed establishment, in brief
104 Inter ___
107 Author Deighton
108 Married mujer: Abbr.
109 Scoldings
112 Advice to Tin Man costume designers?
117 "Good Guys Wear Black" star, 1979
118 Strapped
119 Topsy-turvy
120 Hickman who played 58-Across

DOWN

1 Recording period
2 "Anna Christie" playwright
3 Web site for Charlotte
4 Paper that dishes dirt
5 "Knock it off!"
6 Lumber dimensions
7 "No more, thanks"
8 Shout at a bowl
9 W.W. II command area
10 Voiced, in phonetics
11 Quark/antiquark particle
12 Suffix with cruciverbal
13 Exterminator, often
14 Handel oratorio king
15 Starting stake
16 Bert who was a Leo, aptly
17 Name on the street
18 Algerian port
19 Debugger's mission?
24 Stars can have big ones
26 Free
32 Romance lang.
33 Eye layer
34 Galloping
35 Living ___
37 Touch, e.g.
40 Damage to a paperback edition?
41 Nocturnal fledgling
42 College course, briefly
43 Radar image
44 City near old silver mines
46 Scan for slips
47 "West Side Story" girl

121 Subject of a Scottish mystery, informally
122 Good outcome
123 Carpenter ___

49 ___ of Souls, Na'vi temple in "Avatar"
50 Composer Satie
51 Like a ___ bricks
52 Language from which "sky" and "egg" are derived
53 Skeptical rejoinder
56 Arthur with a racket
61 Shevat or Sivan
62 Poetry contests
64 Exterminator's target
66 ___ Zoo
67 ___ cloud (solar system outlier)
68 Cross out
69 Opposite of stout
70 "Is that ___?"
71 Eric Clapton love song
75 Once, formerly
76 Variety
78 Its crown is in your head
79 Waste line
81 Cocktail party serving
82 College course, briefly
85 Karma
86 ___ avis
89 Pivots
92 Attic scurrier
94 Galoots
95 Ethnic group including Zulus
96 Walked boldly
97 Port sights
98 Nonplussed
100 Duck
101 "This I Promise You" band, 2000
103 Ken of "thirtysomething"
104 Good situation for a server
105 Unattended
106 Imarets, e.g.

by Cathy Allis

ACROSS

1 Letter-shaped woodworking vise
7 Times, e.g.
11 Inuit word for "house"
15 Butchers' offerings
21 Former New Jersey governor James
22 "Typee" sequel
23 Junket
24 Out
25 Rolling in the grass?
27 Party leadership?
29 Comic strip "___ and Janis"
30 Parting locale
31 "Still . . ."
32 Only person to win Emmys for acting, writing and directing
33 1992 Robin Williams movie
34 National Geographic inserts
35 Mall attraction
37 Cookie holders
39 Medium power?
40 Verandas
42 Hypotheticals
43 "___ luego!"
45 Intersection of the x and y axes
49 Biologist Stephen Jay ___
51 Buddhist sect
52 "Who ___?"
54 Kind of artery
55 Cross swords?
56 Oct. ordeal for jrs.
58 Zeniths
61 Lamp locales
63 The Father of Mexican Independence
65 It may rain in these
66 Where a tab goes
67 Botanical balm
69 "Rule, Britannia" composer
70 "The Oblong Box" author
72 Heroin, slangily
73 TV Guide info
76 Stubbornness
79 Quick on the uptake
80 Hinged fasteners
83 Publication founded in 1952 featuring artwork that does the same thing as this puzzle
85 Suisse peaks
87 ___-Kosh B'Gosh
88 Bittersweet performance
90 Run longer than expected
92 Dance move
94 Neither Rep. nor Dem.
95 Headed for overtime
97 PlayStation alternative
98 Monopoly token
102 Nudge
104 Visibly very embarrassed
107 Like tennis serves
109 Shells out
110 Mystique
111 Dumas's Monte Cristo, e.g.
113 Propelled, in a way
114 Flight
115 Musical score abbr.
116 Lacking skill in
117 Become depleted
118 Hanukkah serving
120 Camera type, briefly
122 1950 Asimov classic
124 Whup
127 "Joyeux" time
128 Trillion: Prefix
130 Latin 101 word
131 Bingo call
135 1997 Peter Fonda role
137 Electrician's need
139 Roman's country
141 Five-star review
142 Place for breaking things?
144 Classy publication?
146 First name in soul
147 Morales of "La Bamba"
148 Adequate, old-style
149 Gold Glover Suzuki
150 Narrow waterway
151 Rink fake-out
152 A century in Washington: Abbr.
153 "Roger ___ Book of Film"

DOWN

1 B, essentially
2 Mild cigar
3 Humble
4 Some early New Yorker cartoons
5 1997 Will Smith/ Tommy Lee Jones blockbuster, for short
6 Have-not
7 With 14-Down, what to do on the dotted lines to reveal six hidden things that have something in common with this puzzle
8 Elision
9 All alternative
10 One-piece vestments
11 What "ipso" means
12 Orange spots
13 Woe for Fido
14 See 7-Down
15 Claws
16 World Service airer
17 Labor Dept. watchdog
18 Football Hall-of-Fame coach Greasy
19 Writers Bagnold and Blyton
20 Rein, e.g.
26 Gradually remove
28 Like some elephants and all tigers
36 Come to the rescue
38 Kind of infection
40 "I Shot Andy Warhol" star Taylor
41 The like
44 Pierre's girlfriends
45 Planets, e.g.
46 Casting requirement
47 Prefix with Chinese
48 Valve in some fireplaces
50 Han's hon
51 Veer quickly
53 Polar feature
55 Corey of "Stand By Me"
56 Bamboo lover
57 Vulgar person
58 "Just ___!"
59 Tour de France stage
60 Some Army NCO's
62 Patriotic women's org.
64 Trawler
68 LAX data: Abbr.
71 Bob Marley classic
74 Edition: Abbr.
75 Ham on stage
77 Coquette
78 China's Sun ___-sen
80 R.N. locales
81 Put ___ to (end)
82 Tel Aviv coin
84 "America" singer in "West Side Story"
86 Eda who wrote "When Your Child Drives You Crazy"
89 Mental acuity
91 Fire
93 Correctional
96 Prefix with -gon
99 Brain-busting
100 Lulu
101 Small vortex
103 Jingle writer, maybe
105 Where to find Lux.
106 ___ al-Fayed, companion of Princess Diana
108 Lopsided victory
112 Part of an Ironman competition
115 Mowgli's friend in "The Jungle Book"
116 Cold response?

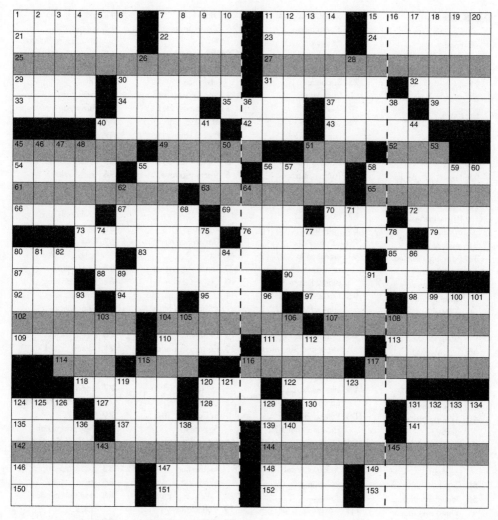

by David Kwong and Kevan Choset

ACROSS

1 Ol' Blue Eyes
8 Forlorn
14 Chatty Cathy
20 Overdress, maybe
21 "Yours" alternative
22 "Bam!" chef
23 Sorcerer behind Amin's rise to power?
25 Brand X
26 Sage
27 "Top Gun" planes
28 Sore
30 "Come ___?" ("How are you?," in Italy)
31 Military wear
33 Dodging midtown traffic?
35 ___ 101, world's tallest building, 2004–07
38 Suicide squeeze result, for short
40 "___ Means I Love You" (1968 Delfonics hit)
41 1964 Cassius Clay announcement?
46 Aspiring atty.'s hurdle
50 Put in
51 Kind of tour, for short
52 Coach Parseghian
53 Something under a tired eye, maybe
54 Suffix on era names
55 Calls of port?
57 Average karate instructor?
61 The Jackson 5 had five
63 "The Black Cat" writer
64 Long-distance call letters
65 "48 ___"
66 "Yummy! Here comes your tuna sashimi!"?
71 Taylor of apparel
73 It's just below les yeux
74 "Catch-22" bomber pilot
75 Boston-to-Washington speedster
76 Lightsaber-wielding hillbilly of TV?
80 CD predecessors
81 Place to watch Truffaut, e.g.
85 Get up
86 Private eye
87 Conditions
89 "Cheers!"
90 ___-Rooter
91 Invitation to cocktails with pianist Ramsey?
95 Film character known for her buns
98 Hoff who wrote and illustrated "Danny and the Dinosaur"
99 Like medieval Europe
100 Rotisserie on a Hawaiian porch?
106 Solzhenitsyn topic
108 Equal: Prefix
109 Judge of Israel, in Judges
110 Eye ___
111 It might hold the solution
116 Graceful women
118 Cranky question on the Himalayan trail?
121 Pigtails, e.g.
122 Out for someone on the inside
123 1964 and 1976 Winter Olympics host
124 Don Quixote's squire
125 Ran off
126 Showy streakers

DOWN

1 Jet-setters' jets, once
2 Blogger's preface
3 "The Seven Joys of Mary," e.g.
4 Part of Lawrence Welk's intro
5 Popular laptop
6 Tract for a tribe, briefly
7 "The Passion of the Christ" language
8 Donna Summer #1 hit
9 Those muchachos
10 Call, as a game
11 "On This Night of a Thousand Stars" musical
12 UPS rival
13 Certain Caribbean, for short
14 Home of the Palace of Nations
15 Like the stranger in Camus's "The Stranger"
16 D.C. V.I.P.
17 Luca ___, "The Godfather" character
18 "We ___ please"
19 Collect slowly
24 7'4" former N.B.A. star Smits
29 ___ meat
32 Farm layer
33 Comic Conway
34 Art exhibition hall
35 List heading
36 Autobahn auto
37 Global warming panel concern
39 Faction
41 1960s–'80s Red Sox nickname
42 Too, in Toulon
43 Former Irish P.M. ___ de Valera
44 Having heat?
45 Thai neighbor
47 Offering at some bars
48 Taiwanese computer maker
49 "Get ___!"
53 Corolla part
55 Synthetic fiber
56 "Holy cow!"
58 Eye-twisting display
59 Civil rights org.
60 Sights on sore eyes?
62 One running a hot business?
66 Bit of gossip
67 One who may have red eyes
68 At attention
69 Chip dip
70 Got in illicitly
71 Almost closed
72 Lancelot portrayer, 1967
77 Capri, e.g.
78 N.Y.C. bus insignia
79 Baby
82 "The Bridges of Madison County" setting
83 Get exactly right
84 Loop loopers
88 Had ants in one's pants
89 High-scoring baseball game
91 Adams of "Octopussy"
92 Land that's largely desert: Abbr.
93 Lions or Bears
94 Narc's org.
96 Pizza slice, usually
97 "Yes, indeed"
100 Features of Castilian speech
101 Refuges

by Tony Orbach and Andrea Carla Michaels

ACROSS

1 Despicable
4 World capital once called Philadelphia
9 Computer book inserts, often
12 Funny fellow
16 "Antiart" art
20 Gold, to Goya
21 1980s–'90s New York governor
22 Actress Thompson
23 Observe
24 Medical sch. topic
25 "The football fan is fingering the buttons on the remote . . . he pushes the ___ and the game is on!"
27 Halfway house
28 "He's prepared a ___ of popcorn for himself . . ."
30 Crunch-time helper
31 ". . . and he's got Budweiser and Michelob on tap — excellent ___!"
34 Form popular among the Romantics
35 No. on a food label
36 Bergen dummy
38 Go off course
39 Thoroughly wets
41 Perfumery bottles
43 Eastern exercise
46 Up to, in brief
48 "Now he remembers setting $10 aside for pizza — he searches his jacket and finds it ___"
50 "But he forgot to place the order — we may be looking at a ___ here, folks"
52 Like birds of prey
54 N.F.L.'er Manning
55 Mountain West Conference team
56 Nastase of tennis

58 Lost power
59 A number of
63 Hiker?
65 Pirate treasure
67 "He phones the pizzeria and tells them he wants full cheese and mushroom ___"
68 Castaway's call
70 Not up
71 Green man?
72 Male meower
73 "The pizzeria's out of mushrooms, though, so he'll need to make a ___"
78 Film producer Apatow
79 Veep Agnew
81 Big holding in Risk
82 Mildness
83 Like cartoon "Melodies"
85 Essayist Didion
86 Lacks, briefly
88 Vaulted recess
89 "O.K., he's ordered the pizza — but now his wife is moving around in front of the TV, making ___!"
91 IntelliStation maker
92 Pertinent, in Latin
94 1978 World Series M.V.P. Dent
95 Bronx cocktail ingredient
96 "He's looking for an opening, but she's doing a tremendous job of ___!"
98 Impure
100 Soft-soap
105 "A Shot in the Dark" star, 1964
106 Muddled situation
107 Fashion's Wang
109 Sufficient, once
110 Battery size
111 Wheeled table

113 "Now he's spotted the pizza delivery boy, who's through the gate and crossing the ___!"
115 "The pizza is $9.75 . . . he hands the $10 off to the boy and waits for the ___"
119 Wee bit
121 Novel ending
122 Amphetamine, slangily
123 Heroic poet of Gaelic legend
125 Ceiling
127 Masked warrior
129 Org. that accredits law schools
130 Suffix with special
132 "Now he's got the pizza — but the TV's showing nothing but snow! He quickly gives it an ___ . . ."
136 Periods of time
137 ". . . and it works — the ___ is good!"
140 Corn site
141 "His posterior goes all the way back into the easy chair — ___!"
143 "It Had to Be You" lyricist
144 Sister of Charles
145 Actor Vigoda
146 '52 campaign name
147 Gettysburg general
148 Keep in
149 Even
150 Bloodshot
151 Unintentional poker table signals
152 P.M. or pres.

DOWN

1 Tosses high
2 Show the ropes
3 Ratty
4 Play a part
5 Newsman Roger
6 Shrubby wasteland
7 Direct-sales giant

8 Light, say
9 Movie snippet
10 Leary of TV's "Rescue Me"
11 Permissible
12 Spoiled
13 "Aladdin" monkey
14 Lie peacefully
15 Gone platinum?
16 Lotion amount
17 Inuit jacket
18 Waste time
19 After much delay
26 Most agile
29 They're drawn in western scenes
32 Nettlesome person
33 Easy-Bake Oven introducer
37 700, once
40 High degree
42 Slicker, in a way
44 Pomade
45 Scarcely
47 Brand name acquired by Toro
49 Vexation
50 French director Besson
51 Crater's edge
53 Carrying a lot
57 Snobbishness
59 Laying down the lawn
60 Sine and cosine
61 Old public squares
62 They may be on the verge of a breakdown
64 Id follower
66 Make one
67 Core military group
69 Bear's partner in investing
71 Frequent partner of Fonteyn
73 Colonial "masters"
74 Aidful
75 "Pepto" go-with
76 Francisco, e.g.
77 Remove a fastener from
78 Spasmodic
80 Some loungewear
83 "'Tis" memoirist

by Patrick Berry

84 Fruit peel
87 Vacation
89 Kind of drug
90 Ivanovic of tennis
93 Another name for the Furies
94 Jet
97 Quilty of "Lolita"
98 Motrin rival

99 Old Ottoman title
101 One way to serve eel
102 Bialy, e.g.
103 Having a big mouth?
104 She that is shorn
106 Battle-scarred
108 Arctic explorer John
111 Cable inits.
112 Fireside recitation

114 Ruckus
115 Up and down
116 Optimistic
117 Iraq War helicopter
118 Salad pasta
120 Harsh decree
124 Daughter of Tantalus
126 Part of L.E.D.
128 Actor Ed

131 "Now!"
133 Exploit
134 Get the best of
135 Food energy unit: Abbr.
138 Talking tree of Middle-earth
139 Letterless phone button
142 Greetings

65

THAT'S AMORE

ACROSS

1 It was once advertised as "Your favorite drink in your favorite flavor"
5 Cigna competitor
10 23-Across . . . according to Shakespeare
15 Mecca trekker
19 Nonexclusive
20 Showed over
21 Sin city
22 Lena of "Chocolat"
23 1993 dance hit, and a question answered seven times in this puzzle
25 "E.T.," e.g.
26 Some da Vinci pieces
27 It's whistleable
28 Kilt accompaniers
30 "What is the sound of one hand clapping?," say
31 Purple or green vegetable
32 . . . according to Joseph Campbell
36 Secret dish in "Sweeney Todd"
37 One ___ (baseball variant)
38 End of shampoo instructions, often
39 Linchpin
41 Martin's partner in 1960s–'70s TV
45 A.A.A. part: Abbr.
46 What some bombs lead to, for short
47 Sherwood Forest sights
50 Like some mutual funds
52 . . . according to St. Augustine
60 Irritated
63 It may be marked on a racetrack
64 Not clerical
65 Literally, "barley"
66 Fresh sets of clothes
68 Lynn Fontanne and her husband
70 Regarding that matter
72 One who's easier to pray for than to visit, according to C. S. Lewis
73 German region occupied by France and Belgium from 1923–25
75 Responses to pleasure or pain
77 "And you'd better listen!"
78 . . . according to Charles Schulz
82 Where some leaves settle
83 Sunfish or moonfish
84 Rep center?
87 Star in the Summer Triangle
90 Slain twin
92 Milanese madames
96 Pioneering 1740 novel subtitled "Virtue Rewarded"
98 Telephone
101 Un-PC behavior
102 . . . according to Frank Sinatra
107 Nary a soul
108 Put one's foot down
109 Actor Jannings, winner of the first Best Actor Oscar
110 Great Scott?
111 Sullen
112 What's said before some numbers
114 . . . according to the Beatles
118 Having given a slip the slip?
119 Apple juice brand
120 E.T., e.g.
121 Early smartphone
122 What bears do
123 . . . according to Neil Young
124 Reagan attorney general
125 U.S.A.F. noncom

DOWN

1 "I said ___!"
2 New Testament book called the "Queen of the Epistles": Abbr.
3 Weapons in Wells's "The War of the Worlds"
4 Senses
5 Hall of "Coming to America"
6 Unagi, in a sushi restaurant
7 Brings (out)
8 Old cruise missile
9 Lacking vitality
10 M.I.T. degs.
11 John who wrote "An Essay Concerning Human Understanding"
12 Teller of a tale "full of sound and fury," per Macbeth
13 Jack Sprat's requirement
14 The saddest key, supposedly
15 Assignations, slangily
16 Ayn Rand and Anne Rice, e.g.
17 Actress Ann
18 It may have an antenna
24 Bungling
29 Lock horns (with)
32 Audio ___
33 Star in the Summer Triangle
34 Like poker faces
35 Maryland fort name
36 Nasdaq, e.g.: Abbr.
40 B or C, but not A or D: Abbr.
42 Edinburgh tourist attraction
43 ___ Romeo
44 Untagged
48 Stereotypical starting job assignment at a corporation
49 "Star Trek" role
51 Blessing preceder?
52 Kind of cartridge
53 Warm welcome
54 Forever, to a bard
55 Kind of sax
56 Philosopher Kierkegaard
57 Pitcher Hershiser
58 Weapons with telescoping bolts
59 Solo
60 Chemicals banned by Congress in '76
61 "This isn't good!"
62 Butler's locale
67 Honeybunch
69 Hiker's map, briefly
71 Bungle
74 Some hot air
76 They may have jets
79 Land of amore
80 One-eighty
81 Kindergartner
84 Heroes
85 The bright side?
86 Flavor-enhancing additive
87 "Scram!"
88 Former chief of staff under Obama
89 Blanket
91 Hash browns, e.g., typically
93 Execute
94 ___ jacket
95 Sets right

by Matt Ginsberg and Pete Muller

ACROSS

1 Trusted one
4 Dairy Queen order
9 W.W. II threats
15 F.D.R.'s mother
19 Eggs
20 Its national anthem is "La Dessalinienne"
21 Unbiased
22 Untouched
23 Anatomical pouch / Run on TV / Consume / Feel sick / Oral history
26 "Big Love" setting
27 Appropriately named monthly of the National Puzzlers' League, with "The"
28 Former Mississippi senator
29 Mamet play revived on Broadway in 2009
31 Periodic table fig.
32 "Whew!"
34 Washington and ___ University
36 Robert Ripley's specialty
39 Joins the team
41 Cry after discovering the furniture's been chewed, maybe
43 Roman goddess of agriculture
44 Christmas season / Greet a villain / Speak aloud / Query / Monthly payment
48 A fist might represent A or S in it: Abbr.
51 Early: Prefix
52 Asian observance
53 ___ kwon do
54 "___ and Prosperity" (Eisenhower slogan)
56 Forum wear

58 Union, of a sort
62 Open
64 Barrel of laughs
65 Indian tea
66 Mideast inits.
67 Least smart / Kitchen worker / Towel word / ___ Fein
71 French article
72 Scottish refusals
73 Crate part
74 Music genre that often includes an accordion
76 Frisk
78 Peloponnesian power
80 Corporate department
81 Japanese tie
82 U.S.S.R. member: Abbr.
83 Blue Cross competitor
85 Traffic warning
86 Trash / Victories / "Get it?" / Do some math / Runs smoothly
93 "___ directed"
94 Strand
95 Egg foo yung and others
99 Obama economic adviser Summers
102 Never, in Berlin
103 McSorley's Old ___ House, New York landmark since 1854
104 North Carolina county
105 World Series manager of 1981 and '88
107 Grayish
109 Fraternity hopeful
111 Blue Bonnet, e.g.
113 Most shaggy / Hotel offering / Actress Goldie

116 Watered down
117 Pickup capacity, sometimes
118 Accumulated, as debts
119 Mens ___ (guilty mind)
120 "My ___" (Clinton autobiography)
121 "You ___ kidding!"
122 Accumulate
123 "Washington Week" airer

DOWN

1 Pretend to be
2 Forward, in 7-Down
3 Ice skate part
4 Thin wedge
5 What's represented by $x^2 = 4py$
6 "I cannot tell a ___"
7 See 2-Down
8 A Jackson
9 What you'll get if you read aloud 23-, 44-, 67-, 86- or 113-Across
10 Neighbor of Braz.
11 ___ Accords of 1993
12 "My bad," for one
13 Ready for bed
14 Three-time Masters champ
15 Amble
16 "Shall We Dance" dancer
17 Inlet
18 Memento of an old flame?
24 "There is no greater ___ than bearing an untold story inside you": Maya Angelou
25 Brother of Prometheus
30 Where 67-Across's face appears
33 Law school newcomers

35 Son — or father — of Henry
37 Contraction before "now"
38 Former part of the British Airways fleet, for short
40 Topnotch
41 Science of duplicating nature
42 It may be made into a meal
45 Buck up
46 Rampaging, after "on"
47 Hannibal Lecter, e.g.
48 Satyajit Ray's "The ___ Trilogy"
49 Satirize
50 Blank space
55 Cupid's teammate
57 Cry accompanying a head slap
58 Sharpened
59 Holder of the alphabet
60 Shortcuts for ships
61 Setter sitter?
63 Skywalker's friend
65 1963 Audrey Hepburn thriller
68 Admitted to the foyer
69 Ga. neighbor
70 Cracker seed
75 Bear, in Baja
77 Emulates a rhabdomantist
78 Entanglement
79 Playwright Fugard
82 Org. for Jimmy Carter, once
84 Many
86 Birth mo. for Coolidge, Ford and G. W. Bush
87 Cable channel
88 Fresh start, metaphorically
89 Bar activity
90 More run-down

by Eric Berlin

91 Yanks and others
92 Playable character in Guitar Hero III
96 Equivalent to F
97 Surfer's place
98 Regarded to be
100 Not in any way
101 Stretch, in a way
103 The "A" of James A. Garfield
106 Prado displays
108 Grooming brand
110 Ones near bases
111 Friend of Pooh
112 Kona keepsake
114 Charged bit
115 ___ high

ACROSS

1 ___ miss
5 Oil holder
9 It's often vaulted
13 Pact of '94
18 Mrs. Shakespeare
19 Shakespearean schemer
20 Bummer
21 Stop overseas
22 Inappropriate on a honeymoon?
26 Parkgoer's charge
27 Italian home of the Basilica of San Francesco
28 Mark Harmon action drama
30 One side in the Pro Bowl: Abbr.
31 Some bank deposits
33 Health club lineup
36 Item at a golf boutique?
40 "Imitation is the sincerest form of television" quipster
42 "Before the Devil Knows You're Dead" actress
43 Shade of green
44 With a run-down look
45 Sperm targets
46 Camera-ready page
48 Microphone tester, perhaps
49 Stub-tailed cat
53 Phnom ___
55 Summer next door to the nudist camp?
57 Solar sails material
58 Set right
60 Things often put in in twos
61 "Butterfly" actress, 1981
62 Hampered

65 Develops an open spot?
66 Datum on an employment contract
67 Some space missions
68 Über ___ (above everything: Ger.)
69 "Falstaff" soprano
70 Late-late-night offering
71 What a pursued perp might do?
73 Eastern noble
77 River deliberately flooded in W.W. I
78 Frequent gangster portrayer
79 Annual awards announced in New York's East Village
81 Chaney of "The Phantom of the Opera"
82 Struggling artists' places
84 ___-chef
85 Explosive event of '54
87 Desert drivers
90 The point when Fido's master starts walking?
92 They may be tickled
93 Filthy quarters
94 Mountain treasure
95 Idea's start
96 City near Bethlehem
99 Film or sculpture
103 Bit of advice when packing anglers' lunches?
108 Possible flight delayer
109 Proceeds
110 Grand
111 Itinerary segments: Abbr.
112 These, in Madrid
113 Convention handout, for short

114 Showed
115 Lows

DOWN

1 TV alien's word
2 Son of Seth
3 Kick in, say
4 Change the focus of, as an argument
5 Face-to-face
6 Bank quote
7 Zero-star restaurant review?
8 Baseballer and O.S.S. spy Berg
9 Carol opener
10 Basketball tactic
11 Pseudonym of H. H. Munro
12 Teamwork thwarters
13 "Uh-uh"
14 The Who's "Who ___ You"
15 Buck's candid conversation opener?
16 Onetime Toyota model
17 Outfit
23 Like some TV interviewers' questions
24 Land with a red dragon on its flag
25 Entered, as a classroom
29 W-2 datum: Abbr.
31 Made it home safely
32 "There there"
34 Dog in a cat comic
35 Nev. neighbor
36 On
37 Go all over
38 Yemen neighbor
39 Loom
40 Dinners likely to have leftovers
41 Some major changes
44 Scoundrel
47 Alternatives to foils
48 Send back to the Hill, say

50 Crooked
51 Former Japanese capital
52 Airport security measure
54 Dating service in a northern German city?
56 Dental hygienists, at times
57 Pronoun designation: Abbr.
59 Bearing
61 1990s war locale
62 Agile, for a senior
63 Los ___ Reyes Magos
64 Days of old
65 Flock sounds
66 Mathematician Pascal
68 Rags-to-riches author Horatio
69 iPod heading
71 Divine
72 Sarge's superior
74 Direction at sea
75 Narrow margin
76 Like many conglomerates: Abbr.
78 One of the housewives on "Desperate Housewives"
80 Thumb's middle?
83 2001 biopic
84 Be sparing
86 John Grisham best seller
87 Smoke
88 Disinclined
89 Gourmet mushrooms
90 Made up (for)
91 It's measured in pound-feet
93 Feed
97 Line at a picnic?
98 Neb. neighbor
99 Accelerated bit
100 Prefix with mom
101 Current: Prefix

by Yaakov Bendavid

68 COME TO ORDER

ACROSS

1 Quarter deck?
7 Cross sites, often
13 "And?"
20 1957 Wimbledon winner Gibson
21 Say "Oh, all right"
22 Folded like a fan
23 Smack
24 More homely
25 Escaped
26 Slogan encouraging binge drinking?
29 Business partner of Marcus
30 Wind up on the stage?
31 Steamship hand
33 Conquers
34 Set straight
38 ". . . ___ saw Elba"
40 French city on the Moselle River
42 What spectators high up in Ashe Stadium see?
45 Tutorial on becoming a resident manager?
49 Congressman who went on to be mayor of New York
50 Make a muffler, maybe
52 By means of
53 Got home in a cloud of dust
54 Like "el" or "le": Abbr.
55 Is light
58 Online "Ha!"
60 Harry's chum at Hogwarts
62 Number of states whose last two letters are its own postal abbreviation
63 Show fear
65 Butterfingers
67 Pickup line locale?
69 Alex Trebek?

73 Eco-friendly computers from Taiwan?
76 1998 De Niro film
77 Character in the Torah
79 Nuts
80 Abbr. on a pay stub
81 Brethren
84 You might bow your head when receiving one
85 Will who played Grandpa Walton
86 Appetizer abroad
90 Casual tops
92 Dictionnaire entry
94 Starchy stuff
96 Explosive mixture
98 Nashville neurosis?
101 Teakettle's sound?
104 Chinese craft
105 Mount ___ (highest point on Baffin Island)
106 Jaded sort
107 Outpouring
110 Head cases?
113 ___ support
115 They point the way
117 Clueless emcee?
123 Giant advantage, scorewise
125 Daniel's mother on "Lost"
126 Even
127 French king called "the Fat"
128 Apple product since 2001
129 Series of notes
130 Put up
131 Comes together
132 Midway enticements

DOWN

1 Jumble
2 Citizen of Sesame Street
3 Surmounting
4 P's, but not Q's
5 Like some plates
6 Colonial word for "master," in India
7 Swiss district known for its cheese
8 ___ Park (Queens neighborhood)
9 Casual reference
10 Conrad of "Casablanca"
11 Month that includes Capricornio
12 Certain crew training
13 Big inits. in news
14 "The Good Earth" heroine
15 Place to sample bouquets of rosés?
16 Portrayer of Cuthbert J. Twillie and Egbert Sousé
17 Damages
18 Really rankled
19 New voters, often
27 Leopold's partner in crime
28 Add zing to
32 More mature
34 "Lemme ___!"
35 13th moon of Jupiter
36 Contents of some cartridges
37 Food whose name means "lumps"
39 Game with racks
41 Franco of "Camelot"
43 On display
44 See 85-Down
46 Skip the service, say
47 Not serious
48 "Waiting for Lefty" playwright
51 "Too bad, so sad!"
56 Like some noodles

57 Franklin who sang "Piece of My Heart"
59 Common Amer. paper size
61 Intl. Peace Garden state
64 Sow sound
65 Some midpoints
66 Bratkowski in the Packers Hall of Fame
68 Rhapsody
69 "___ Remember"
70 Egyptian for "be at peace"
71 Rear-___
72 Wisk alternative
74 Inits. in the classifieds
75 Grammy winner Jones
78 Cotillard's "La Vie en Rose" role
82 Mosqued man?
83 Sexist or ethnically stereotyping
85 With 44-Down, kindness
87 Abbr. at the top of a memo
88 ___ sci
89 Twin vampire in "The Twilight Saga"
91 Having a rhythmically recurrent contraction
93 Diamond holder
95 Bad winner's response
97 Pulitzer winner for "Tales of the South Pacific"
99 Portrayer of Flower Belle Lee and Peaches O'Day
100 Angels are at home there
102 Court reporter?
103 PBS flagship station
107 Shade of black
108 Earlier conviction
109 State one's case

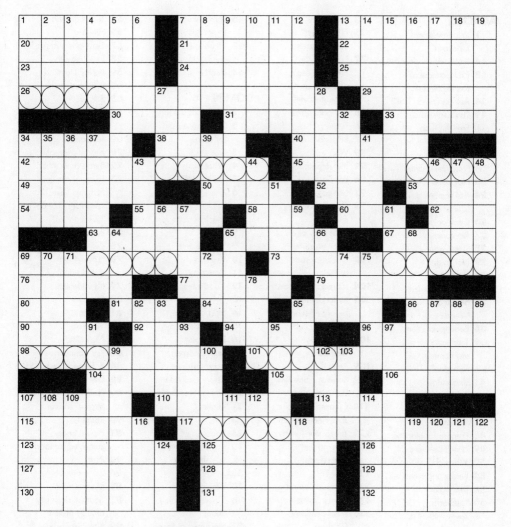

by Tony Orbach and Patrick Blindauer

ACROSS

1 Window boxes, for short?
4 Prefix with business
8 F.B.I. scandal of the 1970s–'80s
14 Actress Fox of "CSI"
19 "Let's Talk About Sex" hip-hop group
22 Tony who directed "Michael Clayton"
23 Not just a little bow
24 Plot of a Willa Cather novel?
26 Cool-looking
27 Río contents
28 "Look what ___!"
29 Not so dry
31 Lb. parts
32 Desert bloomers
35 Ship to the New World
38 Beachgoer's item
39 Tennis star nicknamed "Ice Man"
41 Unabridged version of a Philip Roth novella?
47 Maneuver
48 Prepare for planting
49 "Don't believe that!"
50 Warts and all
54 Bobby and others
56 Drifting
60 "Authority is never without ___": Euripides
61 Pocket edition of a D. H. Lawrence novel?
65 Singer Lambert
66 Trapped
67 Things that go through tubes
68 Analogy part
69 Ed who provided the lead voice in "Up"
71 Eyes

72 Most likely
75 "The Closer" star Sedgwick
77 "Frost/Nixon" director's copy of a Graham Greene novel?
85 No longer fresh
86 Takeoff
87 Bachelor's end?
89 Weary
92 It's molded
96 Ear part
97 Not casual
98 Convertible, maybe
99 Final copy of a Cervantes novel?
103 O.T. book read at Purim
104 It's read to the rowdy
105 Suffix at a natural history museum
106 Literary collections
107 1948 Literature Nobelist
109 Red ___
112 Form of many Tin Pan Alley tunes
114 Creased copy of a Jack Finney novel?
122 Tennis star Tommy
123 One-named supermodel
124 Sky: Fr.
125 C. S. Lewis land
127 Louvre article?
128 Mass producer, for short
130 Himalayan legend
133 Community hangout, informally
134 "Same here"
137 Illustrations in a Leo Tolstoy novel?
142 Sour
143 Brought up
144 1957 film dog
145 How a call may be picked up at the office

146 They get added to pounds
147 "A Serious Man" co-director, 2009
148 Head of state?

DOWN

1 Mineralogist's job
2 String once used for cellos
3 Not sit up
4 Whatever
5 Mailing HQ
6 Altered mortgage, briefly
7 Touch, for one
8 Past
9 Storage unit
10 Plethora
11 Unsettling
12 Blood lines
13 Seer
14 Start of the yr.
15 Suffix with Cray-
16 Fuzz buster?
17 Duke Ellington band instrument
18 Carter and Adams
20 Slightest residue
21 Mimicry
23 Lith., e.g., once
25 Boob
30 Kay Thompson title character
33 Savoy peak
34 Was helpless?
36 "There is ___ in 'team'"
37 Stevenson of Illinois
39 Kind of line
40 Marlon Brando, by birth
42 Neighbor of Swed.
43 Spinner
44 Russian pancakes
45 Some blockers: Abbr.
46 Feel like
50 Too
51 Indian P.M. Manmohan ___
52 Author Calvino

53 Throw around
55 Hit hard
57 Goal-oriented grp.?
58 Shooting site
59 Brought to mind
62 "Gil Blas" author
63 Still
64 Former Wall St. inits.
69 Toy sound?
70 Firefox alternative
72 Byrd's rank: Abbr.
73 Film with the line "Oh, we have 12 vacancies. 12 cabins, 12 vacancies"
74 Beat
76 Celebratory cry
78 "Lovely!," in dated slang
79 It's undeniable
80 Stepped
81 Vagrants
82 Vega of "Spy Kids"
83 Fight announcement
84 Bob Marley, e.g.
88 Deli supplies
89 "Buffy the Vampire Slayer" creator
90 Roughly
91 Flower once cultivated for food
93 Rent
94 ___ mode
95 Marina sight
97 South African city of 2.5+ million
98 Biological bristle
99 Mr. and Mrs.
100 Giving nothing away, in a way
101 Bread with chicken tikka masala
102 College locale
104 Seoul soldier
108 Election winners
110 "I don't need to hear that!," informally
111 "Ciao!"

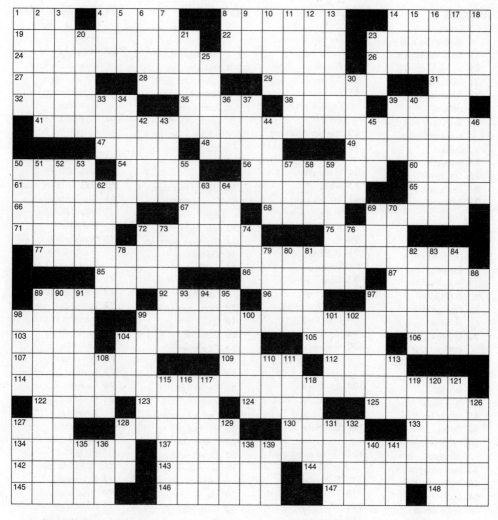

by Caleb Madison

ACROSS

1 Colorful bird
6 Beguiled, maybe
11 Seven-card melds
19 Shortly
21 "All systems ___"
22 Zoo home for gibbons
23 Goes from walk to trot and trot to gallop?
25 Lever in a trunk
26 "You're on!"
27 Flinch, say
29 Tend to a hole
30 Visit
31 S-s-s-subject of a 1918 hit song
33 The "her" in the lyric "I met her in a club down in old Soho"
35 Change south of the border
38 Teaches a ceramics class?
43 Outline clearly
44 Greeting of respect
47 Pour on the love
48 Where Haiku is
50 "Was ___ blame?"
51 Word-processing acronym
53 Dutch construction
56 Not easily stirred
58 Carrier whose name means "skyward"
59 Frist's successor as Senate majority leader
63 Vote in Versailles
64 Bulwark
65 Chow
66 One of two by Liszt
68 James who was C.I.A. director under Clinton
69 Monitors food orders to go?

72 Piscivorous flier
75 Election problem
76 Founder of New York's Public Theater
80 "Onward!," in Italy
81 Narrator in Kerouac's "On the Road"
82 The blond Monkee
83 Potentially going into screen saver mode
84 Less mellow
85 Albatross
87 International food company based in Paris
90 Ky. neighbor
91 Unable to decide
93 Doesn't quite go straight
97 "The Five Orange Pips" sleuth
98 ___ buco
100 Illuminates a Halloween display?
104 San Diego's region, for short
106 Melville work
107 Book after Chronicles
108 Group defeated in '65
111 Eighty-sixes
113 Bridge declaration
115 Wardrobes
119 Ingredient in furniture polishes
122 Puts hats on display?
124 Music Appreciation 101, perhaps
125 Calms
126 Pre-euro coin
127 Big snafu
128 Any member of 4-Down
129 Insurance holder's burden

DOWN

1 Not-quite-ankle-length skirts
2 Make ___ of
3 Free Tibet, e.g.
4 "Chiquitita" group
5 Natural
6 Santa's traditional home, to some
7 Procter & Gamble laundry brand
8 Crack, in a way
9 S-curve
10 Dietary restriction
11 Ones promoting brand awareness?
12 Bee: Prefix
13 Brainiac's put-down
14 Oodles
15 Big do
16 Prepares to play Scrabble?
17 Japanese volcano
18 D.C. V.I.P.
20 Casual top
24 "The Open Window" writer
28 "M*A*S*H" prop
32 General on a menu
34 Coach Parseghian
36 45° wedge
37 Substandard
38 Closely follows secret banking information?
39 Like some emotions
40 Funnywoman Sedaris
41 U.K. reference
42 Solve, in British slang
44 ___' Pea
45 "The Clan of the Cave Bear" heroine
46 It includes a sect. of logic games
49 "Some Like ___"
52 Common place for a pull
54 Whole

55 Gold-certified debut album of Debbie Harry
57 Makes drugs easier to swallow?
60 S.A.S.E., e.g.
61 Nickname for Bjorn Borg
62 Big production company in 1950s–'60s TV
66 Hair care brand since 1931
67 N.F.L. linemen: Abbr.
68 Knowledgeable on arcane details of a subject
70 Maids a-milking in a Christmas song, e.g.
71 It borders the Atl.
72 House add-ons
73 Be that as it may
74 Manages to grab some bullfight attire?
77 First of all?
78 Bend for Baryshnikov
79 Strokes
81 Recording engineer, sometimes
86 ___ admin
88 Cry from one who just got the joke
89 "Eldorado" poet
92 Kia model
94 "Like, totally cool!"
95 Michael Jackson film, with "The"
96 German street
99 Mexican state south of Veracruz
101 Jump #1 in a triple jump
102 Parts of many celebrations
103 Haul
105 Fast times?
108 Skeevy sort
109 Sealy competitor
110 Evaluate

by Adam Fromm

112 Houlihan player on TV
114 Only man to win both a Nobel Prize and an Oscar
116 Swab
117 Its HQ are in Austria, which isn't a member
118 ___ facto
119 One of the Beverly Hillbillies
120 Lighter of the Olympic flame in Atlanta
121 Constitution in D.C., e.g.
123 Hitch up with

WHAT MAKES IT ITCH?

ACROSS

1 "Coffee ___ my cup of tea": Samuel Goldwyn
5 World capital at 12,000 feet
10 Rugby gathering
15 Schoolyard comeback
19 Phone abbr.
20 & 21 Native Oklahoma group
22 Eponymous engineer
23 Problem for a crane operator?
26 Green-light
27 Pillow fill
28 In a lather
29 Get ready to go
31 Noodge
32 ___ culpa
34 Average fellows
36 Haberdashery offering
37 "___ Lincoln in Illinois" (1940 biopic)
38 Exceptional soldier on his only tour?
43 Kvetch
45 Showed over
46 Lead and tin alloy
47 Cuban's home?
51 Food giant based in Downers Grove, Ill.
53 Feigned
54 Chief Norse deity
55 Hot dog topping
57 G.M. tracking system
59 Like many a 36-Across
61 Plug along
62 Motorist's no-no, for short
64 Helps in a heist
66 Get used (to)
67 Rubbish
68 What kind, decent people wear?

72 Colt's fans, for short?
73 Grouchy Muppet
75 Head turner
76 45 ___
77 Leave a mark on
78 Cuddly cat
80 "___ Mucho," #1 hit for Jimmy Dorsey
83 ___ ark
85 Switch add-on
86 Machu Picchu people
88 Wall Street landmark?
90 Arrive unexpectedly en masse
92 Play center, often
93 Dentist's directive
97 iTunes selection
98 Hidden help for one who's trying to quit smoking?
101 Handicapper's hangout, for short
103 Spanish wave
105 Big Apple neighborhood
106 Twice tre
107 Eggy quaff
108 Court figures
111 Scrutinized, with "over"
114 Colorado resort
116 Years, in Rome
117 Instruction #1 for roofers?
121 Beat
122 Centers of early development
123 Wish granter
124 News tidbit
125 Yearn
126 Vocally bother
127 Cry from beyond a closed door
128 Leader of the Untouchables

DOWN

1 Electrical particle
2 Expo '74 city
3 Shirley MacLaine, notably
4 Take a header
5 Keepsake on a chain
6 Volcanic fallout
7 Court transfer?
8 Currency exchange premium
9 Academy Award winner for "Chicago," 2002
10 Hung around
11 Computer screen, for short
12 Jacob who wrote "How the Other Half Lives"
13 Maritime threat of the early 1940s
14 Beggar
15 Off-base in a bad way
16 Hit below the belt?
17 Six-time baseball All-Star Rusty
18 Like universal blood donors
24 Hardly worth mentioning
25 Ahead, but barely
30 Charlie Chan creator Earl ___ Biggers
31 Postman's creed conjunction
33 Courthouse records
35 Gets hold of
39 Member of a strict Jewish sect
40 Hint offerer
41 Follower of Christopher or Carolina
42 Slowing down, in mus.
44 Flip ___ (decide by chance)
48 Tittle-tattle

49 Rugged range
50 Win over
52 Razz
53 Sunscreen additive
55 Conclusion
56 Really angry group?
58 Ohio political dynasty
60 Old Japanese coin
61 Investigated
63 Straighten out
65 Included for free
68 Field ration, for short
69 Some quick-change places
70 Peach and orange
71 It means everything
74 Bygone brand with a torch in its logo
77 Bygone title of respect
79 Bachelor
81 Home of Elmendorf Air Force Base
82 "Fly ___ the Moon"
84 Beastly
87 Filch
89 Google stat
91 Genesis son
92 Sound while jerking the head
94 Tony and Emmy winner Fabray
95 Candleholders on a wall
96 Ticker tape letters?
99 Like atriums
100 Punk's piece
101 City in Florida's horse country
102 Gin's partner
104 Prince Valiant's love
109 "Swoosh" brand
110 One ___ at a time
112 Heavenly place
113 Succinct warning
115 Pest
118 Parseghian of Notre Dame
119 "For shame!"
120 Britannia letters

by Ed Sessa

Bonus question: What word can follow each half of the answer to each starred clue?

ACROSS

1 Economy
6 "Spare" part
9 Direction for violinists
14 Rubbish
19 Relieve
20 "Cold Mountain" heroine
21 Hot stuff
22 High trump card
23 *"Either that ___ goes, or I do" (Oscar Wilde's reputed last words)
25 *Legislative V.I.P.
27 "As You Like It" role
28 Curved nail, perhaps
29 Dentiform : tooth :: pyriform : ___
30 Certain
33 Chin
34 *Object of superstition
38 Wiped out
39 *Annual N.F.L. event
42 Project Blue Book subj.
43 Get a flat
44 "___ Love" (1978 hit for Natalie Cole)
45 German unity
46 Kind of crazy?
47 Org. that gives approval
48 Dirt
50 Obloquy, e.g.
52 ___ dish
53 Print maker
54 *Zigzag trail up a mountain
56 Better writing, e.g.
57 Wry
59 Big band
60 Navigator William with a sea named after him
61 Jazzy Chick

62 Decline in value
63 Sitting around for years waiting to get drunk?
64 Tedious trips
66 Something that might be hard to drink?
68 Open up
71 Jostles
72 *Green Bay Packers fan
74 Chartres shout
75 Femme fatale
76 They may offer rides
77 Site of numerous firings
78 A guard may protect it
79 Imitated
80 Real first name of Alfalfa of the Little Rascals
81 Trouble
82 Bring around
83 Display in the Auckland Museum
84 *Tally
89 Choice
90 *Lamp holder
92 "The Flying Dutchman" tenor
93 Armpits
95 Exotic berry in some fruit juices
96 Missed signals from Little Boy Blue, maybe
97 Director Kurosawa
98 *Lure
102 *Cover-up
106 1986 rock autobiography
107 New addition
108 Lunkhead
109 Babushkas
110 Actress Streep
111 Cultivates

112 Interjection added to the O.E.D. in 2001
113 Land called Mizraim in the Bible

DOWN

1 Harsh call
2 Suffix with boff
3 Purely
4 Birthplace of William Thackeray and Satyajit Ray
5 Wired
6 Spanish fleet?
7 Brain matter?
8 Block
9 June "honoree," briefly
10 Sense of taste
11 Big wind
12 Spanish bear
13 F-14, e.g.
14 1977 Liza Minnelli musical
15 Family name in Frank Miller's "Sin City" series
16 Gary's home: Abbr.
17 "The Purloined Letter" writer
18 Foozle
24 A Baldwin
26 Pages (through)
28 Gregg Allman's wife who filed for divorce after nine days
30 Sudden
31 Oscillate
32 *Wonder product
33 Critical situation
34 Sharp and stimulating
35 *Risking detention
36 Something unprecedented
37 Major party
40 Yahoo
41 Dickens
46 Some naturals

48 Wins everything
49 Cursed alchemist
50 Sands, e.g.
51 Stars in many westerns
52 Stop sign?
54 Cast about
55 One stocking stockings
56 Coat named for a British lord
58 Made an individual effort
60 Scene of confusion
64 "Open ___"
65 Like some earrings
66 Serving from a pot
67 Football do-over
69 Epithet for Elizabeth I
70 Sassy lassies
72 Meat, as in 66-Down
73 Liliuokalani Gardens site
76 Half-circle window over a door
78 Rogue
80 Resident of Daiquiri
81 Frequent disclaimer
84 Like some census categories
85 Closed in on
86 Marks
87 Dashing
88 Out
91 Light brown
94 Galsworthy's Mrs. Forsyte
96 One raised on a farm
97 "Got it!"
98 Empty-headed
99 Rural address abbr.
100 It's in circulation
101 French firm: Abbr.
102 Bankroll?
103 A little or a lot
104 Dupe
105 Pres. with the Marshall Plan

by Bob Klahn

73   TEE TIME

ACROSS

1 Pitch evaluators
5 Children's illustrator Harrison ___
9 "The great aphrodisiac," per Henry Kissinger
14 Easily broken
19 Bathing beauty at a swimming facility?
21 Nicholas Gage memoir
22 Something thrown for a loop?
23 Armistice signed on December 25?
25 Leave-taking
26 Important match
27 Easily attached
28 Allergy medication brand
30 Poultry delicacies
32 Bear Lake State Park locale
33 Excellent summers, for short?
37 Grp. that entertains troops
38 Scottish body of water with beverage concentrate added?
43 Awful illustration from cartoonist William?
48 Mideast capital
49 "Return of the Jedi" moon
50 Something not to be missed?
51 Lone player
52 ___ Field (former name of Minute Maid Park)
53 Discover
55 Reasons to cry
56 Opting not to sunbathe?
60 Readies, as a firearm
63 Reagan-era program, in brief
64 Some of this may be picked up at a beach
65 Better at scheming
66 Union opposer: Abbr.
69 ___ Tribunal (international court)
70 Exactness in giving orders to toymaking elves?
74 Remote button
77 Japanese ruler
79 First lady after Bess
80 Crankcases' bases
83 Civil code entry
86 Minneapolis neighbor
87 Brazilian beach resort
88 What a bunny buyer at a pet shop might want?
90 Choice of songs at a piano bar?
92 It's lode-bearing
93 Pinkish
94 R&B singer Marie
95 12th-century Crusader state
98 Sets free
101 Actor Haley Joel ___ of "The Sixth Sense"
103 Use a cell phone outside one's local calling area
107 ___ rima (verse form for Dante)
108 Hybrid sheepdog that moves ver-r-ry slowly?
113 Oscar : United States :: ___ : Mexico
114 Rack up
115 Drinking and dancing instead of sleeping?
116 Punks
117 "You good to go?"
118 "Nascar Now" broadcaster
119 Conventional explanation for a tragic event

DOWN

1 Scanned lines, for short
2 Hardness scale inventor
3 Tiny perforation
4 Unpromising, as a chance
5 Director's cry
6 Device at a drive-thru
7 Large-scale flight
8 Phrased for a quick answer
9 Lawbreakers
10 Tub filler
11 Remove gradually from, with "off"
12 Med. specialty
13 City that's home to King Fahd Road
14 Like some boots
15 Rush jobs?
16 Like
17 Neutral reaction to a revelation
18 Easily picked up, say
20 TV program set in Vegas
24 Light earth tone
29 Division of an Edmund Spenser work
30 Tiny tiger
31 With all haste
32 Bitterly cold
33 Where some hooks connect
34 Had nothing good to say about
35 Peace Nobelist Sakharov
36 One who's in your business?
38 Swinging dance
39 Sharkey of TV's "C.P.O. Sharkey"
40 Chamber group, often
41 Lessen, as pain
42 Unpaid workers?
44 Yellow-flowered perennial
45 Overwhelmingly
46 "House of Meetings" novelist, 2006
47 Ripped
51 Follower of the philosopher Epictetus
54 Pac-10 competitor
57 Drink from a bowl
58 Puts together, in a way
59 It may be measured by a meter
61 Animator's sheet
62 John ___, villain in the "Saw" films
65 Look-at-me walk
66 "Heaven's Gate" director
67 Is parsimonious
68 Roger on a ship
69 Open to suggestions, say
70 Kept for future use
71 Burnoose wearer
72 Response to the Little Red Hen
73 Speedster's undoing
74 "That's just silly!"
75 Actress Taylor
76 Settled on a branch
78 H.S. exam
81 Epinephrine-producing glands

by Patrick Berry

82 Identified
84 Some Scott Joplin compositions
85 Prominent parts of a George W. Bush caricature
88 Cape Town's home: Abbr.
89 Stephen of "Stuck"

91 Doing time
95 The Eagles of the N.C.A.A.
96 "Ad majorem ___ gloriam" (Jesuit motto)
97 Follow
98 ___ Beach (D-Day site)

99 Historical subject of a Boito opera
100 Vigor
101 Boat in "Jaws"
102 Small earring
103 Sales force member
104 Minnesota's St. ___ College

105 Razor brand
106 Necessity when playing hardball
109 Together
110 Maker of fuel additives
111 Turtledove
112 Smiley dot

ACROSS

1 *Your tongue*
7 Trip preparation
10 Early 10th-century year
14 *Uncle*
19 "Lemme!"
20 Sloping
22 Gland: Prefix
23 *An idea*
25 *The picture*
26 Identify
27 1986 parody of a Sylvester Stallone film series
28 First name among the Axis powers
29 Not going anywhere?
31 Direct to the exit
34 It often follows you
36 Summer coolers
38 Dragon roll ingredient
39 Spots
42 Greek high spot
44 Gambler's hangout, for short
45 Retro upholstery material
48 Dressing choice
49 Contract winner, often
52 Leave in a hurry
53 Opera ___ (complete works: Lat.)
54 TV "Miss"
56 Story accompanier
57 "A Beautiful Mind" star
58 You, in Yucatán
59 Tool for making eyelets
61 Old-fashioned clothes presser
63 Org. with an oath
64 California's ___ Valley
65 Created
67 Old buffalo hunter
69 Closed-captioning problem
71 Expanse
73 Surgeon's tool
77 Kind of ring
79 Rube of bygone funnies
80 Common cricket score
81 Cause of a pain in the neck
82 Yawn producer
83 Pouches
84 Curly pasta
86 Writer Anaïs
87 Like cornstalks after about six weeks
89 Weapon carried in a speakeasy
90 Accommodations with low overhead?
92 Abbr. in many a Québec address
93 Fighter with a shuffle
94 Math operations that yield remainders
97 Shaker ___, Oh.
98 Field tools
100 Moses at the Red Sea, e.g.
102 "In the Bedroom" actress, 2001
106 Rare announcement after balloting
108 Slams
111 *Crow*
112 *A message*
116 Prince Valiant's wife
117 Didn't get a good deal
118 Name associated with fire
119 *The light*
120 Putter (around)
121 Sot's woe
122 *Face*

DOWN

1 Inexpensive pen
2 Joyful cry
3 Author Janowitz
4 Exes, sometimes
5 One ___ (long odds)
6 Eastern path
7 Home of Shalimar Gardens
8 *The point*
9 Like dungeons, typically
10 Some garlic
11 Scorsese subject
12 ___ Kamoze of reggae
13 Big corp. in defense contracts
14 Bob ___, narrator on TV's "How I Met Your Mother"
15 Present-day site of the ancient port city Eudaemon
16 Hirsute Himalayan
17 J. Edgar Hoover used one: Abbr.
18 Fictional terrier
21 1973 NASA launch
24 Gillette's ___ II
28 Major portion
30 Former Chinese Communist military leader Lin ___
32 *A deck of cards*
33 Olympic discus great Al
34 Not straight
35 *The aisle*
37 Announcement at a terminal, in brief
39 Poor support
40 *Sure loser*
41 Sloppy spots
42 ___ Southwest Grill (restaurant chain)
43 A pillow
45 Ticket site
46 *An abacus*
47 "Humpty Dumpty ___ great fall"
50 Angkor ___ (Cambodian temple)
51 *Lunch*
52 Actress Sonia
55 Wharf workers' org.
57 Crossword creator, at times
60 Water source
61 Course calls
62 Part of a tuba sound
66 Dressing choice
68 Spanish bear
69 Theater mogul Marcus
70 Kournikova and others
72 Without breaking a sweat
74 2010 Denzel Washington title role
75 Athletic shoe brand
76 Second place?
78 River of York
80 *Snuff*
84 Far out
85 G.O.P. elephant originator
88 Commit a computer crime
89 Dirt
91 Does very well
94 They may be fed downtown
95 Scots with lots
96 City SSW of Moscow
98 Tuned to
99 Ups
101 Classical sister
102 Seven ___
103 Washed out
104 Suit to ___
105 Field opening?
107 Not much
109 Soccer immortal

by Randolph Ross

110 California's ___
    Valley
112 Nursery rhyme
    boy who "stole
    a pig, and
    away he run"
113 N.Y.C.'s A, B, C or D
114 Night sch. class
115 Rug rat

MONUMENTAL ACHIEVEMENT

When this puzzle is done, the seven circled letters can be arranged to spell a common word, which is missing from seven of the clues, as indicated by [ ]. Connect the seven letters in order with a line and you will get an outline of the object that the word names.

ACROSS

1 Tubs
6 Dead
11 Large amount
15 Imported cheese
19 Tribe of Israel
20 Resident of a country that's 97% mountains and desert
21 Sailor's direction
22 "Here I ___ Worship" (contemporary hymn)
23 [ ]
27 Fling
28 English connections
29 "Le Déjeuner des Canotiers," e.g.
30 You may get a charge out of it
31 Gwen who sang "Don't Speak," 1996
33 Top of a mountain?
35 Saintly glows
37 [ ]
41 Leaving for
44 "Go on!"
45 "A pity"
46 Charles, for one
47 Very friendly (with)
49 Start of a famous J.F.K. quote
52 Price part: Abbr.
55 [ ]
58 Pizza orders
59 Glossy black birds
60 New York City transport from the Bronx to Coney Island
61 Throat soother
63 Like clogs
65 After, in Avignon
66 Paris attraction that features a [ ]
69 Passes over

70 Football shoes
72 Nervousness
73 Low clouds
75 Fannie ___ (some investments)
76 Prenatal procedures, informally
78 [ ]
80 Coast Guard rank: Abbr.
81 Snow fall
82 Run ___ of
84 Willy who wrote "The Conquest of Space"
85 Whites or colors, e.g.
86 NASA's ___ Research Center
87 Trumpet
89 [ ] that was the creation of an architect born 4/26/1917
97 Humdingers
98 Atomic centers
99 Mozart's birthplace
103 Network that airs "WWE Raw"
104 Breakdown of social norms
106 Naval officer: Abbr.
108 Bop
109 [ ]
114 O'Neill's "Desire Under the ___"
115 "___ Death" (Grieg movement)
116 Flat storage place
117 Headless Horseman, e.g.
118 Way: Abbr.
119 Larry who played Tony in "West Side Story"
120 Compost units
121 Professional grps.

DOWN

1 Almanac tidbits
2 "Give it ___"
3 "___ Foolish Things" (1936 hit)
4 Deems worthy
5 Canadian-born hockey great
6 Walter of "Star Trek"
7 "Diary of ___ Housewife"
8 Crash sites?
9 Prefix with sex
10 Cookie holder
11 Seattle's ___ Field
12 Like some cell growth
13 Part of a Virgin Atlantic fleet
14 Prefix with monde
15 "Let's ___!"
16 Composer Shostakovich
17 Like Berg's "Wozzeck"
18 Williams of TV
24 Smallville girl
25 Sudoku feature
26 Genesis landing site
32 "I love," in Latin
33 Tizzy
34 "Krazy" one
36 Financial inst. that bought PaineWebber in 2000
38 Upper hand
39 "I'm impressed!"
40 At ___ for words
41 Suffix with contradict
42 Nutritional regimen
43 Parts of some Mediterranean orchards
47 French pronoun
48 Exists no more
49 High: Lat.
50 It doesn't hold water
51 1980s Chrysler debut
52 April first?

53 Double-crosser
54 Payroll stub IDs
56 Fields
57 History
58 Covered walkways
59 Joltin' Joe
61 "Thin Ice" star Sonja
62 Bars from the refrigerator
64 "___, is it I?"
65 Tip-top
67 Pinup boy
68 "___ Wood sawed wood" (start of a tongue twister)
71 Light lunch
74 Bygone daily MTV series, informally
77 Clapped and shouted, e.g.
78 "___ fan tutte"
79 Ophthalmologist's study
81 Anatomical cavities
82 Both: Prefix
83 Tina of "30 Rock"
85 Baton Rouge sch.
86 "Wheel of Fortune" purchase
87 Wanna-___ (imitators)
88 They're nuts
89 Sitting areas, slangily?
90 How rain forests grow
91 Bells and whistles, maybe
92 Kind of romance
93 Least friendly
94 Valley
95 House keepers
96 Knitting loop
100 Some have forks
101 How some people solve crosswords
102 Singer/actress Karen of Broadway's "Nine"

by Elizabeth C. Gorski

105 Neighbor
   of Sask.
106 Mrs. Dithers of
   "Blondie"
107 Run before Q
110 Ballpark fig.
111 Brown, e.g.: Abbr.
112 Chemical suffix
113 Spanish Mrs.

ANSWERS

1

2

3

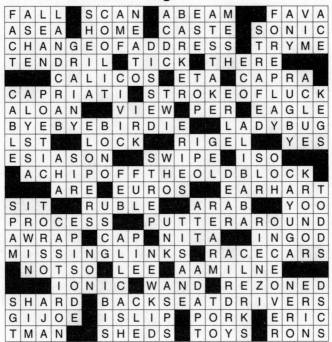

F	A	L	L		S	C	A	N		A	B	E	A	M			F	A	V	A
A	S	E	A		H	O	M	E		C	A	S	T	E		S	O	N	I	C
C	H	A	N	G	E	O	F	A	D	D	R	E	S	S		T	R	Y	M	E
T	E	N	D	R	I	L		T	I	C	K		T	H	E	R	E			
		C	A	L	I	C	O	S		E	T	A		C	A	P	R	A		
C	A	P	R	I	A	T	I		S	T	R	O	K	E	O	F	L	U	C	K
A	L	O	A	N		V	I	E	W		P	E	R		E	A	G	L	E	
B	Y	E	B	Y	E	B	I	R	D	I	E		L	A	D	Y	B	U	G	
L	S	T		L	O	C	K		R	I	G	E	L		Y	E	S			
E	S	I	A	S	O	N		S	W	I	P	E		I	S	O				
	A	C	H	I	P	O	F	F	T	H	E	O	L	D	B	L	O	C	K	
		A	R	E		E	U	R	O	S			E	A	R	H	A	R	T	
S	I	T		R	U	B	L	E		A	R	A	B			Y	O	O		
P	R	O	C	E	S	S		P	U	T	T	E	R	A	R	O	U	N	D	
A	W	R	A	P		C	A	P		N	I	T	A			I	N	G	O	D
M	I	S	S	I	N	G	L	I	N	K	S		R	A	C	E	C	A	R	S
	N	O	T	S	O		L	E	E		A	A	M	I	L	N	E			
		I	O	N	I	C		W	A	N	D		R	E	Z	O	N	E	D	
S	H	A	R	D		B	A	C	K	S	E	A	T	D	R	I	V	E	R	S
G	I	J	O	E		I	S	L	I	P		P	O	R	K		E	R	I	C
T	M	A	N		S	H	E	D	S		T	O	Y	S		R	O	N	S	

4

G	O	D	U	T	C	H		V	A	C	A	T	E	D			B	O	R	G
I	N	U	T	E	R	O		A	R	C	H	I	V	E		A	R	N	I	E
A	F	R	I	C	A	N	A	M	E	R	I	C	A	N		S	E	I	N	E
N	O	E	L		M	E	L	O			K	N	A	P	S	A	C	K	S	
N	O	S	I	R		Y	O	O	H	O	O		D	I	O	C	E	S	E	
I	T	S	T	O	L	D	U	S	I	N	G	A	W	A	T	C	H			
		Y	O	R	E		E	N	O	R	M	E			E	G	O	S		
D	A	P		F	O	W	L		T	R	E	A	T	Y	R	E	S	U	L	T
I	R	O	C		N	S	E	C			P	S	E	U	D		A	D	E	
S	C	O	O	P		E	A	S	E	S		T	I	G	E	R				
C	O	L	O	R	F	O	R	V	A	L	E	N	T	I	N	E	S	D	A	Y
	S	K	I	E	D		D	O	Z	E	S			S	P	I	N	E		
P	H	I		M	E	O	W	S			D	A	M	S		Y	A	N	G	
J	U	D	G	E	S	M	A	T	T	E	R		R	E	P	O		N	O	G
S	M	E	E			C	U	R	L	E	R		A	I	N	U				
	T	H	E	L	O	N	E	L	I	E	S	T	N	U	M	B	E	R		
A	S	T	A	I	R	E		F	O	N	D	U	E		S	L	A	V	E	
P	A	R	C	H	E	E	S	I		U	R	A	L		A	G	O	D		
A	S	Y	L	A		W	O	O	L	F	A	C	E	T	I	O	U	S	L	Y
S	H	O	U	T		A	B	U	S	I	V	E		E	M	O	T	I	V	E
S	A	N	E		Y	E	S	D	E	A	R		R	O	O	S	T	E	D	

5

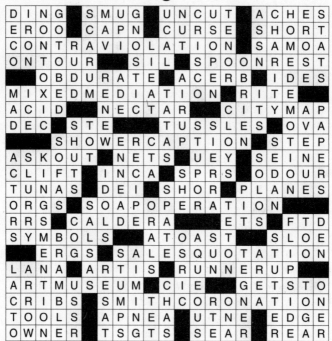

D	I	N	G	■	S	M	U	G	■	U	N	C	U	T	■	A	C	H	E	S
E	R	O	O	■	C	A	P	N	■	C	U	R	S	E	■	S	H	O	R	T
C	O	N	T	R	A	V	I	O	L	A	T	I	O	N	■	S	A	M	O	A
O	N	T	O	U	R	■	■	S	I	L	■	S	P	O	O	N	R	E	S	T
■	■	O	B	D	U	R	A	T	E	■	A	C	E	R	B	■	I	D	E	S
M	I	X	E	D	M	E	D	I	A	T	I	O	N	■	R	I	T	E	■	■
A	C	I	D	■	■	N	E	C	T	A	R	■	C	I	T	Y	M	A	P	
D	E	C	■	S	T	E	■	■	T	U	S	S	L	E	S	■	O	V	A	
■	■	■	S	H	O	W	E	R	C	A	P	T	I	O	N	■	S	T	E	P
A	S	K	O	U	T	■	N	E	T	S	■	U	E	Y	■	S	E	I	N	E
C	L	I	F	T	■	I	N	C	A	■	S	P	R	S	■	O	D	O	U	R
T	U	N	A	S	■	D	E	I	■	S	H	O	R	■	P	L	A	N	E	S
O	R	G	S	■	S	O	A	P	O	P	E	R	A	T	I	O	N	■	■	
R	R	S	■	C	A	L	D	E	R	A	■	■	E	T	S	■	F	T	D	
S	Y	M	B	O	L	S	■	■	A	T	O	A	S	T	■	S	L	O	E	
■	■	E	R	G	S	■	S	A	L	E	S	Q	U	O	T	A	T	I	O	N
L	A	N	A	■	A	R	T	I	S	■	R	U	N	N	E	R	U	P	■	
A	R	T	M	U	S	E	U	M	■	C	I	E	■	■	G	E	T	S	T	O
C	R	I	B	S	■	S	M	I	T	H	C	O	R	O	N	A	T	I	O	N
T	O	O	L	S	■	A	P	N	E	A	■	U	T	N	E	■	E	D	G	E
O	W	N	E	R	■	T	S	G	T	S	■	S	E	A	R	■	R	E	A	R

6

A	R	A	C	H	N	E	■	H	A	R	H	A	R	■	A	G	E	G	A	P
R	E	S	I	D	E	S	■	E	T	H	A	N	E	■	R	O	X	A	N	A
B	A	T	T	L	E	T	H	E	B	U	L	G	E	■	S	O	C	I	A	L
O	T	O	E	■	D	E	A	■	A	M	O	E	B	A	■	G	E	N	T	S
L	A	N	D	P	L	E	N	T	Y	■	■	L	O	C	A	L	E	■	■	
■	■	■	L	E	M	A	T	■	■	B	O	O	K	T	H	E	D	E	A	D
U	T	E	R	O	■	■	E	G	A	N	■	S	I	E	■	■	A	D	O	
C	A	S	T	T	H	O	U	S	A	N	D	S	■	O	M	I	C	R	O	N
L	U	K	E	■	A	U	N	T	S	■	E	A	R	N	■	N	O	T	R	E
A	S	I	■	O	N	C	D	■	E	C	R	U	■	I	F	T	H	E	N	
■	■	M	I	L	K	H	U	M	A	N	K	I	N	D	N	E	S	S	■	
A	D	O	B	E	S	■	L	O	A	D	■	F	A	I	R	■	H	E	F	
B	I	D	E	T	■	B	Y	O	B	■	B	R	O	N	C	■	S	O	Y	A
F	O	O	T	A	G	E	■	D	O	C	T	O	R	L	E	T	T	E	R	S
A	N	G	■	■	A	F	B	■	N	O	U	N	■	■	U	P	S	E	T	
B	E	S	T	F	R	I	E	N	D	S	■	C	L	E	A	R	■	■	■	
■	■	■	A	S	S	T	D	A	■	■	P	O	U	N	D	F	L	E	S	H
S	H	O	R	T	■	S	P	R	I	T	E	■	S	M	A	■	A	S	T	O
H	O	R	T	O	N	■	O	R	D	E	R	T	H	E	G	A	R	T	E	R
E	S	C	A	P	E	■	S	O	I	R	E	E	■	S	I	N	G	E	R	S
S	P	A	R	S	E	■	T	W	O	A	C	T	■	H	O	N	O	R	E	E

7

S	P	U	D		G	O	E	S	G	A	G	A		C	A	S	U	I	S	T

SPUD / GOESGAGA / CASUIST
PESO / UKULELES / OVERDUE
ONEGENERATION / LOTIONS
THREE / ATTIRE / DWI / TUT
REDSEA / DRAWANDONE
HAWK / TRI / KOI / VAL / FOUR
INONEHEAVEN / TARSAL
SEVEN / ANACIN / BAHAI
STEELIEST / ATTHESTART
SISSY / ARVO / ARCSINE
TWP / SAKSONEAVENUE / ROM
ARISTAE / FIVE / COPSE
DIXIECRATS / SOITSEEMS
STYLE / SHEETS / ELIOT
ESTATE / THEONESENSE
ASSN / IRE / MCA / SIX / REST
MEETONEWAY / NOTNOW
EXP / TWO / THRACE / OILED
LITERAL / BEETHOVENSONE
ISADORA / ARMORIES / NINE
ATLASES / TOSSEDTO / TSAR

8

ESTATE / FALCON / ATPEACE
MOORED / ONEDGE / NEUTERS
AUXILIARYVERB / DATASET
ISIS / ERGO / FERRET / LOPE
LENTO / MANE / EARP / PER
ACTIVEVOLCANOES
PBA / TREE / IDIOM / ELAND
CALLOUS / FLOPS / OBLIQUE
PHOEBE / JEERS / INRETURN
ENE / TONYS / ONEA / AMT
ATVARIANCE / ARTICLEVII
VEE / CREE / SNARL / ORI
APRICOTS / LOTTO / SCOTCH
SEASONS / MILLE / SAUSAGE
TESLA / AIMEE / ALIS / EIN
ALESSANDROVOLTA
WAH / SRAS / SNAG / STRAD
ADEE / ALTTAB / ETAS / MEDO
FORMOSA / AFRICANVIOLET
TROTTER / CAESAR / ENSILE
SENSORY / ORDERS / NETTED

9

Puzzle 9:

```
G A R C O N   I T S M E   R B I S   M P S
O M E A R A   S O L A R   O R B E   C A P
W E E D S H A L L O V E R C O M E   E L A
I N K       C E E S     A K A   I K N E W
T R E A D E D   T H E S H O D O F I R A N
H A D L U N C H   L I M P E D   M O L E
      P E N   A T I L T   E S O   J E E R
R I G H T O F W A D E   A R T U R O
A N I   O B L A D I   P E A   L O N E R S
D R A M   L A I   O M O O     E G R E T
N O M O R E M I S T E R N I C E G U I D E
O M B R E       K I S S   M E A   N E B R
R E I S E R   S I C   C W P O S T   P U N
      E L E V E N   C H E E S E T R A D E
O D I C   B A M   W H E E L   D O A
D I N O   A R I O S O   S K I P R O P E
W A N D E R I N G J U D E   I N S A L E S
A R I E L   C O L     I P A D     D R S
L I N   W H O L E N U D E B A L L G A M E
L E G   E U S E   S P I E L   P I D G I N
A S S   S H E S   A N T S Y   S T P E T E
```

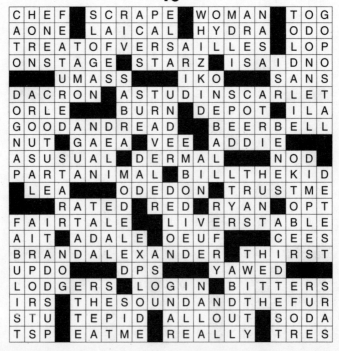

10

Puzzle 10:

```
C H E F   S C R A P E   W O M A N   T O G
A O N E   L A I C A L   H Y D R A   O D O
T R E A T O F V E R S A I L L E S   L O P
O N S T A G E   S T A R Z   I S A I D N O
      U M A S S     I K O     S A N S
D A C R O N   A S T U D I N S C A R L E T
O R L E       B U R N   D E P O T   I L A
G O O D A N D R E A D   B E E R B E L L
N U T   G A E A   V E E   A D D I E
A S U S U A L   D E R M A L     N O D
P A R T A N I M A L   B I L L T H E K I D
  L E A   O D E D O N   T R U S T M E
    R A T E D   R E D   R Y A N   O P T
F A I R T A L E   L I V E R S T A B L E
A I T   A D A L E   O E U F     C E E S
B R A N D A L E X A N D E R   T H I R S T
U P D O       D P S   Y A W E D
L O D G E R S   L O G I N   B I T T E R S
I R S   T H E S O U N D A N D T H E F U R
S T U   T E P I D   A L L O U T   S O D A
T S P   E A T M E   R E A L L Y   T R E S
```

11

12

13

14

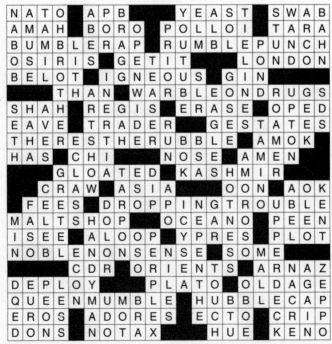

15

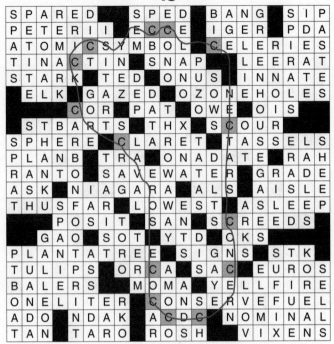

```
S P A R E D   ▓ S P E D   ▓ B A N G ▓ S I P
P E T E R I I ▓ E C C E   ▓ I G E R ▓ P D A
A T O M I C S Y M B O L ▓ C E L E R I E S
T I N A C T I N ▓ S N A P ▓ L E E R A T
S T A R K ▓ T E D ▓ O N U S ▓ I N N A T E
▓ E L K ▓ G A Z E D ▓ O Z O N E H O L E S
▓ C O R ▓ P A T ▓ O W E ▓ O I S
▓ S T B A R T S ▓ T H X ▓ S C O U R
S P H E R E ▓ C L A R E T ▓ T A S S E L S
P L A N B ▓ T R A ▓ O N A D A T E ▓ R A H
R A N T O ▓ S A V E W A T E R ▓ G R A D E
A S K ▓ N I A G A R A ▓ A L S ▓ A I S L E
T H U S F A R ▓ L O W E S T ▓ A S L E E P
▓ P O S I T ▓ S A N ▓ S C R E E D S
▓ G A O ▓ S O T ▓ Y T D ▓ C K S
P L A N T A T R E E ▓ S I G N S ▓ S T K
T U L I P S ▓ O R C A ▓ S A C ▓ E U R O S
B A L E R S ▓ M O M A ▓ Y E L L F I R E
O N E L I T E R ▓ C O N S E R V E F U E L
A D O ▓ N D A K ▓ A C D C ▓ N O M I N A L
T A N ▓ T A R O ▓ R O S H ▓ V I X E N S
```

16

```
T E M P T S ▓ G H A N A ▓ R O A M ▓ D E P
A R A R A T ▓ M O R A N ▓ A T R A ▓ O N O
M A N I L A ▓ A D M I N I S T E R ▓ A D S
▓ I C O N ▓ C A L V I N C O O L I D G E
A S C E N D S ▓ D E E ▓ F A I L ▓ M E A D
L A O S ▓ S E E S T ▓ M A L I A O B A M A
O T T ▓ M I M E ▓ M A N ▓ M U L E S
N A T H A N I E L H A W T H O R N E ▓
E N I A C ▓ Y A R ▓ S E R A ▓ J E T
▓ U R I S ▓ L I M O ▓ A T M ▓ D E E R
B O R N O N T H E F O U R T H O F J U L Y
A L O T ▓ T E A ▓ A S T A ▓ O N E I
Y E W ▓ R E A D ▓ E I N ▓ V N E C K
▓ G E O R G E S T E I N B R E N N E R
T O E A T ▓ T O S ▓ B E E R ▓ D N A
A N N L A N D E R S ▓ S W A T S ▓ T U T U
G E R E ▓ O O N A ▓ C P I ▓ A T F I R S T
L I O N E L T R I L L I N G ▓ A L M A ▓
I D O ▓ M O T O N E U R O N ▓ R A B B L E
N A T ▓ M A I L ▓ A M A N A ▓ E T A L I A
E S S ▓ A D E S ▓ S P L A T ▓ A S L E E P
```

17

```
COIL■ADOBES■PAM■■TDS
ANNI■TIRANE■ENOS■CHET
BLINDEDBYDELIGHT■REAR
■YMCA■SHONE■LAUDABLE
BOI■LSD■SWALLOWDEBATE
INCLINED■STAY■KYL■BIT
ACAI■IBET■NRA■■OMENS
SELL■PUTOFFDESCENT■■
■JOETORRE■SPAZ■VOTE
UPFOR■USAIR■LIE■KIA
GOINGTHROUGHDEMOTIONS
GRR■YOU■SNORT■ONKEY
SEMI■GATE■ENACTING■
■TEACHTODETEST■LOGO
ACTIV■YUP■STAG■EVER
LOO■EPA■DEPP■CRUISERS
QUEENOFDENIAL■SYS■ROO
APPSTORE■IRREG■ESPN■
ELIS■LIVETOTELLDETAIL
DECO■SCOT■GODEEP■LIME
ASK■■AND■INSETS■ODON
```

18

```
BADEN■FACT■SHUT■■LUI
ALAMO■ASHE■WISHI■OARS
AFRICASIARGENTINARUBA
■ATLANTALMAATANDORRA■
■■ITD■GLINTS■LENIENT
IDIOCY■OATES■WINESAPS
PAL■HEB■HEF■MINT■TOP
AGOG■TEK■■PANE■STEPS
NAVAL■FAD■GAD■POV■■
AMERICARIZONALBANIA
■ALGERIALABAMARCADIA
■■ALBERTALAMEDASTORIA
■EEW■TED■SEZ■ALLEN
SHIRR■DOES■■DIP■SILT
HAN■HEWS■BOL■LAC■FLO
ITSADATE■RANIS■CARTON
ABUSIVE■AEGEAN■MRE■
■ALTOONARMENIARALSEA
ANTARCTICALASKANTIGUA
ODER■SEWED■MOET■OZONE
LSD■■SADE■ENDS■NESTS
```

19

W	H	I	L	S	T	■	O	P	T	S	F	O	R	■	M	A	P	P	E	D
C	A	N	O	L	A	■	T	H	E	U	R	G	E	■	I	D	O	I	D	O
S	I	C	K	A	N	D	T	I	A	R	A	E	D	■	D	A	R	N	I	T
■	M	A	I	T	A	I	■	■	T	R	I	E	S	O	N	■	■	A	T	E
■	■	■	K	E	S	T	R	E	L	■	■	E	I	G	H	T	H	S	■	■
C	H	I	A	P	A	S	A	H	O	Y	■	S	A	N	G	R	I	A	■	■
P	A	N	Z	A	■	E	L	I	■	S	P	O	T	■	H	O	T	O	N	E
A	T	T	E	N	■	L	A	N	D	■	I	L	L	■	T	H	E	F	E	D
■	■	R	A	T	■	D	M	V	■	G	O	A	T	S	■	M	B	A	S	■
H	I	B	A	C	H	I	■	A	D	E	S	■	S	O	A	P	■	E	R	E
U	N	A	■	H	A	N	■	N	A	V	A	L	■	R	U	E	■	E	E	L
M	R	T	■	E	T	R	E	■	R	A	T	A	■	I	N	N	A	R	D	S
B	O	H	R	■	W	I	L	C	O	■	A	T	M	■	A	D	S	■	■	■
L	A	T	I	N	A	■	I	A	M	■	Y	E	A	S	■	I	T	S	M	E
E	D	U	C	E	S	■	T	W	A	S	■	F	L	O	■	N	I	K	O	N
■	B	E	H	A	V	E	S	■	P	A	E	L	L	A	G	R	A	N	T	■
C	L	A	R	I	T	Y	■	■	D	I	N	E	S	E	N	■	■	■	■	■
R	E	G	■	■	H	E	A	D	I	N	G	■	■	I	N	A	G	E	S	■
E	C	A	R	T	E	■	C	A	R	D	I	N	A	L	A	S	I	A	N	S
W	H	I	T	E	N	■	A	N	T	O	N	Y	M	■	L	A	R	R	U	P
S	E	N	E	C	A	■	D	A	Y	C	A	M	P	■	S	P	O	N	G	Y

20

A	S	I	A	■	A	M	U	S	E	S	■	G	O	T	O	■	C	A	M	P
I	A	M	S	■	M	A	G	P	I	E	■	A	N	I	L	■	A	G	A	R
X	R	A	Y	M	A	C	H	I	N	E	■	T	E	L	E	P	H	O	N	E
■	I	M	L	A	T	E	■	R	E	F	U	E	L	■	M	A	N	R	A	Y
■	■	■	A	C	E	■	I	R	I	N	A	■	W	I	T	■	A	G	O	■
S	L	O	■	A	U	D	I	T	■	T	O	U	C	H	S	C	R	E	E	N
T	Y	P	E	W	R	I	T	E	R	■	■	H	E	S	H	E	■	■	■	■
O	R	E	L	■	■	S	A	D	A	■	P	E	E	L	■	■	A	S	P	S
W	A	R	M	E	D	A	L	■	H	E	I	N	Z	K	E	T	C	H	U	P
■	■	A	S	T	O	R	I	A	■	V	E	E	■	■	B	A	H	A	M	A
A	V	G	■	H	U	M	A	N	O	I	D	R	O	B	O	T	■	R	A	M
G	O	O	S	E	S	■	■	I	D	A	■	O	N	A	L	A	R	K	■	■
I	C	E	C	R	E	A	M	C	O	N	E	■	S	T	I	R	I	T	U	P
N	E	R	O	■	■	T	E	E	M	■	W	H	A	T	■	■	F	A	T	E
■	■	U	N	I	T	S	■	■	■	W	A	L	L	O	U	T	L	E	T	■
F	E	R	R	I	S	W	H	E	E	L	■	T	E	E	N	S	■	E	S	S
A	N	A	■	G	O	O	■	G	L	I	D	E	■	■	E	E	L	■	■	■
K	E	N	N	E	L	■	B	E	D	L	A	M	■	O	S	M	I	U	M	■
E	S	C	A	L	A	T	O	R	■	I	M	A	X	T	H	E	A	T	E	R
I	C	O	N	■	T	A	X	I	■	E	M	I	L	I	O	■	R	A	G	E
T	O	R	O	■	E	N	Y	A	■	D	E	L	I	S	T	■	S	H	A	Q

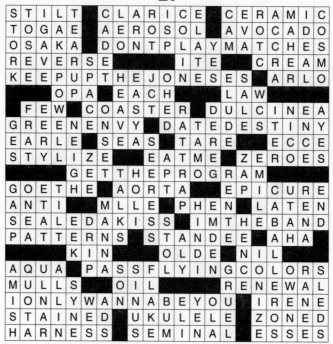

21

STILT · CLARICE · CERAMIC
TOGAE · AEROSOL · AVOCADO
OSAKA · DONTPLAYMATCHES
REVERSE · ITE · CREAM
KEEPUPTHEJONESES · ARLO
OPA · EACH · LAW
FEW · COASTER · DULCINEA
GREENENVY · DATEDESTINY
EARLE · SEAS · TARE · ECCE
STYLIZE · EATME · ZEROES
GETTHEPROGRAM
GOETHE · AORTA · EPICURE
ANTI · MLLE · PHEN · LATEN
SEALEDAKISS · IMTHEBAND
PATTERNS · STANDEE · AHA
KIN · OLDE · NIL
AQUA · PASSFLYINGCOLORS
MULLS · OIL · RENEWAL
IONLYWANNABEYOU · IRENE
STAINED · UKULELE · ZONED
HARNESS · SEMINAL · ESSES

22

COLDCASE · ZAPS · PHASER
OPERATOR · IDEE · PHALANX
CASTLEINSPAIN · SORBETS
ALT · IMS · TIM · SAINTE
EMOTICON · OLDBAG
ATC · HBEAM · TORT · GEORGE
LOAFER · SAFES · ITRY · ORS
URBANE · OTIS · MPAA · WNET
MELD · ANNAN · TEEUP · AXES
NAE · TKOD · AIRER · HERB
ITSRAININGCATSANDDOGS
ITEN · XYLEM · PREY · MOE
MATE · GROPE · CLIME · EBON
ABCS · TEND · FAIR · DWEEBS
DOO · PHIL · KARMA · LEGREE
ADMIRE · INIT · ENDED · SRI
MESMER · NOMINATE
LAUPER · GAD · LGA · LIV
MIRACLE · DEUSEXMACHINA
EPITHET · IGET · EARMARKS
HONEYS · COSY · DRYERASE

23

```
S P R . C P A . M O M E N T . . W I N E D
T H E B A R D . O R A T I O N . A M A T I
R O M A N O V . N I G H T W A T C H M A N
U N I T E D . S I G M A . B U L K I E S T
G O T H M U S I C I A N . A S C O T . .
. . . C O N A N . G R E . . . W R Y
E M I R . T A G . C H I . A P A C H E S
R I T E S . P O A C H E R S . E L A I N E
A N A L O G . F L O R A L A R R A N G E R
S I L I C O N . A R O D . W I C K .
. M O T I V A T I O N A L S P E A K E R
. . A I D A . N I C E . E N Z Y M E S
A L G E B R A T E A C H E R . T A L O N S
P A E L L A . U N C L E S A M . M E T E R
O U T S E L L . T H E . S O O . S E W S
D D S . A S S . E L T O N .
. C H E S T . V I L L A G E I D I O T
S E A H O R S E . O L I O S . P L A Q U E
T V P E R S O N A L I T Y . W A L N U T S
E I S E N . S T R A F E D . B I G G I E S
P L O P S . S T R E S S . C R O . T R A
```

24

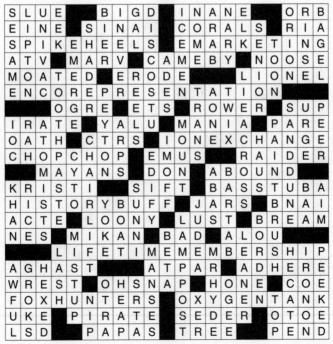

```
S L U E . B I G D . I N A N E . O R B
E I N E . S I N A I . C O R A L S . R I A
S P I K E H E E L S . E M A R K E T I N G
A T V . M A R V . C A M E B Y . N O O S E
M O A T E D . E R O D E . L I O N E L
E N C O R E P R E S E N T A T I O N .
. O G R E . E T S . R O W E R . S U P
I R A T E . Y A L U . M A N I A . P A R E
O A T H . C T R S . I O N E X C H A N G E
C H O P C H O P . E M U S . R A I D E R
. M A Y A N S . D O N . A B O U N D .
K R I S T I . S I F T . B A S S T U B A
H I S T O R Y B U F F . J A R S . B N A I
A C T E . L O O N Y . L U S T . B R E A M
N E S . M I K A N . B A D . A L O U
. L I F E T I M E M E M B E R S H I P
A G H A S T . A T P A R . A D H E R E
W R E S T . O H S N A P . H O N E . C O E
F O X H U N T E R S . O X Y G E N T A N K
U K E . P I R A T E . S E D E R . O T O E
L S D . P A P A S . T R E E . P E N D
```

E	X	T	R	A		S	A	T			D	O	G		A	M	O	E	B	A
W	I	L	E	S		I	V	E			I	K	E		M	A	U	L	E	D
E	X	C	I	T	E	M	E	N	T		G	A	R	D	E	N	T	O	O	L
		N	O	L	O		D	A	I	S	Y		I	S	E	L	I	N		
O	P	S		C	O	N		S	R	I		C	O	S	T	A				
R	O	M		O	P	E	R	A	S	I	N	G	E	R			Y	E	A	H
G	R	O	U	S	E		E	T	E	S		A	D	A	M		S	A	G	O
	C	O	N	T	R	A	S	T			A	S	A	M	A	N		S	R	O
B	I	T	S			C	O	N	C	E	N	T	R	A	T	E		T	O	P
U	N	H	E	A	L	E	D		A	V	E	R	S		R	I	M	E		
D	E	F	A	M	E	D		P	R	I	M	O		S	O	L	A	R	I	A
	A	L	I	A		P	O	E	T	I		G	U	N	S	T	A	N	D	
L	O	B		S	P	L	I	T	S	E	C	O	N	D			A	N	A	S
E	R	R		S	T	E	N	T	S			R	A	S	P	U	T	I	N	
N	C	I	S		O	D	I	E		H	O	U	R		E	N	A	M	E	L
T	A	C	T			P	O	D	D	E	D	P	L	A	N	T		A	L	E
	A	I	D	A	N		E	R	E		R	C	A		L	Y	E			
	V	E	R	S	U	S		S	C	O	U	T		M	I	S	C			
B	I	R	T	H	S	T	O	N	E		M	O	R	A	L	T	E	N	E	T
O	C	E	L	O	T		B	U	N			W	A	D		E	D	U	C	E
B	E	S	E	T	S		S	G	T			S	P	A		D	E	M	O	N

U	S	G	A			I	S	L	A	M		I	O	N		N	E	R	V	E
S	T	O	P	S		L	E	I	L	A		B	R	A	I	N	D	E	A	D
H	O	U	S	E	K	E	E	P	E	R		M	E	R	C	E	N	A	R	Y
E	N	R	I	C	H		D	I	V	E	D		L	Y	E		A	M	Y	S
R	E	D	S	T	A	R		D	E	N	I	M	S		H	A	S			
			K	I	A		G	L	U	E	P	O	T		I	F	I			
O	L	Y	M	P	I	C	C	A	N	O	E	R		B	L	O	W	S	I	T
C	O	O	E	R		K	E	N	O		M	A	S	S	E	M	A	I	L	S
T	O	R	I	I			G	R	E	M	L	I	N			S	T	L	O	
	M	E	R	E	N	G	U	E		M	A	S	T	E	R	T	H	I	E	F
		S	O	N	S		A	B	S		O	W	I	E						
S	T	U	N	T	D	O	U	B	L	E		I	N	S	P	A	D	E	S	
O	O	P	S			M	A	L	L	R	A	T			R	E	G	A	L	
F	R	E	E	S	O	I	L	E	R		M	A	Y	O		U	S	A	G	E
T	I	N	C	A	N	S		A	I	R	P	L	A	N	E	P	I	L	O	T
Y	O	D		D	E	T	E	R	G	E		Y	E	N						
		R	E	M		A	S	H	C	A	N		A	D	M	I	R	A	L	
S	L	O	E		O	N	T		T	I	T	U	S		U	L	T	I	M	O
C	O	W	H	E	R	D	E	R		P	O	K	E	R	P	L	A	Y	E	R
A	N	N	E	M	E	A	R	A		E	N	E	R	O		E	L	A	N	D
G	I	S	M	O		K	Y	D		S	E	D	A	N		O	L	D	S	

27

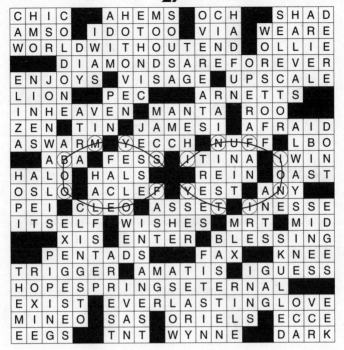

```
C H I C   ■ A H E M S   ■ O C H ■   ■ S H A D
A M S O ■ I D O T O O ■ V I A ■ W E A R E
W O R L D W I T H O U T E N D ■ O L L I E
■ D I A M O N D S A R E F O R E V E R
E N J O Y S ■ V I S A G E ■ U P S C A L E
L I O N ■ P E C ■ ■ A R N E T T S ■
I N H E A V E N ■ M A N T A ■ R O O ■
Z E N ■ T I N ■ J A M E S I ■ A F R A I D
A S W A R M ■ Y E C C H ■ N U F F ■ L B O
■ A B A ■ F E S S ■ I T I N A ■ W I N
H A L O ■ H A L S ■ R E I N ■ O A S T
O S L O ■ A C L E F ■ Y E S T ■ A N Y ■
P E I ■ C L E O ■ A S S E T ■ I N E S S E
I T S E L F ■ W I S H E S ■ M R T ■ M I D
■ X I S ■ E N T E R ■ B L E S S I N G
■ P E N T A D S ■ ■ F A X ■ K N E E
T R I G G E R ■ A M A T I S ■ I G U E S S
H O P E S P R I N G S E T E R N A L ■
E X I S T ■ E V E R L A S T I N G L O V E
M I N E O ■ S A S ■ O R I E L S ■ E C C E
E E G S ■ T N T ■ W Y N N E ■ D A R K
```

28

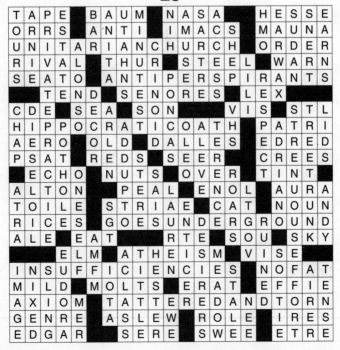

```
T A P E ■ B A U M ■ N A S A ■ ■ H E S S E
O R R S ■ A N T I ■ I M A C S ■ M A U N A
U N I T A R I A N C H U R C H ■ O R D E R
R I V A L ■ T H U R ■ S T E E L ■ W A R N
S E A T O ■ A N T I P E R S P I R A N T S
■ T E N D ■ S E N O R E S ■ L E X ■
C D E ■ S E A ■ S O N ■ V I S ■ S T L
H I P P O C R A T I C O A T H ■ P A T R I
A E R O ■ O L D ■ D A L L E S ■ E D R E D
P S A T ■ R E D S ■ S E E R ■ C R E E S
■ E C H O ■ N U T S ■ O V E R ■ T I N T
A L T O N ■ P E A L ■ E N O L ■ A U R A
T O I L E ■ S T R I A E ■ C A T ■ N O U N
R I C E S ■ G O E S U N D E R G R O U N D
A L E ■ E A T ■ R T E ■ S O U ■ S K Y
■ E L M ■ A T H E I S M ■ V I S E ■
I N S U F F I C I E N C I E S ■ N O F A T
M I L D ■ M O L T S ■ E R A T ■ E F F I E
A X I O M ■ T A T T E R E D A N D T O R N
G E N R E ■ A S L E W ■ R O L E ■ I R E S
E D G A R ■ S E R E ■ S W E E ■ E T R E
```

29

```
ODDEST  POWCAMP  ISLETS
NOIDEA  AREOLAE  CASTRO
NESTED  SCAMMER  OKTHEN
OTC NAME PES URNS ING
WHOS① GOTO③BASE  ⑤ACTS
   THOMSON  ONEIDAS
CAVEART DEOXY  NOVICES
ANOINT BADD  FACEMASK
RAINDELAY OMOO SNORTY
STDS GAR CRISCO UVRAY
   TAKESAⓃSTANCE
DUTCH EXOTIC LIL BATE
ITALIC ATOZ ALTEREGOS
GAMEROOM EASY AUGERS
SHIATSU SPRIT ERNESTO
   NYTIMES RAILSAT
THIS② JULY④BBQS Ⓡ SIDE
TAN SLAT CRU TEMP COD
ONDOPE INHASTE ALIENS
POISON NEUTERS SABINE
SIESTA GAPESAT HYMNAL
```

30

```
GSPOT OXEN UMPS WISES
ALANA MEME NARA ACURA
DOPENDANTS COOLBREEDS
SPEC ENO SCOTT ORATES
  ROOFING IRAE LEG
SALUKI SIDEKICKENERGY
IVORIES NOR TAR ERA
PASSEDMUSTARD KOOLAID
ESSE ONUS IOTA PARED
  DEKE OTTO CETERA
 AMITYVILLEHOARDER
TAPINS EDIE FATS
ELENA ANON ALAN AROD
NARTHEX LEOPARDCOLONY
TMC LEO LEX WARGAME
HOUSEADDRESSED NEEDED
  EXP DELE RAPTORS
ADDLES SHINE MOE HITE
BOULDERHAT SNOWDWIGHT
ULCER AONE PINE ISNOT
TETRA MEGS NLER ISSUE
```

31

O	S	C	A	R		W	H	A	M		H	A	M		W	I	L	D	E
M	A	O	R	I		A	U	T	O	M	A	T	A		B	E	S	E	E	M
I	S	L	A	S		R	E	M	N	A	N	T	S		R	I	L	E	U	P
T	H	E	B	E	N	D	S		G	R	O	U	C	H	O	M	A	R	X
		I	T	E			F	O	C	I		E	D	A	M	
L	O	U	C	O	S	T	E	L	L	O		S	T	A	I	R		U	M	A
A	K	C		S	O	F	A		P	I	E	R	R	E		C	P	U	S
B	R	A	E	S		D	O	G	G	O	N	E	I	T		C	A	S	T	S
S	A	L	V	A	D	O	R	D	A	L	I		B	E	P	O	L	I	T	E
	A	R	I	S		O	N	O		P	E	N	A	L	I	Z	E	S
D	E	S	P	O	T		N	W	T		J	A	S		R	O	G	E	R	S
E	X	T	E	N	S	I	O	N		B	U	Y		E	C	R	U	
P	E	E	R	G	Y	N	T		C	O	N	R	A	D	H	I	L	T	O	N
O	T	R	O	S		F	I	R	E	D	O	O	R	S		N	A	R	C	O
T	E	E	N		Y	E	M	E	N	I		L	E	O	S		A	T	E
S	R	O		M	O	R	E	S		D	Y	L	A	N	T	H	O	M	A	S
		I	R	O	N		A	D	E	S		E	E	N	
	P	A	N	C	H	O	V	I	L	L	A		P	A	P	A	C	I	E	S
I	A	M	T	O	O		I	L	L	E	G	A	L	S		R	A	N	D	I
D	A	E	W	O	O		P	L	A	Y	E	D	U	P		O	L	D	E	N
E	R	R	O	L		S	S	N		R	O	S	S		F	L	Y	N	N

32

S	C	Y	T	H	E		B	E	D	L	A	M		L	O	R	D	J	I	M
T	E	A	R	A	T		A	T	E	A	S	E		O	V	E	R	A	W	E
A	D	M	I	R	A	L	N	E	L	S	O	N		S	O	L	O	M	O	N
T	E	A		A	L	O	G		T	E	N	U	R	E		W	E	N	D
I	N	H	I	S		N	O	H	O			A	T	H	E	N	S
C	O	A	R	S	E	G	R	A	I	N	E	D	W	O	O	D		A	G	E
		K	E	N		A	D	O	R	E	E		M	A	M	M	A	L
L	A	M		R	U	D	E	R		E	M	A	G		E	M	A	I	L	S
A	R	A	G		F	A	L	L	E	N	A	N	G	E	L		N	C	A	A
P	A	N	A	M		Y	I	E	L	D			M	Y	N	A	H
P	L	A	Z	A		S	A	M	S		S	P	E	C		S	T	E	I	N
	G	E	T	U	P			T	E	A	S	E		W	E	N	D	Y
E	M	I	L		P	A	Y	T	H	E	P	I	P	E	R		E	E	L	S
G	U	N	L	A	W		A	R	O	N		S	O	D	O	I		R	Y	E
A	N	G	E	L	A		W	A	L	E	S	A		A	R	T	
D	I	E		P	R	I	N	C	E	T	O	N	S	E	M	I	N	A	R	Y
	D	O	O	D	L	E			M	O	A	B		S	T	L	E	O
I	T	I	S		D	R	A	W	E	E		C	A	S	H		L	I	D
M	A	T	T	H	A	U		T	I	M	O	T	H	Y	Q	M	O	U	S	E
A	M	O	E	B	I	C		T	E	E	N	I	E		M	E	N	D	E	L
C	O	R	R	O	D	E		U	N	R	E	S	T		I	N	T	E	R	S

35

D	E	C	K			U	S	D	A		G	I	B	E		E	S	S	A	Y
I	V	A	N	A		S	T	E	M	C	E	L	L	S		C	O	U	P	E
M	A	N	O	R		B	U	R	Y	A	L	L	A	C	C	O	U	N	T	S
	C	A	R	T	S		P	E	L	T	S		S	A	I	N	T			
F	U	R	R	Y	C	O	O	K			D	E	P	T		H	T	T	P	
R	A	Y			O	R	R		A	C	M	E		E	Y	E	S	O	R	E
A	T	I	S	S	U	E		I	G	U	A	N	A	S		R	E	W	E	D
M	E	N	T	O	R	S		P	A	R	L	O	R		I	N	A	N	E	R
E	S	T	R	U	S		C	U	R	R	A	T	I	O	N	S		W	B	O
		H	E	P		P	O	T		I	D	E	A	L	S		T	I	O	S
	V	E	E		D	E	L		K	E	Y		D	D	T		I	T	A	
L	I	M	P		V	A	L	U	E	D		E	N	S		N	T	H		
I	C	U		U	R	S	I	N	E	W	A	V	E		W	A	H	O	O	S
M	E	R	I	T	S		D	I	P	O	L	E		D	E	N	E	U	V	E
P	R	I	N	E		R	E	V	E	L	E	R		I	N	A	S	T	E	W
I	O	N	E	S	C	O		A	R	F	S		T	E	D			P	R	E
D	Y	E	S		C	A	L	C				O	H	M	Y	G	O	U	R	D
			C	A	N	D	O		B	O	O	Z	E		S	U	P	R	A	
H	O	U	R	L	Y	M	A	T	R	I	M	O	N	Y		T	R	I	T	E
A	E	S	O	P		A	M	B	U	L	A	N	C	E		S	A	T	E	S
G	R	O	W	S		P	S	A	T		N	E	E	T			H	Y	D	E

36

	M	E	D	A	L			O	P	T	I	N			D	I	S	K	S	
T	E	X	A	C	O		U	P	T	O	S	N	U	F	F		O	N	E	N	I	L
E	S	C	R	O	W		G	U	I	D	E	R	A	I	L		S	K	E	I	N	S
C	H	A	I	N		O	L	M	O	S		E	N	R	O	N		I	N	G	O	T
	L	A	N		N	I	P	S			C	E	R	A		N	A	H		
K	A	I	S	E	R	S		SIR	E	S		A	E	SIR		D	O	G	S	T	A	R
N	U	B		C	H	I	C	O		Y	O	N		E	R	I	C	A		S	N	O
O	R	U		T	I	T	A	N		N	A	G		N	I	N	E	R		O	N	T
B	A	R	L	I	N	E	S		N	O	T	I	F		B	E	A	T	I	F	I	C
		A	C	E		S	A	I	D	H	E	L	L	O		N	H	L		
K	O	M	B	U		SIR	I	U	S			Y	E	S	SIR		U	L	T	R	A
E	X	I	S	T		L	O	F	A	T		V	I	D	E	O		R	E	H	E	M
I	C	S		Y	A	O		E	N	V	Y	I	N	G		C	A	S		E	V	E
T	A	T		A	D	I	E	U		S	A	X		E	N	C	Y	C		R	E	N
H	R	S		N	A	N	S		D	E	SIR	E	D		I	O	N	O		O	A	R
S	T	O	C	K		S	A	B	O	T		N	E	A	L	S		U	V	U	L	A
	F	O	E	S		I	R	R			F	G	S		L	R	O	N		
E	N	A	M	E	L		A	M	I	L	A	T	E		E	T	U	D	E	S
J	A	V	A		O	D	O	N		G	A	S		I	S	A	O		S	T	Y	E
E	V	A		S	W	O	R	D	I	N	T	H	E	S	T	O	N	E		A	R	I
C	A	L		Q	U	E	S	T	F	O	R	C	A	M	E	L	O	T		B	I	Z
T	H	O		I	P	S	O		F	R	I	A	R		M	E	R	C		L	E	E
S	O	N		N	S	A		Y	E	A	N	S			R	A	H		E	S	S

37

| M O U T H | ■ | S T R I P E | ■ | A L G A | ■ | A M Y |

- MOUTH STRIPE ALGA AMY
- SUSHI HAIKUS SORT VIA
- GREEKLETTERS KNEESOCK
- FREEBEE PERSIA ONES
- ELOISE IONIA TAU DELTA PHI
- MIRV TI BETA NS PRINCEDOM
- MACED ON THETA KE PORTO RUE
- AMERICAN PI E BLUE PITT
- VASE DRAINS CESAR
- REGISTRY ICED COSTCO
- MOMONEY OINKS TOMCATS
- AMINES BUNS TRADEINS
- LUNGS WARDED OLEO
- ALES HIHO R ALPHA BERNATHY
- WAN PAOLO DU CHI ES SPREE
- INTHEMAIN AI RHO SE PEEN
- OMEGA PSI PHI WORLD JULEPS
- FOAM BEIRUT EMPANEL
- AMNESIAC FRATERNITIES
- CAD MASK FEDORA TONTO
- TRY UNES SYDNEY SNEAD

38

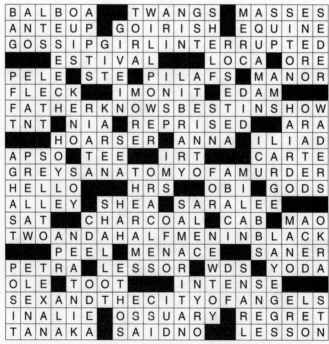

- BALBOA TWANGS MASSES
- ANTEUP GOIRISH EQUINE
- GOSSIPGIRLINTERRUPTED
- ESTIVAL LOCA ORE
- PELE STE PILAFS MANOR
- FLECK IMONIT EDAM
- FATHERKNOWSBESTINSHOW
- TNT NIA REPRISED ARA
- HOARSER ANNA ILIAD
- APSO TEE IRT CARTE
- GREYSANATOMYOFAMURDER
- HELLO HRS OBI GODS
- ALLEY SHEA SARALEE
- SAT CHARCOAL CAB MAO
- TWOANDAHALFMENINBLACK
- PEEL MENACE SANER
- PETRA LESSOR WDS YODA
- OLE TOOT INTENSE
- SEXANDTHECITYOFANGELS
- INALIE OSSUARY REGRET
- TANAKA SAIDNO LESSON

39

T	A	C	K	E	D		R	I	F	T	S		B	I	D	S		F	D	R
H	E	A	R	T	S		U	N	D	U	E		U	T	A	H		R	E	E
E	R	R	O	R	M	E	S	S	A	G	E		R	A	D	I	O	E	R	A
B	O	O	N	E		T	H	I			M	A	S	S	A	P	P	E	A	L
U	S	T	A		I	T	I	S	S	O		W	A	C	S		T	R	I	M
R	T	E		C	O	U	N	T	E	R	P	L	E	A		N	I	E	L	S
B	A	N	G	O	N		S	A	G	A	S			I	N	N	S			
S	T	E	E	R	I	N	G		B	A	N		V	I	S	E		P	U	B
	R	E	C	E	I	V	I	N	G	L	I	N	E		B	O	N	O		
T	U	B	A	L		U	S	E	R	S		E	A	S	E	S	I	N	T	O
A	T	O	L	L	S		E	N	D		W	A	D		A	C	E	S	I	T
R	I	O	D	I	A	B	L	O		H	A	S	U	P		O	N	E	L	S
E	L	K	O		F	I	L	M	D	I	R	E	C	T	I	O	N			
S	E	P		R	E	N	E		E	T	H		T	A	S	T	I	E	S	T
	R	A	M	S		O	A	T	E	N			L	E	A	N	T	O		
U	C	O	N	N		T	E	N	D	E	R	O	F	F	E	R		G	A	M
N	A	P	E		B	O	A	C		R	O	N	E	L	Y		F	I	R	M
C	R	O	S	S	W	O	R	D	S			U	T	A		C	A	R	L	Y
L	A	S	T	C	A	L	L		P	E	C	K	I	N	G	O	R	D	E	R
O	F	A		O	N	E	A		A	L	P	E	S		R	I	A	L	T	O
G	E	L		T	A	R	P		S	M	A	S	H		E	L	D	E	S	T

40

T	E	N	D		P	A	T	H	O		S	T	D	S		O	B	J	E	T
I	T	O	O		E	B	E	R	T		E	R	I	C		L	O	E	S	S
P	R	E	S	S	E	D	T	H	E	F	L	U	S	H		G	R	A	T	E
J	A	X		S	L	U	R		L	A	I	N		M	A	G	N	E	T	
A	D	I	M	E		C	A	S	C	A		S	E	A	U			N	E	S
R	E	T	E		I	T	S	P	A	S	T	M	Y	B	U	D	T	I	M	E
			R	U	N	S		A	C	H	E		A	M	O	R	E	S		
	N	A	I	V	E		N	Y	T		R	I	A		U	R	U			
B	U	T	T	E	R	B	U	S	I	N	E	S	S	B	U	R	E	A	U	
R	G	T		A	T	E	M		O	S	A	K	A			T	I	N	S	
E	G	A	D	S		B	E	E	F	E	A	T	E	R		W	O	R	L	D
D	E	C	O		O	R	I	E	L		D	A	L	I		M	O	A		
	T	H	E	U	M	P	I	R	E	S	T	R	I	K	E	S	B	A	C	K
	S	R	I		C	E	L		E	E	N		T	H	I	N	K			
	T	B	O	N	D	S		N	A	S	L		T	A	I	L				
W	O	R	K	S	W	I	T	H	O	U	T	A	N	U	T		B	E	L	T
A	P	O		A	L	O	E		S	A	X	O	N		V	O	T	E	R	
S	P	I	F	F	Y		P	L	U	S		B	N	A	I		C	M	A	
A	L	L	I	E		T	H	E	L	I	T	T	L	E	R	E	D	H	U	N
B	E	E	N	E		B	A	N	A		E	W	E	L	L		P	E	E	N
I	S	R	E	D		A	T	E	N		L	A	S	S	O		I	D	L	Y

41

42

43

44

45

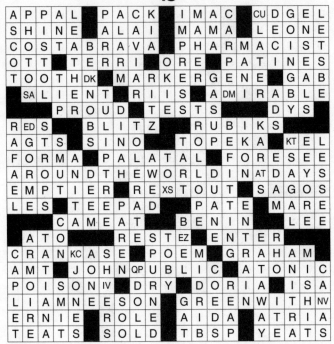

```
A P P A L █ P A C K █ I M A C █ (CU)D G E L
S H I N E █ A L A I █ M A M A █ L E O N E
C O S T A B R A V A █ P H A R M A C I S T
O T T █ T E R R I █ O R E █ P A T I N E S
T O O T H(DK)█ M A R K E R G E N E █ G A B
█(SA)L I E N T █ R I I S █(A)D M I R A B L E
█ P R O U D █ T E S T S █ D Y S
R(ED)S █ B L I T Z █ R U B I K S █
A G T S █ S I N O █ T O P E K A █(KT)E L
F O R M A █ P A L A T A L █ F O R E S E E
A R O U N D T H E W O R L D I N(AT)D A Y S
E M P T I E R █ R E(XS)T O U T █ S A G O S
L E S █ T E E P A D █ P A T E █ M A R E
█ C A M E A T █ B E N I N █ L E E
█ A T O █ R E S T(EZ)█ E N T E R █
C R A N(KC)A S E █ P O E M █ G R A H A M
A M T █ J O H N(QP)U B L I C █ A T O N I C
P O I S O N(IV)█ D R Y █ D O R I A █ I S A
L I A M N E E S O N █ G R E E N W I T H(NV)
E R N I E █ R O L E █ A I D A █ A T R I A
T E A T S █ S O L D █ T B S P █ Y E A T S
```

46

```
M O R T S A H L █ E G G C U P S █ P S S T
T R E A T I E S █ L A R U S S A █ E L E V
S A M U E L A D A M S E S S A Y █ P A R T
█ T E E D █ H O T W A R S █ N E V E R
A N T █ D E C C A █ R O C █ M O L I N A
P O E M █ N O H █ D O N K I N G D E C A Y
I K N O W █ L I A O █ D A M U P █
N I A V A R D A L O S E N V Y █ H E A T H
G A M E R A █ P A R O L E E █ W I R Y
█ I M B U E █ D O W █ D J S █ N O D
Q U E N T I N T A R A N T I N O C U T I E
U R L █ O D E █ L O P █ R A Y O N █
A D E N █ G O T O S E A █ C O V E R T
D U M A S █ T I T O P U E N T E T E P E E
█ M O T I F █ E L I A █ S I E G E
M A X E R N S T E M M Y █ A K A █ L E A N
O U T S E T █ L A A █ A N I M E █ S L Y
S P E A R █ P E A R L E R █ N O N A █
D A R K █ K U R T V O N N E G U T C A V Y
E I R E █ A N T E I N G █ P I N E T R E E
F R A S █ S T E R N E R █ A T T R A C T S
```

47

```
A N G L E ■ ■ W I N ■ H O N U S ■ A D A M
C O O E D ■ J A N E ■ O M A N I ■ G A M E
H A R T E B U R N S ■ W E S T L O N D O N
T H E O R E M ■ O C A N A D A ■ P E A K S
■ ■ F L A P ■ T A B O R ■ C R E W ■ ■
G A F F E ■ S W I F T W A L K E R ■ W H A
I S O ■ S U E M E ■ ■ A S T A I R E S
S N O W W H I T E ■ E T A T ■ I S T I N K
M E T E O U T ■ ■ B E A D E A R ■ O G R E
O R E G O N ■ C A R R P A R K E R ■ H I D
■ B O D ■ P O L E ■ T R O U ■ A I T ■
E M U ■ S T E E L E M A N N ■ D I M P L E
L E N D ■ W I R E D U P ■ M O T O R E D
S A Y I D O ■ C E S S ■ S T O U T K I N G
A R A P A H O E ■ ■ S I O U X ■ C I E
S A N ■ W I L D E S I N G E R ■ G L E N S
■ ■ E S T D ■ A T M A N ■ N E R O ■ ■
C A R L O ■ S C R I P P S ■ I N A S P O T
B R O W N W O O L F ■ P O U N D S T O N E
E L B A ■ T U B A L ■ L U N G ■ P I C K S
R O S Y ■ S L O P E ■ E T C ■ S T O P S
```

48

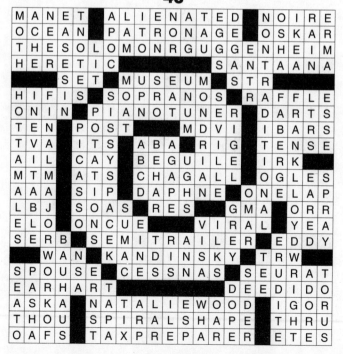

```
M A N E T ■ A L I E N A T E D ■ N O I R E
O C E A N ■ P A T R O N A G E ■ O S K A R
T H E S O L O M O N R G U G G E N H E I M
H E R E T I C ■ ■ ■ S A N T A A N A
■ ■ S E T ■ M U S E U M ■ S T R ■
H I F I S ■ S O P R A N O S ■ R A F F L E
O N I N ■ P I A N O T U N E R ■ D A R T S
T E N ■ P O S T ■ ■ M D V I ■ I B A R S
T V A ■ I T S ■ A B A ■ R I G ■ T E N S E
A I L ■ C A Y ■ B E G U I L E ■ I R K ■
M T M ■ A T S ■ C H A G A L L ■ O G L E S
A A A ■ S I P ■ D A P H N E ■ O N E L A P
L B J ■ S O A S ■ R E S ■ G M A ■ O R R
E L O ■ O N C U E ■ ■ V I R A L ■ Y E A
S E R B ■ S E M I T R A I L E R ■ E D D Y
■ W A N ■ K A N D I N S K Y ■ T R W
S P O U S E ■ C E S S N A S ■ S E U R A T
E A R H A R T ■ ■ ■ D E E D I D O
A S K A ■ N A T A L I E W O O D ■ I G O R
T H O U ■ S P I R A L S H A P E ■ T H R U
O A F S ■ T A X P R E P A R E R ■ E T E S
```

```
A B B A E B A N ■ S D A K ■ C E D R I C
R O I D R A G E ■ A E T N A ■ A Q U I N O
M Y G O A L I N L I F E I S ■ D U N L O P
E L M ■ ■ ■ N A L D I ■ T O B E A C L U E
Y E O M E N ■ ■ D I N A ■ F A T T E S T ■
■ ■ U P T I M E ■ D E S I ■ U T E S ■ ■ ■
I N T H E N E W Y O R K T I M E S ■ G A G
A S H ■ ■ A L E E ■ ■ E O N ■ ■ A I D E
S A S H A ■ C R O S S W O R D P U Z Z L E
■ ■ ■ O R T ■ S H O E ■ E P I T O M E S ■
T O O L B O X ■ ■ I V E ■ ■ I S I D O R E
O X Y M O R O N ■ ■ E L S E ■ A L Y ■ ■
N E V E R T O L D A N Y O N E ■ S E G U E
A Y E S ■ ■ ■ E A R ■ I D L E ■ ■ E S T
L E Y ■ S P O R T S I L L U S T R A T E D
■ ■ ■ S C U M ■ S O L O ■ P A C I N O ■
■ S A V A N N A ■ N O V A ■ ■ H O O V E S
P E T E R K I N G ■ S A P O R ■ ■ E T H
■ A D E L I E ■ T H A T B U T I T S T R U E
V A S T E R ■ S I G I L ■ T E S T R I D E
E N T E R S ■ ■ J E T E ■ O N E L I T E R
```

```
C A P S ■ B A T T ■ A B H O R ■ ■ C D S
A P O C R Y P H A ■ P I A N O ■ T W E E T
R E T R O S P E C T A C L E S ■ V I L L E
■ ■ B A T E ■ S K A T ■ F L E W A K I T E
E L E P H A N T O M ■ S P O R A D I C A L
A I L S ■ ■ Y A N ■ C O R T E S ■ P A S ■
R E L ■ C R A G ■ W A D I ■ D O T E ■ ■
P S Y C H E D E L I C A C Y ■ N O D I C E
■ ■ A A H ■ ■ A L A ■ E A T ■ M I S O S
C O N T R A B A N D O N ■ L I P B A L M S
U T A H ■ S E D G E ■ E F I L E ■ T A M E
O H F A T H E R ■ R O U L E T T E R M A N
M E T R O ■ R A J ■ A M O ■ ■ I C I ■
O R A T O R ■ G U I T A R I S T O C R A T
■ ■ I L A Y ■ S V E N ■ N O E L ■ E G O
■ R E C ■ L E C T E R ■ S T L ■ A F E W
P E R H A P S O D Y ■ F O R E V E R I E S
H I R O S H I M A ■ Z O L A ■ A S A N ■
O S A K A ■ C E N T I P E D E S T R I A N
T E T E S ■ A R D E N ■ M A K E H A S T E
O R A ■ N S Y N C ■ N Y E S ■ T H A W
```

51

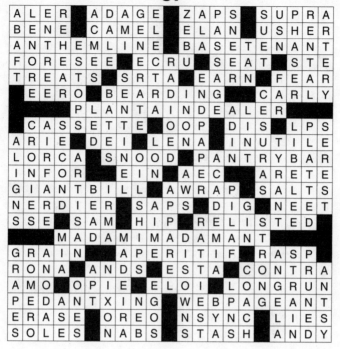

```
A L E R   A D A G E   Z A P S   S U P R A
B E N E   C A M E L   E L A N   U S H E R
A N T H E M L I N E   B A S E T E N A N T
F O R E S E E   E C R U   S E A T   S T E
T R E A T S   S R T A   E A R N   F E A R
  E E R O   B E A R D I N G   C A R L Y
    P L A N T A I N D E A L E R
  C A S S E T T E   O O P   D I S   L P S
A R I E   D E I   L E N A   I N U T I L E
L O R C A   S N O O D   P A N T R Y B A R
I N F O R   E I N   A E C   A R E T E
G I A N T B I L L   A W R A P   S A L T S
N E R D I E R   S A P S   D I G   N E E T
S S E   S A M   H I P   R E L I S T E D
    M A D A M I M A D A M A N T
G R A I N   A P E R I T I F   R A S P
R O N A   A N D S   E S T A   C O N T R A
A M O   O P I E   E L O I   L O N G R U N
P E D A N T X I N G   W E B P A G E A N T
E R A S E   O R E O   N S Y N C   L I E S
S O L E S   N A B S   S T A S H   A N D Y
```

52

```
A N J O U S   D E B S     H A V A
G O E A S T   B E S O T   M E D I A T E D
O N E F O R M Y B A B Y   C O A L Y A R D
R E P S   A O R T I C   T A N G E R I N E
A T E   F I D O S   A C I D S   I L E R
  R O T T E N   A T S E A   T I D
  I S L S   L I B S   A T M   O N E B C
O N C D   E T C E T C   O S L E R   R O W
B O R E A S   F A H D   A R I Z O N A
O R E   S T E N O   A U T E U R   S A C K
I D E A S   M O O N R I V E R   L A D L E
S E P T   W I L L Y A   S K A T E   W A N
T R E F O I L   E D I T   B E H A V E
S T R   F L Y A T   E L A N D S   E Y E D
  O S M I C   M U D   E R E I   A M S
  A D O   O R O U T   O R M O L U
A C C T   S U N I N   A C E I T   S I N
G R E A T G U N S   C A N O L A   A I R E
H E A D W E S T   J O H N N Y M E R C E R
A S S O O N A S   A L O I S   I N L A N D
S T E R     G A Y E   S T O L E S
```

53

B	A	M	B	I		S	M	O	K	E		I	R	E	S	T		L	G	A
I	L	I	A	D		E	S	S	E	X		N	E	C	C	O		O	R	S
T	I	C	K	E	T	A	G	E	N	T		S	M	O	O	T	H	O	U	T
			L	A	U	D		S	O	C	I	A	L	W	O	R	K	E	R	
E	T	T	A		R	O	L	O		R	I	T	T			S	I	L	O	
D	R	I	V	I	N	G	I	N	S	T	R	U	C	T	O	R		E	S	S
S	E	D	A	N	S		M	E	E	S	E		H	E	R	E	S			
E	V	A		A	R	A	B	L	E				A	G	I	T	A	T	E	
L	I	L		I	E	S		B	R	A	N	C	H	M	A	N	A	G	E	R
	B	A	R	D	O	T		R	H	E	A		N	A	C	R	E	S		
I	R	A	N		F	I	L	E	C	L	E	R	K		K	E	N	T		
S	Y	S	T	E	M		F	I	S	H		M	I	S	U	S	E			
U	N	I	O	N	O	F	F	I	C	I	A	L		L	A	T		S	H	E
P	E	N	N	A	M	E			K	E	N	O	B	I		W	A	Y		
			E	R	M	A	S		A	S	I	D	E		E	L	A	I	N	E
G	A	T		M	A	R	K	E	T	I	N	G	D	I	R	E	C	T	O	R
E	V	A	N			E	G	O	S		E	S	T	S		T	H	I	S	
R	E	C	O	R	D	K	E	E	P	E	R			L	A	F	F			
B	R	O	W	B	E	A	T	S		N	O	V	E	L	W	R	I	T	E	R
I	S	M		I	N	L	E	T		O	N	E	N	D		A	V	I	A	N
L	E	A		S	T	E	R	S		R	A	T	S	O		Y	E	A	R	S

54

D	O	C	S		S	P	O	O	L		Z	I	N	E		V	I	S	E	
O	P	A	H		P	L	A	N	A		T	O	N	A	L		I	N	C	A
S	Q	U	E	A	L	O	F	A	P	P	R	O	V	A	L		S	M	O	G
	S	P	R	I	T		I	D	E	A	M	A	N		S	H	A	W	L	
O	N	E	H	I	T	T	E	R		T	I	E	D		G	E	N	T	L	E
R	O	W	E		S	E	X		W	I	L	D	E	B	E	Q	U	E	S	T
G	U	A	R	D		D	E	B	I	T			E	M	U					
S	N	Y	D	E	R		C	O	D		O	M	A	N		E	V	I	A	N
		S	N	I	P		B	E	A	V	I	S		F	L	A	N	G	E	
S	K	I	P		S	I	P	S		B	E	N	I	C	E		N	C	A	A
L	O	C	I		Q	U	E	A	S	Y	R	I	D	E	R		Q	U	I	P
I	R	A	Q		U	S	A	G	E	S		G	E	R	M		U	R	N	S
D	A	N	U	B	E		L	E	T	S	G	O		T	A	T	I			
E	N	T	E	R		B	E	T	H		A	L	I		T	A	S	M	A	N
			E	A	U			I	N	F	R	A		C	H	I	C	A		
Q	U	A	L	M	S	G	I	V	I	N	G		O	U	T		I	S	M	S
U	N	D	I	E	S		M	E	R	E		I	N	D	I	A	N	T	E	A
A	S	H	E	N		A	P	R	O	P	O	S		I	M	A	G	O		
F	E	E	L		Q	U	A	I	N	T	M	I	S	B	E	H	A	V	I	N
F	A	R	O		B	E	L	L	Y		A	T	O	L	L		C	E	D	E
S	T	E	W		S	L	A	Y		R	I	L	E	Y		T	R	O	D	

55

S	C	A	L	E	D			G	I	M	L	I			C	O	B	R	A
C	A	R	N	E	R	A		E	A	T	O	U	T		B	L	A	R	E	S
C	H	A	N	G	I	N	G	G	R	O	O	M	S		L	A	T	E	N	T
C	A	N	A	A	N		E	R	N		S	P	O	R	T	S	S	C	A	R
P	R	E	L	L		S	T	E	E	L		P	A	S	S		H	M	O
A	S	S	A	U	L	T	T	R	I	F	L	E	S		C	I	T	E	S
	G	R	A	Y		B	R	A	N		P	L	O
S	T	A	T	E	L	Y		T	W	E	E	D		F	O	O	T	E	R
P	I	L	E	S		G	E	H	R	Y		N	E	W	W	A	G	E	R
I	M	I	N		G	L	O	R	I	A		W	O	V	E	N		O	D	E
R	E	B		T	R	O	O	P	P	L	E	A	D	E	R	S		T	W	A
A	L	A		H	E	A	D	S		M	A	T	E	R	S		G	R	I	P
L	A	B	B	R	A	T	S		L	I	S	T	S		S	E	I	N	E
	G	A	R	E	T	H		B	O	N	E	S		W	H	E	L	P	E	D
	Y	E	S		P	R	O	D		V	E	E	P
G	H	A	N	A		C	A	R	P	E	N	T	E	R	R	A	N	T	S
R	O	T		M	A	I	N		D	E	E	R	E		R	A	H	A	B
A	T	O	M	I	C	C	A	G	E		E	N	D		P	A	T	R	I	A
M	A	N	A	G	E		M	I	X	E	D	D	E	M	O	T	I	O	N	S
P	I	A	N	O	S		A	S	P	E	N	S		E	L	E	V	A	T	E
A	R	L	E	S		S	H	O	R	T		R	E	S	E	T	S

56

A	T	H	E	A	R	T		P	A	P	A	W		D	E	E	P	E	N
T	O	O	L	B	A	R	S		E	L	I	T	E		I	N	D	I	R	A
T	A	B	L	E	T	O	P		D	O	N	T	B	E	S	T	U	P	I	D
I	M	A		L	E	W	A	Y	R	E	S		S	U	P	E		S	E	A
C	A	R	B		D	E	T	O	O		A	I	R	E	R	S
A	N	T	I	C		L	E	N		H	E	C	T	O	R		E	L	M	O
	T	A	R	S		C	A	B	L	E		S	O	C	I	A	L
R	I	B	I	S	I		F	L	A	T	B	U	S	H	A	V	E	N	U	E
A	T	O	N	I	C		O	Y	L		A	L	A	D	D	I	N
G	O	O	G	O	O	D	O	L	L	S		A	S	K		L	E	A
A	R	K		H	I	D	E	A	N	D	S	E	E	K		H	I	P
	T	I	S		A	S	S		L	A	P	I	S	L	A	Z	U	L	I
S	T	I	N	T	O	N		W	I	N		I	C	O	N	I	C
W	I	T	H	A	V	E	N	G	E	A	N	C	E		N	A	N	T	E	S
I	M	L	A	T	E		O	A	S	I	S		M	E	R	E
T	E	E	N		R	A	T	T	E	D		F	R	I		D	R	A	M	A
	D	O	W	S	E	S		C	L	A	N	S		S	P	O	T
I	C	E		T	R	I	P		B	O	L	O	T	I	E	S		T	N	T
P	O	T	A	T	O	F	A	M	I	N	E		I	M	P	O	L	I	T	E
O	M	E	L	E	T		D	E	L	T	A		O	U	T	L	I	V	E	S
D	E	S	I	R	E		S	A	L	O	N		M	I	D	E	A	S	T

57

Puzzle 57 grid solution:

```
W A A H   I S I A H   T I D A L   S H A M
A L B A   R O D E O   O L I V E   M E S A
R A I N F O R E S T   P L A I N F O L K S
T I E D I N T O   S C R U M   D A L L A S
      S T O O L S   H O S   A L L D O N E
M C C A I N F O L L O W E R S   S E A T S
S H A W N   G O U P   E K B E R G
D A I S   D A Y A N   S O D O I   A A A
O R R   V E T   N A P K I N F O L D I N G
S T O V E P I P E   A I D E   E R N I E
    I N T E R   P T S   C O N A N
B R E S T   I M I T   O K E Y D O K E Y
R E G A I N F O O T I N G   D E S   R A E
O X O   E L R O Y   O D I S T   R O T S
    C L A W A T   S T E N   R E N E E
S M E A R   T O P S P I N F O R E H A N D
C O N S O R T   A H A   S E N A T E
U N T A M E   A G O R A   R E F R A I N S
B A R G A I N F O R   J O I N F O R C E S
A M I N   M E A D E   A B O I L   S O W N
S I C A   S T R A D   M E R L E   E N T S
```

58

Puzzle 58 grid solution:

```
C H E E R S   A C R A B   C L I N K S
H A L L O W   M A U R A   H O L L I S
A R S E N A L   O B I E S   R O S I E S T
  I A M D R I N K I N G T H E S T A R S
      O M N I   N G O   A B E T
S T A B S   E L O   P H I   O I L U P
I O N E   O N E T O   L E A D A   T A N S
N O T N O W   S I S S I E S   G A S K E T
  K I E F E R   C H A M P   S U N T E A
L A H D I D A H   A G N   G O E S W E S T
A C E I T   C O O   E   Q U A   A E R I E
N A R C   M E R C E   B U N K O   L I E N
  B O T T O M S U P   W I N E L O V E R
    I N H E E L S   A V E R A G E
M A G N U S   L A O   N E D   N E O C O N
A P O E T   F I R M   A R F S   E C O N O
D O O M   O A K   O L A   L R O N
  D O M P I E R R E P E R I G N O N
P H O N I E S   B A T E D   G N O C C H I
J U N K D N A   I M A R I   H U L K O U T
S H E   I S L   S A L U T   T S O   B E T
```

59

```
ENYA   OPEC   BASS      COBRA
MOOR   VETO   LMNOP     AXIOM
TRUMPETHPLAYERS      LONGI
  DRYER   ISIS   EDSEL    GES
    GTO     CELEBRITYDIETH
STRANGE      USD   EIN
IRAN   ETE   STOA      BIJOU
ROCKETHSCIENTISTS      CUT
  TESLA   OHMS     RAH   SRTA
    ANA   LITTERBASKETH
SPASTIC   OASIS   OTTAWAN
PICKETHFENCES   TSO
ELOI   COO   ODES   HOARS
NAM   SHOESTRINGBUDGETH
TRANQ     THEN   TAG   GNAT
    TUG   ARI     SECRETS
AFGHANBLANKETH     LAG
NAE   DUEBY   ESAU   NOVEL
TUNIC   BUCKETHBRIGADES
ELIZA   EMAIL   OBIT   TOOK
STEER     STDS   EAVE   ENVY
```

60

```
STEELER   AGHAS   SHADES
NOSCORE   RHONE   TAPESUP
ALTOONA   MOTOR   ELANTRA
PLANNED   RUEDE   PARTIAL
ESSO     SMELLING   STUM
    MAP   ISS   ZERO   RANG
BEMYGUEST   PERON   TETON
ETO   ATMS   SRS   WINO   ETA
LUNAR   ITALO   FLOOREDIT
LITH   BLEWOVER   NOSE
ASHORE   PRAIRIE   SOREAT
    RATA   ANNMARIE   IAGO
ORGANSTOP   CARON   LEGAL
MHO   DYES   DES   DUPE   LIE
SETBY   OTOES   REPRESENT
KOOL     FITS   DEN   EST
    SODS   ATOMISTS   ACHS
CALCIUM   ALERO   WEATHER
ELEKTRA   WATER   ANTIART
SLEEKLY   ATEST   GOTOSEA
  SPRAYS   NERTS   SLYNESS
```

61

62

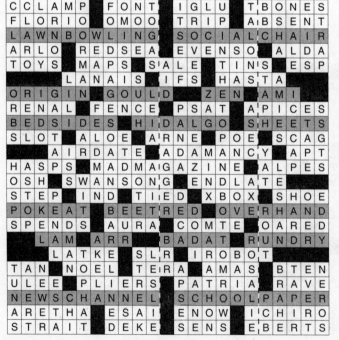

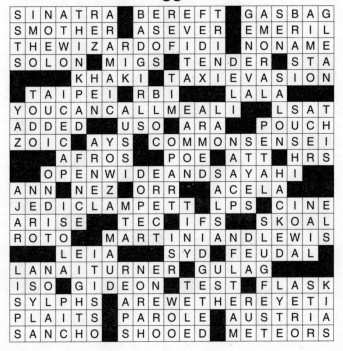

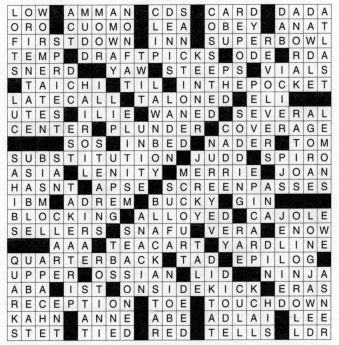

65

N	E	H	I		A	E	T	N	A		B	L	I	N	D		H	A	J	I
O	P	E	N		R	E	R	A	N		S	O	D	O	M		O	L	I	N
W	H	A	T	I	S	L	O	V	E		S	C	I	F	I		O	I	L	S
		T	U	N	E		T	A	M	S		K	O	A	N		K	A	L	E
	F	R	I	E	N	D	S	H	I	P	S	E	T	T	O	M	U	S	I	C
M	E	A	T	P	I	E		O	C	A	T				R	E	P	E	A	T
K	E	Y	S	T	O	N	E		R	O	W	A	N		A	S	S	N		
T	D	S			E	L	M	S		N	O	L	O	A	D					
			T	H	E	B	E	A	U	T	Y	O	F	T	H	E	S	O	U	L
P	U	T	O	U	T		M	I	L	E		L	A	I	C		O	R	Z	O
C	H	A	N	G	E	S		L	U	N	T	S		T	H	E	R	E	I	N
B	O	R	E		R	U	H	R		O	O	H	S		O	R	E	L	S	E
S	H	A	R	I	N	G	Y	O	U	R	P	O	P	C	O	R	N			
			T	E	A	P	O	T		O	P	A	H				G	Y	M	
	V	E	G	A		R	E	M	U	S		S	I	G	N	O	R	A	S	
P	A	M	E	L	A			R	I	N	G		L	E	E	R	I	N	G	
A	M	A	N	Y	S	P	L	E	N	D	O	R	E	D	T	H	I	N	G	
N	O	N	E		T	R	O	D		E	M	I	L		D	R	E	D		
D	O	U	R		H	I	T	I	T		A	L	L	Y	O	U	N	E	E	D
A	S	E	A		M	O	T	T	S		A	L	I	E	N		T	R	E	O
S	E	L	L		A	R	O	S	E		M	E	E	S	E		S	S	G	T

66

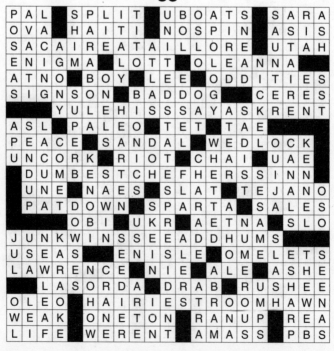

P	A	L		S	P	L	I	T		U	B	O	A	T	S		S	A	R	A
O	V	A		H	A	I	T	I		N	O	S	P	I	N		A	S	I	S
S	A	C	A	I	R	E	A	T	A	I	L	L	O	R	E		U	T	A	H
E	N	I	G	M	A		L	O	T	T		O	L	E	A	N	N	A		
A	T	N	O		B	O	Y		L	E	E		O	D	D	I	T	I	E	S
S	I	G	N	S	O	N		B	A	D	D	O	G			C	E	R	E	S
			Y	U	L	E	H	I	S	S	S	A	Y	A	S	K	R	E	N	T
A	S	L		P	A	L	E	O		T	E	T		T	A	E				
P	E	A	C	E		S	A	N	D	A	L		W	E	D	L	O	C	K	
U	N	C	O	R	K		R	I	O	T		C	H	A	I		U	A	E	
	D	U	M	B	E	S	T	C	H	E	F	H	E	R	S	S	I	N	N	
	U	N	E		N	A	E	S		S	L	A	T		T	E	J	A	N	O
	P	A	T	D	O	W	N		S	P	A	R	T	A		S	A	L	E	S
			O	B	I		U	K	R		A	E	T	N	A		S	L	O	
J	U	N	K	W	I	N	S	S	E	E	A	D	D	H	U	M	S			
U	S	E	A	S		E	N	I	S	L	E		O	M	E	L	E	T	S	
L	A	W	R	E	N	C	E		N	I	E		A	L	E		A	S	H	E
	L	A	S	O	R	D	A		D	R	A	B		R	U	S	H	E	E	
O	L	E	O		H	A	I	R	I	E	S	T	R	O	O	M	H	A	W	N
W	E	A	K		O	N	E	T	O	N		R	A	N	U	P		R	E	A
L	I	F	E		W	E	R	E	N	T		A	M	A	S	S		P	B	S

67

Puzzle 67 grid solution:

```
NEAR  DRUM  APSE  NAFTA
ANNE  IAGO  DRAG  ARRET
NOTFORTHEWEEKOFHEART
USERFEE   ASSISI   NCIS
    AFC SILTS  LOCKERS
AROMATICTEE  FREDALLEN
TOMEI  MOSS  SEEDILY
OVA  REPRO ROADIE  MANX
PENH PEEKSEASON  MYLAR
   AMEND CENTS  ZADORA
STYMIED BALDS  BASEPAY
PROBES  ALLES  ALICE
RERUN  FLEECOLLAR  RANI
YSER  BOGART OBIES  LON
   GARRETS SOUS  HTEST
CAMELEERS ATIMETOHEEL
IVORIES   STIES  ORE
GERM   EASTON  ARTFORM
  REELMENDONTEATQUICHE
 SLEET  TAKE  THOU RTES
 ESTOS  SKED  CAME MOOS
```

Puzzle 68 grid solution:

```
HEARTS  GRAVES  NOWWHAT
ALTHEA  RELENT  PLICATE
SMOOCH  UGLIER  RANFREE
HOPSTILYOUDROP  NEIMAN
   OBOE STOKER  BESTS
ALIGN EREI  EPINAL
TENNISBELOW  SUPERDEMO
EDKOCH  KNIT  PER  SLID
MASC OWES  LOL RON  ONE
  COWER KLUTZ  DEPOT
THEHINTMAN  GREENACERS
RONIN  ALEPH KOOKS
YTD KIN LEI  GEER  TAPA
TEES MOT SAGO  AMATOL
OPRYMANIA  FLOWWHISTLE
  SAMPAN  ODIN  CYNIC
SPATE  CRANIA  TECH
ARROWS  AHOSTINTHEDARK
BIGLEAD ELOISE  INATIE
LOUISVI ITUNES  MELODY
ERECTED MERGES  PRIZES
```

Puzzle 69 (solution grid):

```
A C S   A G R I     A B S C A M     J O R J A
S A L T N P E P A   G I L R O Y   S A L A A M
S T O R Y O F O P I O N E E R S   S N A Z Z Y
A G U A     I D I D     W E T T E R   O Z S
Y U C C A S   N I N A   P A I L   B O R G
  T H E L O N G G O O D B Y E C O L U M B U S
    P L O Y   T I L L     I T S A L I E
A S I S   O R R S   A I M L E S S   H A T E
L I T T L E W O M E N I N L O V E   A D A M
S N A R E D   O V A   I S T O   A S N E R
O G L E S   A P T E S T     K Y R A
  H O W A R D S E N D O F T H E A F F A I R
      G A M Y     P A R O D Y   A L T A R
  J A D E D   C L A Y   C O B   D R E S S Y
S O F A   T H E L A S T D O N Q U I X O T E
E S T H   R I O T A C T   S A U R   A N A S
T S E L I O T   H O T S   A A B A
A W R I N K L E I N T I M E A N D A G A I N
  H A A S   E M M E   C I E L   N A R N I A
L E S   J S B A C H   Y E T I   T H E Y
I D O T O O   A R T O F W A R A N D P E A C E
M O R O S E   R E A R E D   O L D Y E L L E R
O N T W O   S T R A Y S   C O E N   E S S
```

70

Puzzle 70 (solution grid):

```
M A C A W   L E D O N   C A N A S T A S
I N A B I T   A R E G O   A P E H O U S E
D O U B L E S P A C E S   T I R E I R O N
I T S A D E A L   R E A C T   D A R N
S E E   K A T Y   L O L A   P E S O S
    T R A I N S P O T T E R S   E T C H
S A L A A M   D O T E   M A U I   I T O
W Y S I W Y G   D I K E   S T O L I D
E L A L   R E I D   N O N   S H I E L D
E A T S   C O N C E R T O   W O O L S E Y
    P O L I C E S T A K E O U T S
P E L I C A N   M I S C O U N T   P A P P
A V A N T I   S A L   T O R K   I D L E
T E N S E R   O N U S   Y O P L A I T
I N D   T O R N   Y A W S   H O L M E S
O S S O   L I G H T S W I T C H E S
S O C A L   O M O O   E Z R A   C S A
    A X E S   I P A S S   A R M O I R E S
J A P A N W A X   S H O W S T O P P E R S
E L E C T I V E   T A M E S   P E S E T A
D I S A S T E R   S W E D E   C O P A Y
```

71

I	S	N	T		L	A	P	A	Z		S	C	R	U	M		A	M	S	O
O	P	E	R		O	S	A	G	E		T	R	I	B	E		W	A	T	T
N	O	W	I	N	C	H	S	I	T	U	A	T	I	O	N		O	K	A	Y
	K	A	P	O	K		S	O	A	P	Y		S	A	D	D	L	E	U	P
N	A	G		M	E	A		J	O	E	S		T	I	E		A	B	E	
O	N	E	H	I	T	C	H	W	O	N	D	E	R		C	R	A	B		
R	E	R	A	N		T	E	R	N	E		C	I	G	A	R	C	A	S	E
		S	A	R	A	L	E	E		P	U	T	O	N		O	D	I	N	
C	H	I	L	I		O	N	S	T	A	R		S	T	R	I	P	E	D	
P	L	O	D		D	U	I		A	B	E	T	S		I	N	U	R	E	
R	O	T		M	E	N	S	C	H	F	A	S	H	I	O	N		N	R	A
O	S	C	A	R		B	E	A	U	T		R	P	M		S	C	A	R	
B	U	R	M	E	S	E		B	E	S	A	M	E		N	O	A	H	S	
E	R	O	O		I	N	C	A	S		N	E	W	H	I	G	H			
D	E	S	C	E	N	D	O	N		A	C	T	I	I		R	I	N	S	E
		S	O	N	G		P	A	T	C	H	O	N	T	H	E	B	A	C	K
O	T	B		O	L	A		S	O	H	O		S	E	I		N	O	G	
C	O	U	N	S	E	L	S		P	O	R	E	D		A	S	P	E	N	
A	N	N	I		G	E	T	A	L	O	A	D	O	F	T	H	A	T	C	H
L	I	C	K		U	T	E	R	I		G	E	N	I	E		I	T	E	M
A	C	H	E		Y	A	P	A	T		E	N	T	E	R		N	E	S	S

72

C	O	A	C	H		R	I	B		U	P	B	O	W		T	R	I	P	E
A	L	L	A	Y		A	D	A		S	A	L	S	A		H	O	N	O	R
W	A	L	L	P	A	P	E	R		F	L	O	O	R	L	E	A	D	E	R
		C	E	L	I	A		C	L	A	W		P	E	A	R				
A	S	S	U	R	E	D		C	H	A	T		B	L	A	C	K	C	A	T
B	E	A	T		C	O	L	L	E	G	E	D	R	A	F	T		U	F	O
R	E	N	T			O	U	R		E	I	N	S		S	T	I	R		
U	S	D	A		S	M	U	T		A	B	U	S	E		P	E	T	R	I
P	A	W		S	W	I	T	C	H	B	A	C	K		R	E	V	I	S	E
T	W	I	S	T	E	D		H	O	R	D	E		B	A	R	E	N	T	S
		C	O	R	E	A		S	A	G		A	G	I	N	G				
S	C	H	L	E	P	S		C	I	D	E	R		B	L	O	S	S	O	M
E	L	B	O	W	S		C	H	E	E	S	E	H	E	A	D		C	R	I
S	I	R	E	N		F	A	I	R	S		K	I	L	N		S	H	I	N
A	P	E	D		C	A	R	L		A	I	L		C	O	A	X			
M	O	A		R	U	N	N	I	N	G	S	C	O	R	E		A	O	N	E
E	N	D	T	A	B	L	E		E	R	I	K		A	X	I	L	L	A	S
		A	C	A	I		B	A	A	S		A	K	I	R	A				
D	R	A	W	I	N	G	C	A	R	D		W	H	I	T	E	W	A	S	H
I	T	I	N	A		H	I	R	E	E		A	S	S		N	A	N	A	S
M	E	R	Y	L		T	E	N	D	S		D	O	H		E	G	Y	P	T

The word is BOARD

73

U	M	P	S		C	A	D	Y		P	O	W	E	R		F	R	A	I	L
P	O	O	L	C	U	T	I	E		E	L	E	N	I		L	A	S	S	O
C	H	R	I	S	T	M	A	S	T	R	E	A	T	Y		A	D	I	E	U
	S	E	M	I			S	N	A	P	O	N			A	C	T	I	F	E	D
			C	A	P	O	N	S			I	D	A	H	O		
C	P	A	S		U	S	O			L	O	C	H	N	E	S	T	E	A
H	A	N	N	A	B	A	R	B	A	R	I	T	Y		T	E	H	R	A	N
E	N	D	O	R		P	A	Y	M	E	N	T		S	O	L	O	I	S	T
E	N	R	O	N			F	I	N	D	O	U	T			W	O	E	S
K	E	E	P	I	N	G	P	A	S	T	Y		C	O	C	K	S
S	D	I		C	O	L	O	R			S	L	I	E	R		C	S	A
		H	A	G	U	E		S	A	N	T	A	C	L	A	R	I	T	Y
P	L	A	Y		E	M	P	E	R	O	R			M	A	M	I	E
O	I	L	P	A	N	S		S	T	A	T	U	T	E		E	D	I	N	A
O	L	I	N	D	A		R	A	B	B	I	T	W	A	R	R	A	N	T	Y
H	I	T	O	R	M	I	S	T	Y		O	R	E		R	O	S	E
		T	E	E	N	A			E	D	E	S	S	A
U	N	B	I	N	D	S		O	S	M	E	N	T		R	O	A	M
T	E	R	Z	A		T	O	R	T	O	I	S	E	S	H	E	L	T	I	E
A	R	I	E	L		I	N	C	U	R		U	P	T	O	P	A	R	T	Y
H	O	O	D	S		R	E	A	D	Y		E	S	P	N		F	A	T	E

74

B	I	T	E	I	T		L	S	D		C	M	I	I		S	A	Y	I	T
I	W	A	N	N	A		A	T	A	S	L	A	N	T		A	D	E	N	O
C	O	M	E	T	O	T	H	I	N	K	O	F	I	T		G	E	T	I	T
	N	A	M	E		R	O	C	K	Y	V	I			B	E	N	I	T	O
		I	N	P	A	R	K		L	E	A	D	O	U	T
	A	R	E		I	C	E	T	E	A	S		E	E	L		A	D	S
M	T	O	S	S	A			O	T	B		B	A	R	K	C	L	O	T	H
O	I	L		L	O	W	B	I	D		B	O	L	T		O	M	N	I	A
E	L	L	I	E		A	R	T		C	R	O	W	E		U	S	T	E	D
S	T	I	L	E	T	T	O		F	L	A	T	I	R	O	N		B	S	A
	N	A	P	A		W	R	O	U	G	H	T		O	T	O	E
L	A	G		O	P	E	N	A	R	E	A		H	E	M	O	S	T	A	T
O	N	I	O	N		A	B	N	E	R		N	I	L		N	O	O	S	E
E	N	N	U	I		S	A	C	S		R	O	T	I	N	I		N	I	N
W	A	I	S	T	H	I	G	H		G	A	T		A	T	T	I	C	S
	S	T	E		A	L	I		M	O	D	U	L	O	S		H	T	S
		S	C	Y	T	H	E	S		P	A	R	T	E	R
S	P	A	C	E	K		I	T	S	A	T	I	E		R	I	P	S
E	A	T	I	T		T	A	K	E	I	T	O	R	L	E	A	V	E	I	T
A	L	E	T	A		O	V	E	R	P	A	I	D		S	T	E	L	M	O
S	E	E	I	T		M	E	S	S		D	T	S		L	O	S	E	I	T

The New York Times

Crossword Puzzles

The #1 Name in Crosswords

Available at your local bookstore or online at nytimes.com/nytstore

St. Martin's Griffin